Film Viewing in Postwar Japan, 1945–1968

An Ethnographic Study

Jennifer Coates

EDINBURGH
University Press

For my family, with love.

Edinburgh University Press is one of the leading university presses in the UK. We publish academic books and journals in our selected subject areas across the humanities and social sciences, combining cutting-edge scholarship with high editorial and production values to produce academic works of lasting importance. For more information visit our website: edinburghuniversitypress.com

© Jennifer Coates, 2022, 2024

Edinburgh University Press Ltd
The Tun – Holyrood Road
12 (2f) Jackson's Entry
Edinburgh EH8 8PJ

First published in hardback by Edinburgh University Press 2022

Typeset in Monotype Ehrhardt by
Manila Typesetting Company

A CIP record for this book is available from the British Library

ISBN 978 1 3995 0103 3 (hardback)
ISBN 978 1 3995 0104 0 (paperback)
ISBN 978 1 3995 0105 7 (webready PDF)
ISBN 978 1 3995 0106 4 (epub)

The right of Jennifer Coates to be identified as author of this work has been asserted in accordance with the Copyright, Designs and Patents Act 1988 and the Copyright and Related Rights Regulations 2003 (SI No. 2498).

Contents

List of Figures	iv
Note on the Romanisation of Japanese Words	vi
Acknowledgements	vii
Introduction: Feelings without Words	1
1. What Do We Talk About when We Talk About Cinema?	24
2. The Cinema as a Place to Be	52
3. Times Past and Passing Time at the Cinema	75
4. Stars, Occupiers, Parents and Role Models: Cinema as a Way of Being (Japanese)	96
5. Gender Trouble at the Cinema	120
6. Organised Audiences and Committed Fans: Cinema, Viewership, Activism	138
7. Crafting the Self through Cinema Culture	159
Conclusion: Giving an Account of Oneself through Talking About Cinema	183
Bibliography	193
Index	206

Figures

1.1	Kobe Meriken Park entrance	37
1.2	Kobe Meriken Theatre monument commemorates the first film screening from overseas	38
1.3	A sculpture in Kobe Meriken Park commemorates the location's important place in Japanese cinema history	38
1.4	Stones in Meriken Park commemorate important figures in Japanese cinema, such as Ozu Yasujirō	39
1.5	Stones in Meriken Park commemorate important figures in Japanese cinema, such as Kyo Machiko	39
1.6	A monument near Kyoto's Nijō castle marks the spot of an early film studio	40
1.7	A monument near Kyoto's Nijō castle marks the spot of an early film studio (close-up)	40
1.8	A sign outside Kyoto's Rissei elementary school commemorates the 'birth of the Japanese cinema'	41
1.9	A sign outside Kyoto's Rissei elementary school commemorates the 'birth of the Japanese cinema' (close-up)	41
2.1	An outdoor screening on the bank of the Kamogawa river near the Delta, home to the Shimogamo studios	55
2.2	An interviewee holds a picture of her father, trained in traditional ceramic production, working as a background actor	68
3.1	Koyama san brought photographs and printed film posters to her interview	84
4.1	Signed photograph of Hara Setsuko	97
4.2	A fan's scrapbook showing stars Ri Kōran and Hasegawa Kazuo	103
5.1	The Senbon Nikkatsu cinema theatre on Senbon street, now a 'pink' cinema theatre	121
7.1	The Motono house, home to the Kinugasa eiga kai until 2018	178

7.2 The Kinugasa eiga kai hosts a screening of *Godzilla* (1954) and *Shin Godzilla* (2016) 178
7.3 On Senbon street, a plaque commemorates the 'father' of Japanese cinema, Makino Shōzo 179

Note on the Romanisation of Japanese Words

Japanese names are given in the Japanese format of family name first, followed by given name. Where a Japanese academic publishes in English and uses the anglophone convention of given name followed by family name, I have written their name in the same order. Interviewees are referred to by surname and the honorific 'san' (loosely equivalent to Mr or Ms). All names of study participants are pseudonyms.

In the romanisation of Japanese words in the text, macrons indicate long vowels, but are not given in words commonly used in English (for example, 'Tokyo' rather than 'Tōkyō'). All translations are my own unless otherwise indicated.

I have used the standard English translations of the titles of the films under discussion; where a film was distributed under an alternative English title, I have cited it as 'a.k.a.'. The Japanese film title is given in brackets at the first mention of each film, alongside the date of release in Japan.

Birth and death dates (where known) of filmmakers, actors and artists are similarly given in brackets after their first mention in each chapter. Where the known dates are unclear, they are cited as 'c.'.

Acknowledgements

This project owes a huge debt of gratitude to so many people. First thanks must go to my study participants, without whom this book quite literally would not have been possible. Thanks for your time, for sharing your memories and your wisdom and for your friendship. I learned so much about life, and not just about cinema, from our time together.

My family have also shaped this project significantly by joining in my fieldwork and helping me to see new angles to the project. Thanks to Dad, one of my most frequent fieldwork visitors, for joining me on trips and at dinners and building friendships with many of my study participants. It was a real joy to share this experience with you. Thanks to Mum for hosting (and singing with!) my participant friends and for your support during research and writing, as well as your reminders to take breaks. Charlotte, thanks for your companionship as we were walked around most of Kyoto and fed everything and anything – you have the endurance of an ethnographer and the patience of a saint! Chris and Gill, I really appreciate your insights on the project and the research process more broadly. It's a real gift to have so many problem solvers in the family. Laurie, thanks for the long chats about cinema and everything else. And Jamie, your influence and inspiration is everywhere in this book – thanks for working together with me at every step.

Mentors and friends have been invaluable advisors and confidantes. Thanks go to Isolde Standish for setting me on this path and talking through the project, to Hideaki Fujiki and Alastair Phillips for your kind support and mentorship, and to Hiroshi Kitamura for sharing your ideas and some great dinners. Thanks to David Desser for your tireless encouragement, and to Sharon Hayashi for expanding my thinking in so many new directions. Kanako Terasawa kindly shared her path-breaking PhD thesis with me before this project had even begun, and this book would have been unimaginable without it.

Kyoto University Hakubi Center for Advanced Research was an invaluable incubator for this slightly odd project, and Yoshitaka Hori, Katsura

Koishi, Hisayo Mizuno, Kiyokazu Okita, Hemant and Bibu Poudyal, Niels Van Steenpal and Ikuko Wada offered advice and friendship that made Kyoto life so rich. Thanks to Nozomi Matsuyama for your great work on the project as research assistant, and for your own inspirational filmmaking practice. Across the university, I benefited greatly from the mentorship of Yuka Kanno, Chika Kinoshita, Yoshihiko Sugimoto and Mitsuyo Wada-Marciano, and the kindness and friendship of Deanna T. Nardy and Yutaka Kubo. Members of the Kyoto-based Emosense group, including Andrea De Antoni, Eyal Ben-Ari, Caitlin Coker, Emma Cook, Paul Dumouchel, Andrea Giolai and Shiori Shakuto, expanded my thinking during the research and early writing stages, and became great friends. Thanks to Irina Holca and Carmen Tamas for their friendship and deep knowledge of Osaka restaurants, as well as for finding so many opportunities to work together. Itsushi Kawase, Yushi Yanohara and the scholars at Minpaku modelled enthusiastic, ethical and boundary-pushing visual ethnography approaches and shared so much of their experience and ideas, which enriched this project and my wider thinking on ethnohistorical approaches. Bunpaku staff and patrons, and particularly Kiyotaka Moriwaki at the Kyoto Film Archive, provided invaluable feedback and support for the project from its earliest stages.

At the School of East Asian Studies, colleagues who are also friends contributed hugely to this project and the conditions which made it possible. In Kate Taylor-Jones, I couldn't have asked for a better friend and champion. It's been a privilege to work together on so many projects and I look forward to the next. Mark Pendleton made these collaborations and so much more possible – thanks for everything. Clea Carroll, thanks for your friendship, kindness and fellow food fandom. Across academia, I've learned so much from the company and understanding of so many friends, as well as from your excellent work. Julia Alekseyeva, Alejandra Armendáriz-Hernández, Erica Baffelli, Oleg Benesch, Eveline Buchheim, Leloy Claudio, Aya Ezawa, Irene Gonzáles-López, Laura Haapio-Kirk, Alexandra Hambleton, Iris Haukamp, Fusako Innami, Iza Kavedžija, Ran Ma, Noriko Morisue, Fuyubi Nakamura, Lindsay Nelson, Mara Patessio, Maisha Wester and Victoria Young – both my work and daily life are richer for your friendship and wisdom.

I am grateful for the kind efforts of staff at Edinburgh University Press: thanks to Gillian Leslie for her invaluable support for this project, Sam Johnson and Eddie Clark for such careful management of the production process, and Caitlin Murphy for her wonderful work on the cover. Thanks also to Ian Brooke for excellent copyediting.

Introduction
Feelings without Words

> Some films can skilfully show those feelings that so many people have inside, that can't be expressed in words (*kotoba de ienai kanji*). (Kishida san, born 1952)

How can we understand what cinema means to others? One of the biggest issues in audience and reception studies is the ultimate unknowability of the processes going on in the mind and body of another person as they watch a film. This has implications for our understanding of how these processes contribute to meaning making, in relation to how viewers understand the events and images onscreen to relate to, inform or contrast with their own lives and understandings of the world. This book approaches the question of viewers' relationship to film from a different angle, asking instead what it means to engage discursively with one another *through* cinema. What does talking about the cinema do?

This is more than a simple curiosity. Over more than a century of cinema, grassroots popular support for the movies has waxed and waned, peaking in countries as diverse as the USA, the UK and Japan in the 1950s and 1960s at the height of the organised studio systems. In the same century, many corners of the world have seen the cinema co-opted by governments and organisational institutions, which imagine film technologies as a means to influence those same grassroots audiences. The consistent use of cinema, among other popular entertainments, to persuade or attempt to manipulate viewers keeps the question of what (and how) cinema means to viewers at the forefront of inquiry. This book takes postwar bureaucratic interventions into Japanese cinema production and exhibition as the starting point for an exploration of the roles that cinema can play in our lives, as viewers, citizens and humans.

Postwar Japanese cinema presents an ideal case study for this investigation due to a coincidence of particular socio-political, historical and structural factors occurring in the first decades after 1945. Japan was a relatively early adopter of film technology, beginning in the 1890s, contemporaneous with many countries around the world and not far behind France and the USA. At the same time, the early Japanese cinema industry was in many ways expressly local. Borrowing technologies and tropes from North America and Europe, Japanese cinema developed into an organised system which by the 1920s had begun to bear a resemblance to Hollywood (H. Kitamura 2010: 13). By wartime, this organised studio system was ripe for conscription into the Imperial propaganda effort to mobilise mass publics in support of expansion and war (Fujiki 2019). After 1945 the same studio system, superficially reorganised (Standish 2005: 272), became a major component of the Allied Occupation forces' attempt to remodel postwar Japan in the image of a modern democratic capitalist nation state.

While 1945 and the rapid changes that this year brought provide the starting point for this study, it should be noted that the period covered by this book, 1945–68, is by no means a homogenous one in terms of political structure, social change and economic conditions. Rather, 1945 and 1968 should be understood for the purposes of this study as two bookend years of major rapid change, on either side of a period in which change may be said to have been the only constant. A number of important historical shifts are encapsulated within this span of twenty-three years, and the chapters to follow weave these socio-political and historical changes into the narrative of memories of film viewership presented by participants in this study.

The year 1945 was a watermark year for cinema in Japan, as well as historical and political change more broadly. In a 'Memorandum Concerning Elimination of Japanese Government Control of the Motion Picture Industry' circulated on 16 October 1945, the General Headquarters of the Supreme Commander for the Allied Powers (hereafter SCAP GHQ) directed an end to wartime censorship, 'to permit the industry to reflect the democratic aspirations of the Japanese people' (Allen 1945: 3). A new Occupation censorship process was designed to channel viewers' conscious and unconscious responses, aiming to shape film viewers into modern subjects, imagined in the democratic capitalist mode modelled by the Occupiers themselves. But could cinema really have such an impact? Do we form ourselves through engagement with popular media to this extent, and can that same media change our self-formation? Taking the Allied intervention in film production and exhibition as a starting point, this book presents an ethno-history of film viewing and cinema culture in Japan from 1945 to 1968, exploring how we interface with and through cinema, and what that means for our understandings of our place in the world. Throughout the manuscript, the structural interventions of government, Occupation forces, political movements and education are discussed in tension with the various modes of self that were developed and discussed in the postwar period.

The research on which this book is based was conducted from 2014 to 2018 using mixed methods, including interviews with film viewers who attended the cinema regularly between 1945 and 1968, a long-form questionnaire project involving eighty-seven participants and participant observation conducted at several cinemas and film groups specialising in Shōwa-era film (1926–89). Analysing how viewers' memories of attending the cinema in postwar Japan intersect with their current attitudes and life projects, this book challenges the idea of the cinema as a tool for producing controlled changes in social attitudes. By exploring viewers' memories of how SCAP's cinematic interventions played out in real film theatres and informal screening spaces across the Kansai area of Western Japan, we can see how everyday hopes and expectations clash or merge with governmental and top-down views of social change. An ethnographic approach to viewership practices outside the Occupation-centred Tokyo area helps us to understand the role that cinema played in forming a self fit for the new postwar world.

Setting the Scene: Kansai

The location of this study in the Kansai region allows for an ethnography of life in a cinema-producing area, as the area hosted a number of film studios and location shooting in the period under study. Throughout this book, an account of the industrial conditions of the Kansai region in the postwar period, particularly in regard to exhibition and distribution, is interwoven with discussion of the everyday lived experiences of study participants, which in many aspects is specific to the area.

The Kansai region comprises the cities of Kyoto, Osaka and Kobe, as well as a number of rural areas in between those entertainment centres. Reflecting the formative role that these three cities played in the development of Japanese cinema culture, there are an increasing number of publications and scholarly works in Japanese that explore local film industries outside Tokyo (Kondo 2020; Itakura 2019; Takabe 2016). While Chapter 2 discusses the role of each Kansai city in the foundational narrative of cinema in Japan in greater detail, this short section gives an overview of the major role played by this area in the production and exhibition of Japanese cinema, as a reminder of the necessity of scholarship that does not focus solely on Tokyo.

Director Ichikawa Kon noted the attraction of 'Kansai as material' for many Japanese directors, suggesting that a number of the major titles of

Japanese cinema history, both from a commercial and an artistic perspective, 'could only have been set in Kansai' (2001: 412). Ichikawa notes the importance of the 'customs and mores' of the region to authenticity in the filming of major literary works which are themselves set in the area. Describing the area as 'the heart of Japan' and also 'the money center' (2001: 413), its importance to entertainment and commerce is clear. While the region had long been used as a setting for period dramas due to the large number of older buildings and nature spaces, the film industry moved to Kansai in earnest after the Great Kanto Earthquake of 1923. Due to widespread destruction of buildings and systems, major Tokyo-based film companies began to move production facilities and personnel to Kyoto, Osaka and Kobe soon after the disaster. Even Shōchiku and Nikkatsu, whose Tokyo studios had not been extensively damaged by the earthquake, nonetheless moved their film personnel to Kyoto temporarily, making Kansai 'the new center of Japanese motion picture production' (Lewis 2019: 35). This was the first time that the major studios of the pre-war era, Shōchiku, Nikkatsu, Teikine and Makino, had operated from the same area, which was widely compared to the migration of New York film companies to Los Angeles in the US. From 1924 until the end of the decade, film production in Kansai surpassed that of Tokyo, and Kyoto was discussed as 'the Hollywood of Japan' (Lewis 2019: 35). The Japanese offices of American companies Paramount, Fox and United also relocated to Kansai after the disaster (Lewis 2019: 57).

Shōchiku returned to its original base at Kamata in early 1924, but no other major studio reopened its Tokyo premises until 1934 (Lewis 2019: 58). Even so, the Shōchiku Shimogamo studio in the Kamogawa Delta in the heart of Kyoto continued to operate, specialising in period drama. Kansai kept its particular relation to cinema production throughout wartime and into the postwar era. In fact, as Occupation control of cinema content extended to a ban on representations of the Occupation itself, Kansai became a popular filming location due to its distance from GHQ in the Tokyo Ginza area. Long established as a popular secondary film industry even before the influx of Tokyo personnel after the earthquake, postwar Kansai enjoyed significant status as both subject of and production site for postwar Japanese cinema. Director Yoshimura Kōzaburō complained that thanks to the rebuilding efforts that had left many postwar Japanese cities looking homogenous, Kyoto, Kanazawa and Nara now dominated the 'exotic' filming locations available (1952: 36). While Kansai was anything but exotic for many of the participants in this study who had been born and raised in the area, it was nonetheless a point of pride that the region had played such a significant role in Japanese cinema history. In the following chapters, we can see the activities of the Japanese cinema industry playing out in the background of participants' lives as they narrate their particular relationship to film viewing, exhibition and production.

Cinema Viewership as Ethnographic Encounter

This research was inspired by studies published in the 1980s and 1990s in English which reshaped scholarly understanding of the methods available for the study of popular media and literature. Developing contemporaneously with the ascendance of British Cultural Studies, Anglophone Film Studies and English Literature turned to the question of reception and began to employ ethnographic methods drawn from the field of Anthropology to collect and analyse the responses of popular-culture consumers. Janice Radway's *Reading the Romance: Women, Patriarchy, and Popular Literature* (1984), Ien Ang's *Watching Dallas: Soap Opera and the Melodramatic Imagination* (1985), Jackie Stacey's *Star Gazing: Hollywood Cinema and Female Spectatorship* (1994) and Annette Kuhn's *Dreaming of Fred and Ginger: Cinema and Cultural Memory* (2002) opened up new methods and questions for the study of literature, television and film. These key works focused firmly on the reader or viewer and drew attention to the utility of the analytic methods of close reading and discourse analysis for understanding audience-produced texts such as letters, questionnaires and interviews.

In placing the viewer at the centre of my study, and applying discourse analysis to viewer-produced letters, emails, questionnaires and interviews, this work follows the lead of the scholars named above. Applying this method to the context of the second 'Golden Age' (*ōgon jidai*) of Japanese cinema is timely, as while contemporary studies of Japanese fan cultures make varied use of ethnographic techniques (for example, Allison 1996, 2002; Galbraith 2013), the hybrid methods used by scholars of Anglo-European popular culture have not yet been extended to Japan's peak period of film production and viewership. Including casual viewers as well as fans in the ethnographic material analysed in the following chapters further broadens extant scholarship on the period and its entertainments. In many ways then, this study connects the Japanese Golden Age of cinema to its contemporaneous eras in North America and Europe, while also linking contemporary Japanese fan studies to this earlier era of consumption and production.

Designed as an ethno-history, this study most closely resembles Annette Kuhn's ethno-history of 1930s cinemagoing in Britain (2002). Yet several key differences became apparent from the first stages of fieldwork. Like

Kuhn's interlocutors, participants in this study first attended the cinema at a time with relatively few other entertainment options. The ways that participants watch films have also changed greatly, as run-on programme viewing, the 'stuffing system' (*tsumekomi shiki*) of packing theatres and standing and temporary seating no longer feature in today's mainstream cinemas. Both ethno-histories present a cinema culture now past. While Kuhn's interlocutors have largely retired from cinema culture, watching favourite films at home on television rather than attending public screenings, a number of participants in this study were still actively involved in public cinema cultures into their seventies, eighties and nineties. In fact, I first encountered many participants at public retrospective screenings and film clubs. Furthermore, while only two of Kuhn's interlocutors were members of film clubs or fan appreciation societies, a large number of the participants in this study met regularly with other viewers to watch and discuss films in the 'circle' (*sākuru*) group structures particular to modern Japan. Chapter 6 will explore the historical background and contemporary development of these informal film-screening organisations, while Chapter 7 investigates the role of cinemagoing and film-screening club organisation in participants' everyday lives during their retirement years, analysing how participation in cinema culture can provide fulfilment and interest perceived to be missing from one's life after leaving the workplace. In this sense the ethno-history presented here stretches up to the present day, revealing how elderly film fans in Western Japan continue to engage with cinema in their daily lives.

Yet no matter how many viewers we interview, no matter how many letters or questionnaires we collect, we will never be able to surmise with any degree of certainty what exactly a viewer is experiencing in the cinema. Kuhn and Stacey raise the question of memory in relation to this problem; after all, a viewer's account of their experience is necessarily a question of recall, whether the memory in question is from five minutes or fifty years before the interview. My participant observation at retrospective film programmes and in film circles suggests that personal memory plays a key role not only in the encounter between interviewer and interviewee but also in discussions between viewers before or after a screening.

Memory, like sensory perception, is something the researcher can only ever understand from the outside, unless of course we follow Kuhn and Stacey in their practices of auto-ethnography. Refocusing on audience experiences outside the personal experiences of the researcher, I consider what exactly we *can* know about another's viewing experience from ethnographic study. It seems that all we can apprehend with any certainty is that an interlocutor has brought themselves to the moment of the encounter in order to communicate something, perhaps with the intention or hope of producing some kind of mutual understanding or collective meaning. This is true of the face-to-face encounter in an interview situation, whether formal or informal, and also true of encounters conducted by email or by post. It is also the case in participant observation, where viewers have chosen to attend a public screening despite the availability of the same film online, and in DVD rental stores, libraries or shops. This study focuses on these encounters in order to understand how accounts of cinema viewership can become tools to communicate both to another and to oneself.

In asking the question 'What does cinema viewership do?' then, I am really asking how we use the cinema in our daily lives, and what kinds of avenues of expression, communication, meaning making and understanding film viewership affords. The goals of the Allied Occupation censorship process explicitly connected these aspects of film viewership with ways of being, suggesting that the way of being Japanese in everyday postwar life could be fundamentally changed by exposure to specific film content. Like the phenomenological and memory-related experiences discussed above, being falls within the category of something we cannot know with certainty in relation to another. Yet the ethnographic encounter can tell us something about the tropes and stories that viewers use to try to communicate their experiences of being, and changes in the state of being, to others. In speaking with film viewers about their experiences and memories of postwar cinema, I had a strong sense that cinema discourse often became a tool to convey personal, perhaps unrelatable, experiences and feelings, and to make those experiences mean something, both socially and historically. I wondered if my interviewees and fellow viewers were even drawn to the cinema for this particular affordance. Was the cinema a window that viewers used to try to make sense of deeper questions of being, both for themselves and for others? Can we make ourselves more knowable to others by thinking and communicating through accounts of cinematic engagement?

Encountering the Audience

I have attempted throughout this book to lead from the words of my research participants into the descriptive and analytic material that follows, mirroring the emic imperative of anthropological study. In practice, this means using the terms and phrases spoken and written by my research participants, rather than imposing categories and words of my own. In the remainder of this introduction, I will outline the development of the study before giving some historical and scholarly background in Chapter 1. Historical information on viewership practices in the Kansai region, including amateur viewership organisations, arrives as it is introduced in the memories of my interlocutors, rather than in chronological order. I hope that readers will bear with this unfolding in the interests of allowing the voices of research participants to drive the structure and development of my argument.

I began research for this volume with two years of participant observation at the retrospective screening programmes held at the Kyoto Bunka Hakubutsukan (Kyoto Culture Museum), known locally as the Bunpaku. This large museum was situated on the central Sanjō street, just off Karasuma street in downtown Kyoto. On the third floor, a film theatre with a capacity of 180 seats hosted two daily screenings at 1:30pm and 6:30pm. Programmes ran for around one month, and programme themes ranged from a focus on the work of a particular director, scriptwriter, camera operator, composer or cinematographer to more abstract concepts such as 'Eating on Film' (*Taberu eiga: eiga de no shoku no yakuwari*, 10–29 November 2015). With the exception of specially organised events such as an annual student film festival, and the rare programme devoted to European art-house cinema, all programmes featured Japanese studio films made between 1910 and 1980. Each film was repeated four times in a programme, twice per day on two days of a single week. Tickets were comparatively cheap at 500 yen ($4.50 US) for non-members and 400 yen ($3.60 US) for members, or 4,000 yen ($36.50 US) for a yearly pass, whereas a single commercial cinema ticket would have been closer to 2,000 yen. Viewers were relatively free to come and go as they pleased, though two yellow-jacketed attendants attempted to discourage visitors from entering the theatre during the last thirty minutes of a screening.

The museum housed an archival collection of materials related to Kyoto's film history. A scholarly approach was also apparent in the changing displays in the small lobby area in front of the theatre entrance, which showcased archival materials related to the screening programme, including contemporary posters, magazine articles, critical coverage, published interviews with directors and stars and on-set photographs. The changing lobby displays also provided an opportunity to observe how viewers interacted with film materials other than the film texts themselves, and the roles film ephemera played in interpersonal conversations between viewers.

The location, surroundings and access arrangements of the Bunpaku film theatre ensured a diverse audience in terms of personal interest and expertise as well as class, educational and financial background. The central area of Kyoto city is quite easily accessible and the film theatre has disabled access, which is not guaranteed in the smaller commercial cinemas.

Viewers with mobility impairments attended Bunpaku cinema theatre screenings regularly. In its position on the third floor of a large museum which featured a permanent exhibit on Japanese culture and history as well as several temporary exhibits on topics as diverse as The English Country Garden (May 2016) and classical Japanese painting, the Bunpaku film theatre also attracted patrons who had not come to the building with the specific intention of watching a film, but found the theatre an interesting or convenient place to visit after an exhibition. Patrons purchasing tickets for any exhibition could enter the cinema theatre for free. The low price of tickets and availability of an affordable yearly pass further suggested that viewers at the Bunpaku theatre ranged from dedicated film fans to first-time visitors, and people attended the screenings for reasons of personal convenience and curiosity as much as long-term interest in Japanese cinema. As a participant at the Bunpaku film theatre, I was able to observe the viewing practices of both regular and occasional viewers. The range of casual and committed viewers who visited the Bunpaku presented a rare opportunity to incorporate casual viewer participants into a study of cinemagoing.

After two years, I obtained permission to conduct a questionnaire survey at the Bunpaku film theatre. In consultation with a local research assistant and museum staff, I developed two versions of a questionnaire. Janice Radway's survey materials included in the appendices of *Reading the Romance* originally inspired my questionnaire format, yet the challenge of conducting a questionnaire survey in Japanese required certain modifications. Radway's extensive questionnaire asks participants to tick boxes next to statements with which they feel the strongest affinity. I was reluctant to circumscribe participants' responses in this way for several reasons. As a native English speaker with Japanese as a second language, I was hesitant to impose my own word choice on participants, and had some concerns about missing key points or patterns in the responses collected due to unnatural or misleading phrasing. As this is the first ethnographic study of general cinema viewership practices in Japan to be written in English, I sought to impose as few of my own assumptions on the language as possible. I attempted to keep the phrasing of the questions neutral, aiming to generate free responses from which I could identify recurring patterns in word choice and viewer preferences. The planning of the questionnaire took six months, after which I conducted a one-week survey at the Bunpaku film theatre from 18 May to 24 May 2016. Stamped addressed envelopes left in the museum lobby, and word of mouth transmission of the project's goals, enabled me to continue collecting questionnaire responses for three months after the Bunpaku survey ended, and introduced me to the film-screening clubs that would become my next sites of participant observation.

Making Contact and Making Mistakes

The questionnaire survey at the Bunpaku film theatre revealed many new elements. The first surprise was the gender of respondents. Depending on the day, the audience of the Bunpaku theatre was either gender-balanced or around 60 per cent male and 40 per cent female. There was a large gender bias in favour of male viewers in the final collection of survey responses. Though the questionnaire format was designed to be anonymous, the majority of respondents waived anonymity in favour of signing their names. From these details, as well as observations of respondents depositing questionnaires in the return box, the gender disparity was clear. Furthermore, in the interview stage of the project described below, far more men than women volunteered to participate in a filmed or recorded interview.

The historical background to this gender disparity is explored at greater length in Chapter 5, but I would like to briefly indicate some context here. Male patrons often came to the Bunpaku cinema alone, while women more frequently attended in couples or groups. Of the mixed-gender couples observed, women were often dissuaded or distracted from completing a questionnaire by the needs or preferences of their male partners. Several male attendees refused to wait while their female partners completed a questionnaire, requiring the women to abandon the project or take the half-completed questionnaire home to return at a later date. As the greater number of questionnaires submitted by post were from male respondents (judging by the senders' names), few of these half-completed efforts seem to have been submitted. A number of female attendees cited chores waiting at home as a reason for their lack of time to participate in the project. Further, female participants recalled that in the early postwar years it was difficult for a woman to attend the cinema alone (Coates 2017), as the cheaper seats and venues were considered unsafe due to the darkness of the theatre, and the location of many cinemas in areas 'full of temptation', as Koyama san described it in an interview, rendered going to the cinema alone a challenging prospect for many young women. While the household duties which preoccupy many women even (or perhaps especially) after a male partner has retired from work cause a disparity in available leisure time between the genders in the senior demographic which made up the largest number of participants in this study, this historic detail also suggests that perhaps women did not form cinema-going habits in the same numbers as men, and subsequently may not feel today that they have the expert status required to teach a foreign researcher about the history of Japanese cinema.

In order to achieve a gender balance among participants in the research project, I added further participant observation sites to the study, and conducted repeated informal interviews with a core group of twenty women who met regularly to participate in various cultural activities around Kyoto, including cinemagoing. As we established a friendship and began to meet several times each week in smaller groups, many of these female research participants expressed a sense of uncertainty in the questionnaire stage of the project. In particular, opening questions about the age of their first cinema visit and the number of times per week that they had visited the cinema made many women feel that their lesser cinema participation, compared to men of the same age, meant that they were not the target audience for my study. A number declined to complete a questionnaire in the first weeks of the project out of concern that their perceived non-standard cinema experiences would give me misleading information. Over the course of our friendship, which in many cases outlasted the duration of the project, I was able to better explain the breadth of the study. When my participant-friends felt comfortable enough to complete questionnaires and informal interviews, I learned that the design of this early questionnaire model had unintentionally excluded a number of women who were glad to participate after confirming that weekly cinema attendance was not a prerequisite for participation. While this error in design had risked recruitment to the project, it led in the end to the findings detailed in Chapter 5, which explores the gender of the cinema audience from 1945 to 1968. This mistake also demonstrated the accuracy of Bunpaku staff members' warnings that some research participants could be dissuaded from completing a questionnaire by the concern that they did not have the perceived 'right' answers.

Further to the pre-prepared questionnaires, an accompanying information sheet invited participants to send letters and emails to my university office. The first letter arrived on the second day of the survey, hand delivered by a lady who had completed the questionnaire the day before. Her letter, and those which followed, confirmed a tendency also evident in the questionnaire responses to draw a strong connection between memories of cinema and events in the respondent's personal life. This connection was so strongly assumed by participants that many began both letters and questionnaires with a version of the *jiko shōkai*, or self-introduction used when meeting a new person in Japan. This standard format includes the following personal information: name, place of birth, place of residence, and perhaps year of birth or job description. It seemed surprising that questionnaire respondents would volunteer this information despite my repeated promises, both verbal and in printed information materials, to anonymise personal data. Several participants and interviewees also produced personal life narratives structured like published biographical information presented in a magazine or newspaper, delivered by post or in person, with an accompanying personal letter or a completed questionnaire. Study participants would regularly contact me to correct details that they had misremembered, particularly in relation to the name of a film or actor. The materials generated by study participants are discussed more closely in Chapter 7, which considers the role of amateur creative activities in the development of a public identity as lay expert or keeper of cinema memories. Before narrowing down to the narratives of passionate 'expert fans' of Golden Age Japanese cinema, however, I will explore some common themes and overarching trends in the questionnaire responses which informed the extended interviews and discussions that followed the questionnaire survey described above.

Extending the Encounter

Approaching the collected questionnaires from the perspective of grounded theory, I generated interview questions from the recurring themes emerging from the questionnaire responses. I intended to film interviews for a documentary film project that developed alongside this study, and it occurred to me that a methodological innovation could be made by analysing the filmed interview footage using an iconographic method similar to that used for film text analysis. I proposed to structure the interviews quite freely, and to analyse not only my interviewees' words but also their physical modes of expression and the locations they chose for the interview.

Twelve Bunpaku patrons volunteered to take part in a filmed interview lasting around two hours, and everyone initiated lengthy communication by telephone, post or email in the months between first contact and interview. In addition to conversational emails and letters, interviewees also sent unsolicited life narratives, most often organised in the form of a biographical chart, as well as clippings from newspapers and publications that the participant perceived to be relevant to my study. One man with a high-profile public persona sent clippings and a DVD of his own media appearances, while another interviewee sent a package of academic articles on the topic of Kansai film clubs that became the basis of a literature review for Chapter 6. Several interviewees introduced me to friends who were also willing to be interviewed, to film centres and archives around Kansai, and to perceived-expert interviewees such as producers and actors active in the period 1945–68.

While none of the interviewees or questionnaire respondents were professionally active in commercial filmmaking, three interviewees organised *eiga sākuru* (film club) meetings in the Kansai area. Takeda san ran the Kinugasa eiga kai (film meeting), a monthly film screening near Ritsumeikan University's Kinugasa campus in the north-west of Kyoto. He invited me to join the meetings, which typically attracted 10–20 participants each month from a larger group of 150 contacts. The meetings ran for five to six hours, with a rotating volunteer *zachō* (session leader) selecting two or three films for screening and discussion. The regular organisation of the group was managed by Takeda san, born in 1943, Watanabe san, born in the 1950s, and Kubo san, born in 1923. On average, attendees were aged between seventy and eighty in the period I attended the screenings, from 2016 to 2018. The post-screening discussion was a particularly rich participant observation experience, as opinions were traded freely and often clashed. The Kinugasa eiga kai became my second field site for participant observation, and so opinions voiced at Kinugasa, and the summary emails Takeda san wrote each month to the whole group, have made a great impact on this study.

As Chapter 6 details, *eiga sākuru* are rarely productive of longer-term friendships outside the screening group. However, during the first meeting I attended, one member approached me to discuss her friend's experience of marrying an assistant director at Tōei film studios in the 1960s. We arranged a lunch meeting with this friend, and through both women I came to know a large group of sixteen female friends aged between seventy and eighty, connected by their experiences of working in the arts and marrying filmmakers. Their husbands have mostly now passed away, but the group kindly met with me monthly to discuss my project, and many sent materials from their husbands' collections, including film journals and personal records. This informal group, along with several study participants who adopted a mentoring role in relation to the project, forms a third layer of more casual ethnographic encounters loosely evolving around discussions of postwar Japanese cinema.

Across these three field sites, I followed the memory-work approaches developed by Kuhn and Stacey to address the question of what cinema meant to the first postwar generation of Japanese viewers. The recollections presented and analysed in this book should not be taken as historical fact. Rather, participants volunteered narrative communications focused on conveying the affect of the very particular moment in time that was post-defeat Japan to someone from a different generation and part of the world. Taking seriously the role of 'feelings without words' in the encounter between viewer and film text, I edited the filmed interviews described above into a short documentary film in order to capture and convey the affect of these interviews visually, as well as descriptively in the chapters to follow. These chapters include visual analysis of this footage, layering this information over the more classical discourse analysis of interview transcripts, letters and email communications about postwar cinema. In the final part of this introduction, I'd like to explore where this kind of analysis could lead.

Cinema Ethno-history as a Grounded Theory of Affect

Cinema is commonly understood as an affective medium, moving the bodies and minds of viewers. But when we speak with audiences about their experiences with cinema, how do we assess the affect of that experience and the resonances of its memory? How can we analyse affective response and how can we communicate our findings? I have no intention of attempting to compress the many definitions and complex histories of 'grounded theory' and 'affect' into one short section here. For the purposes of this introduction, I employ the basic definition of grounded theory as theory deduced from data collected, and I understand affect as defined by Gregory Seigworth and Melissa Gregg: 'vital forces insisting beyond emotion – that can serve to drive us toward movement, toward thought and extension' (2010: 1).

In considering how research on affect-laden narratives might generate something like theory, Dorinne Kondo emphasises 'the complexity and richness of experience', suggesting that 'to examine that complexity and richness in its specificity leads toward a strategy that expands notions of what can count as theory, where experience and evocation can *become theory*, where the binary between "empirical" and "theoretical" is displaced and loses its force' (Kondo 1990: 8). Foregrounding the voices, expressions and communicated feelings of my study participants, I aim to trouble this binary distinction and position experience and evocation closer to the heart of Japanese film theory.

At the same time, I am mindful of the warnings issued by audience studies researchers such as Ien Ang that 'material obtained by ethnographic fieldwork or depth-interviews with audience members cannot simply be treated as direct slices of reality' (1996: 39). Ang argues that viewers' statements are neither 'self-evident facts' nor 'immediate, transparent reflections of those viewers' "lived realities" that can speak for themselves' (Ang 1996: 39). By incorporating memory work, testimony and participant observation, I focus on the narratives created by audience members *around* the cinema, rather than attempting to reconstruct a factual historical account of the era.

In interviews and questionnaire surveys, I repeatedly encountered the phrase 'feeling without words' (*kotoba de ienai kanji*) in relation to the experience of cinema. This would seem to cohere with dominant understandings within the 'affective turn' of affect as extra- or pre-linguistic (Ahmed 2004). Yet this insistence on the insufficiency of words to communicate feelings or affects around the cinema causes problems when we attempt to map these affects in the form of academic writing. Incorporating not only linguistic accounts of affective experience but also observational detail from filmed interviews and participant observation appeared to be a way to address the difficulty of translating these 'feelings without words' into academic language.

These observational details take the form of a close reading of the performances of interviewees in filmed interviews. Following anthropologist Peter Stromberg's identification of 'enacted culture' within interviewee narratives, I apply a film studies-style close reading to the physical communications performed by speakers in recorded interviews. Stromberg argues that 'iconic manual gestures, direct quotation, emotional expressions, and facial portrayals' are tools used within the telling of a narrative 'to elaborate, enhance, and generally present [the speaker's] take on what that knowledge and its significance are' (2021: 429). Grouping these behaviours together as 'enacted culture', Stromberg notes that such performances 'can be used to channel emotional arousal into a particular perspective on reality and thereby either validate or transform conventions or experience' (2021: 428). Exploring how my interviewees used narratives about film viewership and cinemagoing to communicate their beliefs and experiences, I attempt to map where and how affect is generated and projected in these stories by analysing gesture and expression as the kind of augmentations to denotational speech which Stromberg argues are 'typically laden with affect' and thereby used to 'recruit listeners to the speaker's perspective' (2021: 428).

Participants in the interview sections of this study invested their stories with affect through their use of gesture in part as a demonstration of the repeated characterisation of cinemagoing and film viewership as something that generates 'feeling without words' or sensations that could not be verbally described. Yet despite their insistence on the inability of conveying their feelings about cinema in words, many participants returned again and again to the question of language, not only in our communications but also in the events and encounters they created around the cinema. Attending a number of regular cinema-related meetings, I was struck by how many incorporated some reference to talking into their titles, from the Eiga o kataru kai, or 'Meeting to Talk About Cinema', to the monthly film-watching club that suggested banning members from skipping the discussion session (*zadankai*) after the long day of screenings. Study participants' relation to cinema appeared to exist somewhere in the tension between 'feelings without words' and constantly *talking* about cinema.

Kondo warns that 'what counts as experience is itself a discursive production underlain by certain theoretical assumptions, and what is conventionally considered "theory" is always already a position in which a positioned subject has "personal" stakes' (1990: 303–4). How, then, can we generate a grounded theory of affect drawn from study participants' memories of their experiences? Following the style of Kathleen Stewart's *Ordinary Affects*, Ian Skoggard and Alisse Waterston have argued for an 'evocative ethnography' as a means of avoiding 'the danger in trying to grasp intellectually what is fundamentally felt and sensed' (2015: 111). They argue that 'affect theory must come to life by means of an integration of abstraction and illustration' (2015: 111). If we imagine the concrete elements of a spoken narrative that seeks to present an account of a lived experience as the abstraction of lived experience into communicable words and phrases, we can think of the accompanying gestures and expressions as illustrations which imbue the story with affect. Folding analysis of a speaker's gesture and expression into the study of the narrative told is one means of generating an evocative ethnography that attempts to communicate the feeling of being there when the story is told. We can never capture in words 'what transpires in the affective bloom-space of an ever-processual materiality' (Seigworth and Gregg 2010: 9). Yet in approaching gesture and expression as elements of 'enacted culture' which are part of thinking, understood as a 'public activity that engages with the environment' rather than an interior process hidden from the interlocutor (Stromberg 2021: 427), we can get a little closer to an understanding of the human processing of material encounter. Borrowing my study participants' particular phrasing and combining these with accounts of their expressions, gestures and a sense of their physical presences, I have tried to evoke not only the historical moments they described but also their feelings about these moments, both as their remembered emotions at the time and their feelings today, at a significant temporal distance from their childhood and teen years.

In the essay 'Thinking About Feeling Historical', Lauren Berlant emphasises that the historian not only thinks but also feels. The ethnographer of cinema cultures thinks *and* feels, of course, but also sees. Honing in on this last faculty, we can collect and organise affect-related material, and then generate theory, from the ethnographer's visual perception. After all, the etymological roots of theory point us towards the spectator, from *theōros*, through *theōria*, contemplation or viewing, to theory. This suggests the importance of visual perception to our assessment. While the documentary film that I produced alongside this study is of course a different kind of text from this book, the contribution of the film to the book should not be understated. In making and editing the film, I was engaged in an attempt to generate some theoretical position through visuality alone, and the details observed during this process have greatly informed the writing of this book.

David MacDougall, among others, has argued for the act of making ethnographic films as a mode of 'visual reasoning' (2005: 5). Referring specifically to the act of framing a shot in visual ethnography practice, MacDougall suggests that 'filming, unlike writing, precedes thinking', producing 'intensifications and reinforcements of perception' (2005: 4–7). This intensification sounds a lot like Seigworth and Gregg's affect, and indeed MacDougall is proposing that we expand our ideas of how to use images beyond simply 'adapting them to the rules of scholarly writing' (2005: 2). I want to suggest that we might think beyond the act of filming, of framing the shot, through to the editing process of filmmaking as a place to observe affect. Film editing as a process provides a means of studying expressions and mannerisms up close, and repeatedly. In the editing suite, the ethnographer can study the production and communication of affect extra-linguistically. 'If we are to gain new knowledge from using images,' MacDougall argues, 'it will come in other forms and by different means' (2005: 2).

Editing and screening early cuts of my documentary film, I noticed that my concurrent ethnographic writing project was becoming strongly influenced by the filmmaking process. I played short clips over and over, scrutinising participants' faces and micro-expressions as they recalled their memories of going to the cinema in the early postwar era. I manipulated these images through cutting and placing, with the goal of creating a certain affect for viewers of the documentary film; I wanted them to feel warm and nostalgic while watching, a feeling I imagined would match that experienced by the study participants both in their encounters with cinema and while recollecting those early experiences. To do this, I both thought carefully and guessed instinctively about the visual images and sounds that would create a sense of nostalgia. While I developed this project with the generous input of a number of visual anthropologists, my background in film studies has also influenced the process, resulting in a hybrid method in which I manipulate and read the images I have created with my research participants in the manner of a film analyst. Along the way, I began to feel a sense of something like theory emerging extra-linguistically. Throughout the chapters which follow, I incorporate visual analysis of filmed interviews and hand-drawn materials created by my study participants to bring a Film Studies mode of analysis into conversation with Anthropological ethnographic engagement. This blend of Film Studies visual analysis with Anthropological ethnography is an original methodological contribution of the study, proposing a particular kind of visual turn in ethnographic research and analysis to produce new kinds of insights, data and knowledge. Bringing analyses of gestural expression and narrative construction, including word-choice and emphases, together to create an evocative ethnography reveals the deep significance of the cinema, and talking about cinema, in the life experiences and memories of this generation.

Making the Historical Personal

While the voices and opinions of critics, journalists, directors, producers, camera operators, actors and other professionals proliferate, we have not yet heard directly from the postwar Japanese viewer. This book aims to place the voices of film viewers at the centre of a new account of postwar Japanese cinema. I distinguish the viewer from the audience here, and the viewers' own voices from third-person accounts of viewership. Following Fujiki Hideaki's path-breaking work (2019; 2011) and building on preceding Japanese-language accounts of viewership in Tokyo and Kyoto (Ueda 2007; Ueda 2012), I offer the first grounded ethnography of the Japanese cinema audience of the peak period of production and cinema attendance, alongside an account of their memories of the era.

Through the memories and opinions gathered here, I aim to build an ethno-history of postwar Japanese cinema that challenges several assumptions in current understandings of the period. For example, the account of the cinema theatres of Kansai as spaces where women often felt ill at ease alone runs counter to the expectations of many involved in the Allied Occupation of Japan (1945–52), when cinema was imagined as an accessible tool for social reform, and particularly those social reforms aimed at women and gender relations more broadly. Clearly the cinema was a more accessible space to some than others. And yet, although we may think of economic circumstances as a constraint for postwar cinema attendance, this seems to have been less of an impediment than previously assumed, as suggested by several male study participants who shared with me stories of obtaining entrance to cinema theatres without paying, particularly in their younger years. The picture of just who made up the audience in postwar Japan is in need of added nuance.

The close associations that research participants demonstrated between cinema experience and personal, historical and even national circumstances further tie this study to historical concerns at the collective, national and international levels. Connecting these large-scale political and social issues with more personal experiences through accounts of cinema viewership, in the chapters that follow I suggest some of the roles that cinema can play in building a sense of being, as well as meaning, in the world. Viewers interpret historical and news events through cinema content, and at the same time see the cinema not only as social education but also as a means to think, and feel, more freely. The dual questions, 'What kind of person is attracted to the cinema?' and 'How can the cinema make a certain kind of person?' are interwoven throughout the personal accounts and analysis that follow.

The first chapter develops a theoretical approach in response to the motivating concern that while ethnographic cinema projects have considered the question of memory (Stacey 1994), and cinema memories as ethno-history (Kuhn 2002), the *act* of discussing film-related memories itself has not been fully interrogated. This book's innovation is its focus on what we talk about when we talk about cinema. In this chapter, I propose an understanding of film-related memory as a mode of 'giving an account of oneself' (Butler 2005). Chapter 1 argues that talking about film offers people a way to negotiate their individual subjectivity and experiences as viewers, within the normative social frameworks modelled by classical cinema narratives. At the same time, performing a passionate relationship with a film text, creator or moment in cinema history allows the speaker a mode of distinguishing themselves as an individual subject. This chapter lays the ground for understanding the narratives that follow as at once performances of compliance with social norms, and at the same time as claims for recognition of an individual self with particular tastes, preferences and memories. Participants discussed specific films, situated memories relating to particular places and people, and more general memories of the times, including recollections of sudden historical and social change. In this aspect, the experiences of everyday life at key moments of the ever-changing postwar era are interwoven throughout this chapter and those which follow.

Chapters 2 and 3 consider the importance of the cinema as a place to be for the postwar viewer, understanding place as a geographical, historical and temporal location. This chapter situates different 'tiers' of cinema theatre within different areas of particular cities (for example, theatres that were perceived to be dangerous or lowbrow were often situated in entertainment districts with gambling and sex work establishments). Engagement with the cinema as a geographical place includes treating the space as a convenient place to rest, as well as a space of entertainment. The geographical locations of the cinema theatre itself had significance for participants in the study, particularly in the divisions between countryside, suburb and town, and between high-class and lower-class cinemas and areas. Talking about cinema can also be a way to represent and explore regional diversity, as well as memories of areas and spaces that are now greatly changed. Yet cinemagoing in postwar Japan also enabled viewers to see other areas of the world through imported films, both fictional and documentary. In the last section of this chapter, cinema viewership is discussed as a mode of being in the world, and a way for postwar viewers to situate Japan in the larger global context.

Postwar Japan as a particular historical location is explored through the viewers' memories that are analysed in Chapter 3. The film theatre is literally a place to spend time, but film content also inspires viewers to situate their memories in a particular time and place, for example during or after wartime. For the younger generation of participants in this study, born in the 1950s, Shōwa-era cinema (1926–89) provided a sense of a connection to parents and older family members. This is also true of the earlier generation, who described a sense of achieving a deeper understanding of their early childhood years during wartime by watching films set in that era. The use of repeated viewing as a way to manipulate or even freeze personal time reveals a mode of engaging with cinema as a memory aid, linked to place and family. The second part of Chapter 3 posits the sense of a memory fostered by cinema viewership as a kind of 'prosthetic memory' (Landsberg 2004), which allows viewers born into the aftermath of Japan's wars to find a personal mode of engaging with the events that shaped their early lives. This engagement with Japan's difficult wartime and early postwar histories introduces the use of cinemagoing as a mode of developing a postwar Japanese sense of self, explored in detail in the next chapter.

Chapter 4 develops a concurrent argument for talking about cinema as a device for communicating a way of being, by analysing study participants' accounts of learning new ways of living, being and thinking of oneself through cinema. For the generation who came of age in the 1950s and 1960s, the high-art element and international recognition of later postwar cinema led to a sense of Japan as a leading artistic force, generating positive associations with being Japanese. In contrast, the elder generation recounted a perception of Japan as being behind an imagined international standard cinematically in the early years of the postwar era, for example, importing films years after their distribution in other countries. While cinema was discussed as a mode of marking Japan's relative advancement or developmental lag related to other parts of the world, film viewership was also understood by many research participants as a mode of improving the individual, as well as the national, self. Chapter 4 takes a philosophical approach to the discussion of self and its formation and performance, which is not solely focused on the national. The second part of this chapter develops an account of viewership as a means of seeing and feeling surprising or emotional things, to argue for a dominant understanding among committed film fans of the viewing experience as a sensory invitation to sympathetic or ethical co-feeling and to historical understanding. The limits of this invitation to expand the self are considered in Chapter 5, which explores the restrictions that different demographics experienced accessing the cinema and its stories in postwar Japan.

This chapter explores the gender of the early postwar cinema audience and its implications for the sharp decline in cinema attendance that set in after 1958. During the Allied Occupation of Japan (1945–52), female audiences, particularly children and teenaged girls, became the imagined market for censored cinema content designed to support the democratic re-education of the Japanese populace. Yet an ethnographic approach gives a more conflicted picture of the cinema audience who viewed these narratives, demonstrating that an easy inference of mass female viewership from female-oriented film content, marketing and censorship is not supported by the memories of many female viewers. Analysing the memories of female viewers who engaged with the cinema and its stories between 1945 and 1968, this chapter posits some nuanced suggestions for the steep decline in cinema attendance into the 1960s. Contrasting the political goals that the Occupation forces expressed for cinema culture with the everyday restrictions experienced by female cinemagoers, this chapter reveals some structural limitations of using cinema narratives to generate political change. In the next chapter, the relationship between a political or politicised sense of self and cinema narratives is further explored, using the example of a dedicated politicised film club.

Chapter 6 turns to the dedicated cinemagoer with an account of historic film-related grassroots organisations in postwar Kansai. Beginning with the activities of the Kyoto Kiroku Eiga o Miru Kai (Documentary Film Viewing Group), an amateur film-appreciation group who attempted to produce their own film, this chapter traces the increasingly political activities of film clubs and circles in Kyoto. As we move into the 1960s, the second part of this chapter considers the relation of the kinds of selves developed through film viewership to the activism of the decade. Exploring how viewers found models for activist conduct, and also spaces and reasons to abstain from activism, in the very same cinema, we can see how cinema is used as a flexible signifier in discourse, particularly in relation to giving an account of one's personal politics.

Broadening out to consider the period 1945–68 more widely, Chapter 7 explores how the self is crafted through the narration of a relationship to cinema, investigating the creation and running of film clubs as a creative activity. Creative production around the cinema is extended to include the contemporary materials and collections of ephemera which interviewees brought to the interview, or gifted later, including copies of memos, notes or timelines of their lives, or copies of photographs and posters. The narration of the self is literally crafted in the hand-drawn maps and diagrams that participants shared with me, and in the social activities, media appearances and dedicated speaking events that key participants organised to share their stories about the cinema, prompting me to think about how viewers integrate their lives into cinema discourse. This final chapter argues for the study of discourses and communication practices, including the creation and collection of film ephemera, as an essential element in our understanding of film history.

The book concludes with a consideration of how to generate a new understanding of spectatorship in postwar Japan using hybrid methods drawn from Film Studies and Anthropology, as well as Memory Studies and oral history. Examining what the testimony of viewers can tell us suggests that audience members' memories can complicate extant scholarship. This short conclusion considers how we can account for the relationships between viewer organisations, industry and social organisations, arguing that English-language scholarship is missing a grassroots account of the impact of cinema on everyday life in Japan, both at the individual and the community organisational levels. How can we understand media reception as part of a larger project of constructing the self, and at the same time as a mode of being constructed by our socio-political and historical environment?

Koyama san, a stylish lady in her mid-seventies with a lifelong love of cinema, was among many research participants who expressed hope that film viewing might be a means of fostering more engaged, expansive and generous modes of relating to our histories and futures. Choosing her words carefully, but nodding to emphasise her point, she suggested that 'Japan's history and its postwar recovery can be felt through stories on film. It can be a good way to study the past, and I think that if children can watch good films that touch their hearts, they can become people capable of being moved emotionally.' Koyama san clearly associated cinema viewing with becoming a person who can be emotionally affected by others' stories, and she situated cinema as a technology which can develop these feelings. In the chapters to follow, participants express varied relationships to cinema, theatres, film content and narratives and particular actors and directors. Yet underpinning these diverse memories of cinemagoing is this foundational belief, that the cinema is somehow good for us, and that while the feelings evoked through cinema viewership may not be easily expressed in words, they are essential for our self-formation.

CHAPTER 1

What Do We Talk About when We Talk About Cinema?

> I agreed that what really matters is what you like, not what you are like . . . Books, records, films – these things matter. (Stephen Frears, *High Fidelity* 2000)

The opinions of the hapless protagonist of Stephen Frears' film adaptation of Nick Hornby's novel *High Fidelity* (1995) often set him up for ridicule, particularly those opinions, such as the above, that are shared by his arrogant friend and co-worker. At the same time, it's hard to argue with the sentiment at work in the claim above. From the position of the audience for Frears' film, which we may guess to include viewers who have chosen to engage with a film, based on a novel, about the formative role of music in one man's life, it would be difficult to argue that these things definitively *don't* matter. Yet Frears' protagonist misses the point by assuming that the popular culture materials that a person surrounds themselves with can tell us some fundamental truth about that person. Rather, this book argues that it is the way that people choose to represent their interest in these materials and their experiences of engagement with cinema culture that gives us some insight into how they build a public-facing self. Examining how people talk about cinema shows us how people use popular culture to communicate personal information such as personality, politics and formative anecdotes.

It may seem a little odd to begin a chapter on cinema viewing in postwar Japan with a quotation from a contemporary North American film adaptation of a British novel. As the following chapters will show, the idea that film connects viewers to worlds apart from their own was a central theme in research participants' accounts of their relationship with cinema culture in Japan. Film was seen by many as a means of engaging with other geographical locations and historical periods, and in this spirit many participants in this study were keen to emphasise their regular viewing of European and American cinema, as well as a tendency to keep up to date with contemporary films. Interest in US film narratives was particularly acute among the generations which made up the larger number of interviewees and questionnaire respondents, in part due to the formative cultural influence of the Allied Occupation of Japan (1945–52) and its legacies. Participants regularly quoted American cinema texts as indications of attitudes and sentiments that they believed to be also true of, or present in, Japan. At heart, the presumption of Frears' protagonist that the cultural texts we engage can tell us something about our own character is a claim encountered in many contexts. The purpose of this book is to explore how discourses such as this one form a network of claims about cultural engagement that reveal how selves can be communicated about through discussions of popular culture passions.

Of course, the researcher of cinema cultures is also such a viewer, who communicates through narratives about film engagement. Judith Mayne has perceptively pointed out that a major blind spot in the application of ethnographic methods to audience and reception studies is the tendency to forget that the researcher is also a viewer (1993: 84). Today, we are viewers and audiences almost from birth, long before we develop an interest in researching viewership, though the two are rarely unconnected. Ethnographers in fields such as Anthropology might argue a similar point – we have been ethnographers long before we begin fieldwork for a paper or a thesis. Growing up, we develop a mode of being in the world through observation and trial. And we must begin all over again when we enter a new language, country or culture, observing the people around us to understand how to manage our daily encounters.

Alongside its ethno-historical focus on the everyday experiences of cinema in postwar Japan, this book is also an ethnographic study of the role that discursive accounts of film viewership play in our self-representation in everyday encounters. In focusing on the encounters in which cinema is discussed, I situated myself not only as a fellow viewer but also as a fellow communicator. This chapter may as well have been called 'We Have Always Been Ethnographers', or even 'We Are All Interlocutors in the Cinema'.

As it is, I have settled on an adaptation of the much-borrowed title from a Raymond Carver short story (1981). Carver's original title, *What We Talk About When We Talk About Love*, has been adapted for projects as diverse as alt-country and rock albums, marathon memoirs and studies of love, hip-hop, war, god and Anne Frank. The short story is a recurring theme in Alejandro Gonzáles Iñárritu's *Birdman* (2014), in which the main character attributes his acting career to a note written on a napkin by Carver himself. What these adaptations have in common is a sense of inability to communicate emotion-related experience – how can we understand something as immense as war, as exceptional as Anne Frank's life, as phenomenological as another's experience of running, or hip-hop, or god? It may be significant that the original title of Carver's story was *Beginners*, taken from the line, 'It seems to me we're just beginners at love' (Carver 1981: 56). Many of us are also beginners when it comes to finding the words to communicate abstract feelings. Nonetheless, those who have borrowed Carver's title have attempted to communicate something to an audience through music, speaking or writing, just as Carver's characters attempt to communicate through stories about romantic engagement. While I believe it is impossible to fully understand or communicate the affective relation of film viewers to the cinema, participants in my study nonetheless managed to communicate an account of their most formative encounters with cinema through words and gestures at the moment of our own encounter, and I hope to communicate them to you in the chapters that follow. I don't expect to achieve this with any totality, so I have rephrased Carver's title as an open question.

This study explores the ways that film viewership becomes a discursive tool in the encounter – both the encounter with another, or others, and the encounter with the film text and its ideological content. By questioning what we talk about when we talk about cinema, I investigate how viewership and its related practices can play a part in the development of a self in conversation with other selves. Discourse on film viewership can therefore be understood as a mode of giving an account of oneself.

Giving an Account of Oneself

> When the 'I' seeks to give an account of itself, it can start with itself, but it will find that this self is already implicated in a social temporality that exceeds its own capacities for narration; indeed, when the 'I' seeks to give an account of itself, an account that must include the conditions of its own emergence, it must, as a matter of necessity, become a social theorist. The reason for this is that the 'I' has no story of its own that is not also the story of a relation – or set of relations – to a set of norms. (Butler 2005: 7–8)

This book considers both cinema content and the scene of communication about the cinema as sets of norms from which the story of the 'I' is, in part, constructed. Extending Michel Foucault's understanding of the formation of the subject, Judith Butler's *Giving An Account of Oneself* seeks to uncover 'a desire to know and understand that is not fuelled by the desire to punish, and a desire to explain and narrate that is not prompted by a terror of punishment' (2005: 11). Taking this line of inquiry into the leisure space of film viewership suggests how pleasure, rather than punishment, factors into the human desire to know, to understand and to explain and narrate the self.

Here we must recognise the associations of particular terminology for film studies and cultural studies, where the same terms carry different implications and meanings than in anthropological ethnographic practice, and in philosophical studies and the study of rhetoric. Judith Mayne argues that the insistence on 'real viewers', as distinct from the Film Studies and Media Studies 'subject', has generated some confusion in audience and reception studies as to whether the spectator may be 'readily defined as "either" a real person "or" a position, a construction' (1993: 32). While I refer to my study participants, interviewees and questionnaire respondents as viewers, I intend the simplest understanding of that word: people who regularly watch films in a variety of contexts, including the cinema theatre (historical as well as contemporary), formal and informal association meetings, on television, on DVD and on Internet streaming sites. These viewers are 'real' in the basic sense that they are individuals I have personally encountered, rather than composites or hypothesised viewers, yet at the same time my focus on film viewership as a technology in the ongoing project of self-construction posits this reality as less than total.

Mayne refers to the 'subject' of Media and Film Studies as a position or construction in the sense that the subject has often been hypothesised as 'subject to' media technologies. Theories such as the hypodermic syringe hypothesis (Lowery 1995: 400) imagined viewers as passive, absorbing the ideological content of popular media without resistance. Studies such as Ien Ang's *Watching Dallas* (1985) challenged this assumption by using ethnographic methods to argue for the viewer of film and media as a resisting subject, acting against ideological dictates such as the division of 'high' and 'low' culture. Yet Mayne warns that work that argues for an eternally struggling subject, as in some cultural studies and ethnography, can 'foreground yet another problem, and that is the tendency for the researcher to construct an image of the "spectator" or the "real viewer" every bit as monolithic as the "subject" of dominant ideology' (1993: 61).

The historical context of the ethnographic material discussed here spans the end of Japan's failed war and expansion (1931–45), through Occupation (1945–52), into Japan's economic growth and political activism of the 1960s. As such, study participants generally demonstrated an understanding of viewers' relation to media that phases in and out of the two positions outlined above. Most participants displayed awareness of the propaganda measures in place in the production and exhibition of cinema in Japan during the war and Occupation. At the same time, almost all at one time or another recounted their own experiences and awareness of responses that diverged from the imagined 'correct' attitude towards a particular text, theme or actor. Though several participants in the study appeared tempted to approach propaganda and state control of media during wartime as a means of understanding how so many in Japan's population became complicit with a fascist regime and colonial policy, cohering this claim with personal experiences of viewership presents challenges. It is in this space between imagination and experience, and between the national and the personal, as well as the past and the present, that I locate the complicated business of giving an account of oneself through discourse on cinema.

The 'subject' is therefore deployed in the fields of Media and Film Studies with rather different associations to the use of the same term in Anthropology and Cultural Studies. Butler's *Giving an Account of Oneself* presents an understanding of the 'subject' drawn from postwar Anglo-European philosophy, specifically the later writings of Michel Foucault. Butler interprets Foucault's subject as self-forming 'in relation to a set of codes, prescriptions, or norms' (Butler 2005: 17). This self is formed 'in ways that not only (a) reveal self-constitution to be a kind of *poiesis* but (b) establish self-making as part of the broader operation of critique' (Butler 2005: 17). *Poiesis*, from the Greek 'to make', is another borrowed and interpreted term, used not only in philosophical discourse but also in such diverse fields of study as Biology and Literature. As such, it is a particularly helpful image for thinking about a subject simultaneously brought into being and constructing itself through the norms and codes communicated by cinema, and in the practice of communicating that experience to another. The subject of Butler's philosophical argument is at once more active and engaged, and at the same time more potentially conflicted than the subject of classical Film and Media studies.

Furthermore, 'self-making as a part of the broader operation of critique' is an excellent description of what occurs in the encounters related in the following chapters, where study participants use discourse on cinema viewership to endorse, negotiate or reject certain social norms:

> The norm does not produce the subject as its necessary effect, nor is the subject fully free to disregard the norm that inaugurates its reflexivity; one invariably struggles with conditions of one's own life that one could not have chosen. If there is an operation of agency or, indeed, freedom in this struggle, it takes place in the context of an enabling and limiting field of constraint. This ethical agency is neither fully determined nor radically free. Its struggle or primary dilemma is to be produced by a world, even as one must produce oneself in some way. (Butler 2005: 19)

We can understand the encounter with a film text as the kind of 'enabling and limiting field of constraint' in which the struggling subject is contextualised. While Miriam Hansen argued for classical narrative cinema as 'the single most inclusive, cultural horizon in which the traumatic effects of modernity were reflected, rejected or disavowed, transmuted or negotiated' (2000: 333), Hideaki Fujiki has recently challenged film scholars to go beyond 'the conventional view that sees a film as the reflection, representation or mediation of history and society' in order to 'take into account a film's dynamic relations with diverse social and ecological dimensions that may include politics, economics, aesthetics, education, ethics, psychology, technology, and even the material existence of the object itself' (2020: 53). Thinking of the film viewer as a subject much like Butler's, who negotiates ethical agency in a context of often clashing norms and codes, we can see 'film's dynamic relations with diverse social and economic dimensions' (Fujiki 2020: 53) as the shifting terrain upon which this negotiation plays out.

Of course, the accounts of viewers' experiences presented here are filtered through a double layer of encounter and negotiation, in that participants in this study have encountered a film text, memorialised certain aspects of the encounter and then communicated this experience to me, and to one another, in subsequent interpersonal encounters, separated by a significant temporal distance from the original viewing experience. Butler frames the attempt to give an account of oneself in these terms:

> An account of oneself is always given to another, whether conjured or existing, and this other establishes the scene of address as a more primary ethical relation than a reflexive effort to give an account of oneself. Moreover, the very terms by which we give an account, by which we make ourselves intelligible to ourselves and to others, are not of our making. They are social in character, and they establish social norms, a domain of unfreedom and substitutability within which our 'singular' stories are told. (Butler 2005: 21)

I aim to take seriously the ethical implications of participants' accounts, at the same time understanding that the terms of our encounter will have rendered a degree of 'unfreedom and substitutability' to the telling of my interlocutors' stories. Butler suggests that 'what I can "be," quite literally, is constrained in advance by a regime of truth that decides what will and will not be a recognizable form of being' (2005: 22). In the chapters which follow, the question of what constitutes a 'recognizable form of being' is perhaps further problematised by the positionality of study participants relative to myself, as each encounter brought together a Japanese native speaker born between 1930 and 1955 with a Scottish woman born in 1985, raised outside Japan and communicating in her second language. What I may have assumed as a 'recognizable form of being' is perhaps quite different to the forms of being recognised by an interlocutor born in a different time and place, and raised in a different language. At the same time, my 'outsiderness' may have contributed to the recognition of some marginalised, non-normative or less recognised forms of being, and to study participants attempting to clearly articulate ways of being that a native speaker-listener may be expected to understand without explanation.

In the next section of this chapter I will briefly sketch some background for understanding the conceptualisation of the self and questions of being in the Japanese language context. An exhaustive handling of this broad topic is outside the scope of this study. Nonetheless, I wish to contextualise Butler's theory within recent socio-political and historical developments in understandings of self and selfhood in Japan. Throughout the chapters that follow, I aim to maintain an awareness of the self as something always compromised, always in process and often conflicting.

The Self in Japan and the 'Japanese Self'

The 'Japanese self' has been a popular topic in studies of philosophy, history and Japanese studies, as well as the focus of self-help books and theories of 'Japaneseness'. The ethnographic method of this particular study precludes any concept of a monolithic national self. However, I would like to sketch some key historical developments in popular understandings of the concept of the self in order to contextualise what 'self' might mean to my study participants. I am particularly interested in highlighting public debates of the postwar era that formed the environment in which participants in my study developed both a personal sense, and perhaps an ideological concept, of the self.

In the early 'feudal' history of Japan, Timothy Iles argues that social order was conceptualised as 'dividual' in that 'each member of society receives his or her sense of identity precisely from his or her role and function within that society' (Iles 2008: 37). With the end of the Edo period (1603–1867), and following the Meiji Restoration (1868), the question of the definition of 'the individual' and 'the individual's place in society' generated some public consternation, perceptible in social discourse as well as popular media (Iles 2008: 39). From the early Meiji era through to Japan's militarisation and Imperial expansion at the turn of the century, popular discussion centred on 'self-awareness, self-identification, and self-realization' (Jansen 1965: 88). While there is certainly a connection between national, and nationalist, rhetoric and conceptions of the self, it should be noted that multiple modes of conceiving and discussing selfhood tend to coexist. For example, the early twentieth century also saw a turn to discussion of the 'somatic self' imagined as a self in need of care. Nitobe Inazō's *Shūyō* (*Self-Cultivation*), published in 1911, furthered this kind of early 'self-help' approach to conceptions of selfhood. Paul Roquet has argued that the trend for self-cultivation and self-improvement of which Nitobe's text is exemplary was connected to a stall in upward mobility (Roquet 2016), as the workplace became flooded with educated young men. Discourses of self-improvement, promoted as a good in and of itself, as well as a means to promotion and personal success, became a dominant motif in many popular texts, such as the novels of Kikuchi Kan.

As militarisation gathered pace, however, discourses that focused on the individual came into conflict with the increasing nationalisation apparent in government rhetoric. The ruling classes began to interpret individuation as 'a symptom of political and social disintegration', and the expression 'individualism is a greenhouse for all radical ideas' became popular (Maruyama 1965: 527). The Imperial Rescript for promoting the National Spirit, issued in 1924, supported this interpretation of signs of individuation, or individualism, as 'subversive'. The 'subversive way of life' involved 'frivolous radical tendencies' and 'the habit of luxurious indulgence' (Maruyama 1965: 528), associating ideas of the self as individual with softness and waste, in contrast to the hardy aspirational rhetoric used to describe the ideal Imperial Japanese citizen. While *nihonjinron* (theories of Japaneseness) and popular literature tend to base claims of Japanese uniqueness on earlier periods of Japanese history, I am most concerned here with situating the memories recalled by my study participants within historical discourses of the era.

Many conceptualisations of the self that were offered in the first years of defeat and Occupation after August 1945 drew from an imagined historical or traditional Japan. This was true not only for discussions among the Occupied but also of the rhetoric of the Occupiers. In the context of a perceived hollowing out or death of the wartime Japanese self, the 'Japanese image' as imagined by the Occupiers offered a ready-made alternative. Psychologist Robert Lifton noted that survivors of the atomic bombings used the term '"*muga-muchū*," meaning without self or without a centre' to describe their personal state in the immediate aftermath of the war (Lifton 1967: 26). In this context, it is perhaps not surprising that Takie Lebra reports on the popularity of Ruth Benedict's *The Chrysanthemum and the Sword: Patterns of Japanese Culture* (1946) with everyday readers in Japan as well as (or perhaps more than) Japanese academics. Though

Benedict had not visited Japan at the time of her anthropological study, drawing on interviews with Japanese prisoners of war in the US for her government-commissioned work, 'many readers claim that they discovered their Japanese selves through this revelatory analysis from the United States, when postwar defeat had left them in a state of bereavement over their true identity' (Lebra 2004: 276). Benedict's survey made waves in Japan even before its translation was published in 1948, when Tsurumi Kazuko published a sharp critique in the popular journal *Shisō* (1947). Despite Tsurumi's criticisms of cherry-picked supporting evidence and a lack of historical context, *The Chrysanthemum and the Sword* sold well in Japan, and was re-released as a pocket-sized edition in 1967 for convenient personal use. An estimated 2.3 million copies have been sold in Japan (Fukui 1999: 73) and Benedict is quoted in Japanese high-school textbooks (Lummis 1982: 2). The influence of this study of 'the Japanese' has reached well beyond the academy in Japan, though US markets showed less popular interest.

Of course, postwar Japanese writers and thinkers generated their own theories of the Japanese self. In the context of defeat and public debates on war responsibility generated by the war crimes trials held in Tokyo and in former colonies, many saw an opportunity for self-definition (Kersten 1996: 42). Tsurumi claims this was the case for 'the majority of the Japanese', for whom the punishment of war criminals became 'a substitute for self-examination of their own responsibilities for the war' (Tsurumi 1970: 174). One result was a newly strengthened discourse of post-defeat humanism, imagined as a 'belief in the individual's capacity for self-cultivation and improvement' (Standish 2005: 220). Postwar Japanese humanist discourse propagated the view that 'each human is an autonomous being capable of self-determination and the assumption that through an individual's choices he/she can alter society and effect the course of history' (Standish 2005, 220). While many interpreted this idea in terms of social responsibility, directed both towards fellow citizens and in the construction of a 'good' nation within the global sphere, others felt the state–citizen relationship to be utterly tainted after the war:

> Immediately after the war, people were infuriated by the principle of 'sacrifice of the self in service to the state,' for this was the very principle that had led eventually to tragedy. As a result, the young totally ignored the prewar slogan and plunged into 'indulgence of the self, neglect of the public' – the ethic of the black market. At the same time, there appeared a new form of 'sacrifice of the self in service to the state.' Sacrifice was redirected from the special attack [*kamikaze*] unit to the Communist Party. (Hidaka 1984: 68)

Mostly born between 1935 and 1945, the participants in my study would have been 'the young' to which Rokurō Hidaka refers, though many were in fact too young in 1945 to have actively participated in the 'indulgence of the self'. Born in 1917, and aged twenty-eight in 1945, Hidaka is most likely referring here to the sentiments of his own generation rather than the group I have interviewed. It is possible, however, that children of this era absorbed some sense of the change in the relationship between state and self, growing up around this kind of discourse. Many of my study participants expressed conflicted feelings about the Communist Party, for example; Otsuka san and Yamashita san, born in 1943 and 1946 respectively, bitterly complained about having been made to watch Soviet films at school in Kyoto, where they claimed that 'all the teachers were Communists!'.

While the particular rhetoric of the concepts of self discussed here may have gone over the heads of young children in 1945, these same discourses shaped the postwar education system, particularly where grassroots or philosophically generated ideas chimed with the Occupation agenda. Two more conceptualisations of the postwar self dominated public discourse on the topic, along with the discourses on humanism, independence and Japanese uniqueness discussed above. The 'victim consciousness' stance identified by historian Narita Ryūichi approaches the period 1945–60 as a point when the historical narrative focused on the question of who was responsible for the catastrophe that 'we Japanese' had to endure (1999). In this formulation, the Japanese people are imagined as a collective, yet distinct from their 'bad government', who had deceived the people into collaborating in an aggressive and wrong war. James Orr argues that this ideological stance even casts the 'victim as hero' (2001), in accounts of suffering endured at home under fascist rule that suppressed individuality and starved the people literally and figuratively for the cause of over-extending resources in the colonised areas. Quite where the line between 'the people' and an imagined bureaucratic war machine was to be drawn remained unclear, yet this position propagated the idea of the Japanese people as a collective and suffering self. SCAP GHQ, keen to foster a more critical grassroots approach to government ideologies and 'Emperor worship' in the early years of the Occupation, supported this popular discourse.

At the more philosophical end of the spectrum emerged the '*shutai-sei* (subjectivity) debate', peaking around 1947–8 and reflecting a growing concern with the self in postwar Japanese intellectual culture. Concerned with philosophical issues of idealism and determinism, the *shutaisei* debate in Japan shared much with its European counterpart (Kersten 1996: 91). Umemoto Katsumi (1912–74), for example, argued that subjectivity was the missing link of Marxist theory. Suggesting that the autonomous actions of individuals motivated by commitment to a goal was consistent with Marxism's humanistic orientation, he argued for the incorporation of this idea into Marxist theory (Kersten 1996: 93). Conversely, Maruyama Masao argued that true autonomy required a whole new 'referential axis' to imagine a new kind of self which was not expressed by cultural productions, but was instead concurrent with it, as a 'supra-traditional, supra-cultural mechanism' (Kersten 1996: 114). The question of where exactly the 'self' was located in Japan, and how this concept could square with the recent fascist collaboration of Japanese citizens, gave rise to a range of discourses comparing Japan to an imagined 'West'. For example, Takeuchi Yoshimi argued that 'the fact that there was no resistance means that Japan is not Eastern, and at the same time, the fact that Japan made no demand for self-preservation (has no self), means that Japan is not European. In other words Japan is nothing' (Kersten 1996: 121).

While the *shutaisei* debate was by no means resolved by the 1950s, as Occupation ended and Japan began to grow more economically prosperous, as well as closer politically to the US, the idea of a 'Japanese self' as defined against other selves in other parts of the world began to change. As the 1964 Tokyo Olympics approached and Japan negotiated membership of the Organization for Economic Co-operation and Development (OECD), the *Asahi Shimbun* reported on new developments in citizens' consciousness of self as Japanese (1963). The Japanese government focused on Japanese advances and accomplishments, painting a picture of Japan as a leading nation. Focus on the relationship between the citizen self and government bureaucracy was maintained by the high-profile demonstrations against the US–Japan security treaty (Anpo), and the student movement. At the same time, however, the Japanese self was considered as part of an international community, on more equal terms than in the comparisons between Allied or American and Japanese bodies and selves at the beginning of the Occupation (Orbaugh 2007: 88).

My interlocutors grew up surrounded by the discourses sketched above. They also experienced a boom in discourses of self-improvement, self-help and self-care, notable in Japan's first 'self development seminar' (*jikokeihatsu seminā*), which was held in 1977. While the memories that participants have contributed to this study are limited to the period 1945–68, the language in which they were communicated has been shaped by discursive trends popularised since. Individual preferences became more central to discourses of cultural consumption as the mass culture discussed in the 1950s and 1960s transformed into the 'micromasses' of the 1970s (Roquet 2016). Before moving on to the conceptualisation of the viewer as a 'self' in Japanese audience and reception studies, I would like to take a brief look at the language this focus on the self in 1970s popular culture introduced, through psychological, linguistic and sociological discourses which fed into the mainstream.

From the 1970s, many Japanese psychiatrists and psychologists became concerned with the idea of Japan as a uniquely inter-personal society. From Doi Takeo's work on the concept of *amae* (loving dependence), which he considered particularly 'Japanese' (1973), to Kimura Bin's *Hito to hito to aida* (*Between Individuals*, 1972), scholars with a popular audience began to narrate the Japanese self as inter-dependent. This trend is also evident in linguistic studies, such as Suzuki Takao's claim that the Japanese language, unlike Indo-European languages, does not have a history of personal pronouns to distinguish between 'I' and 'you', 'we' and 'them'. Suzuki argues that Japanese language use implies that both the speaker or self, and the addressed, or other, are nonetheless members of the same group or culture (Suzuki 1984: 116). Emiko Ohnuki-Tierney similarly notes that the *kanji* compound used for the word 'human' (*ningen*) is in fact a composite of the character for 'person' and the character for 'among'. Ohnuki-Tierney argues that a Japanese vision of society does not consist of atomised individuals; 'instead, *ningen* is dialectically defined by both humans and society . . . Such a society consists of interdependent individuals' (1990: 207).

Kimura was most interested in a common term for 'self': *jibun*. He understood *jibun*, composed of characters signifying 'self' and 'part', as a concept which was not fixed or continuous, but dynamic and dependent on others. Hamaguchi Eshun (1977) and Murakami Yasusuke, Kumon Shumpei and Satō Seizaburo (1979) similarly conceptualised the self as always in relationship to others, and criticised Benedict's scholarship on collectivist ideologies as distinct from individualist. Though these scholars disagreed with Benedict's distant analysis of Japanese culture, it is interesting to note that the popularity of her book in Japan in fact supports their argument for a Japanese self as something that comes into being through encounter with others, residing conceptually in the spaces between people, between words and ideas, and perhaps also between cultures. The next part of this chapter deals with how this self has been discussed and understood throughout more than a century of Japanese popular film culture.

Cinema and the Self in Japan

Cinema Arrives in Kansai

The cinema is intimately tied to concepts of the self, in Japan as in many other corners of the world. The development of cinema technologies roughly simultaneously in France and the US became an occasion for those two nations to claim technical prowess as a national characteristic. Early adopter nations of cinema technologies such as Japan congratulated themselves on their proximity to and adaptation of this technological development. Yet at the same time, popular discourse expressed lingering concerns about a perceived Japanese inferiority, related to the identity of adopter or adapter nation understood in opposition to the technological global leadership demonstrated by Europe and America. As the first cinema apparatus appeared some thirty years after the modernisation drive of the early Meiji era, Japan's reliance on adopting technologies from the dominant Anglo-European world could be interpreted as a failure of Japanese modernity. On the other hand, skilful adaptation of this same technology could prove that Japan had adapted to the modern world.

In fact, this technology became an opportunity to define regional modernity in the Kansai area as much as Japanese national identity in relation to the rest of the world. Japanese publications, including popular books and newspapers, had been reporting on Thomas Edison's work as early as 1890, before his Kinetoscope was even patented (Gerow 2014: 159). The history of the introduction of cinema, as both concept and apparatus, has been thoroughly documented by Tsukada Yoshinobu in his *Nihon eigashi no kenkyū* (*A Study of Japanese Movie History*, 1980), which contains newspaper and magazine articles reporting on the early stages of Edison's work. While Tsukada's account is near exhaustive, here I want to draw attention to the importance of this moment in cinema history for defining regional identity, a motivating aspect of many of my study participants' interests in cinema.

This slice of Western Japan, encompassing the cities of Kyoto, Osaka and Kobe, is home to a diverse range of regional identities, accents, histories and politics. Though the borders of Osaka and Kyoto are blurry, and you can travel from the centre of one city to the other in under one hour by train, the cities are fiercely competitive. Everything from sports teams to dialect, accent to social norms, is daily drawn into a discourse of 'Kyoto versus Osaka'. Kobe, though not geographically distant, is often spoken of as a place from another time, largely rebuilt after a major earthquake in 1995. Though I met most of my study participants at three field sites in Kyoto, an equal number live in Osaka, Kobe and the regions in between, travelling to cinema theatres and events in Kyoto several times each month. Japan's cinema culture is yet another opportunity for inter-regional rivalry, particularly around the question of where Japan's cinema history can be said to have 'begun'. This depends not only on regional loyalties but also on a personal definition of what counts as 'cinema'.

Edison's Kinetoscope arrived in Kobe in November 1896. The Kinetoscope was not a movie projector as we know the device today, but allowed a single viewer to look through a peephole to see moving images, similar, as commentators noted at the time, to the Japanese *gentō* or moving-picture lantern. Edison's exhibition remained open for five days from 25 November 1896. Kobe city built a commemorative theatre in Meriken Park in 1987, complete with a plaque claiming the site as the birthplace of cinema in Japan (see Figures 1.1–1.5).

By January 1897, however, this technology was superseded by Edison's newer Vitascope and the Lumière brothers' Cinématographe, which allowed for large-scale projection, meaning that several viewers at once could take part in these cinematic experiences. While the team bringing Edison's Vitascope to Tokyo hosted a premiere at the Kinkikan Theatre on 6 March 1897 (Komatsu 1996: 433), the Lumière Cinématographe was brought to Japan by businessman Inabata Katsutarō (1862–1949) in

Figure 1.1 Kobe Meriken Park entrance.

Figure 1.2 Kobe Meriken Theatre monument commemorates the first film screening from overseas.

Figure 1.3 A sculpture in Kobe Meriken Park commemorates the location's important place in Japanese cinema history.

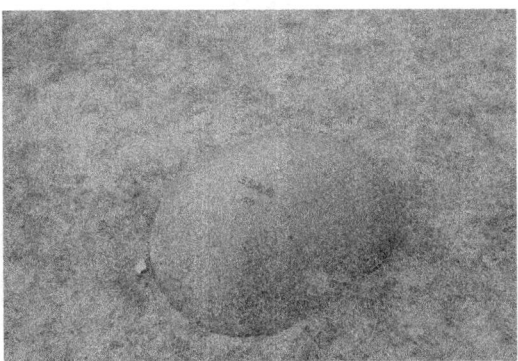

Figure 1.4 Stones in Meriken Park commemorate important figures in Japanese cinema, such as Ozu Yasujirō.

Figure 1.5 Stones in Meriken Park commemorate important figures in Japanese cinema, such as Kyo Machiko.

January of that year. For many of my interlocutors, Inabata's screening was considered the first true instance of cinema in Japan. But which screening? Though Inabata hosted the first open commercial screening at the Nanchi Enbujo Theatre in Osaka from 15 February 1897, he had first stopped in his hometown of Kyoto for a trial screening lasting for around two weeks from 20 January 1987, where Inabata and François-Constant Girel (1873–1952), a Lumière cinematographer, addressed difficulties including the special installation of electricity at screening sites (Inabata 18 March 1897/Letter 1: 1). The commercial Kyoto screening later opened to the public from 2 March 1897, and Inabata wrote to the Lumière brothers of the screening's success, with an average of one thousand viewers per day paying 10 sen each in admission fees which, he noted, was 'all that we can charge Kyoto residents' (*c'est tout ce que l'on peut faire payer pour la poche*

Figure 1.6 A monument near Kyoto's Nijō castle marks the spot of an early film studio.

des habitants de Kyoto) (Inabata 18 March 1897/Letter 1: 2). Needless to say, both Kyoto and Osaka city governments have also erected plaques claiming their respective sites as 'the birthplace of the Japanese cinema' (see Figures 1.6–1.9).

Representing the Japanese Self Onscreen

Aaron Gerow writes of the reporting and study around this early period of cinema as 'a discursive history' (2014), and it is in the spirit of discourse analysis rather than in pursuit of historical accuracy that I want to consider how the beginnings of film in Japan are discussed in Western Japan today. While Edison is known to have employed a Japanese assistant at Menlo

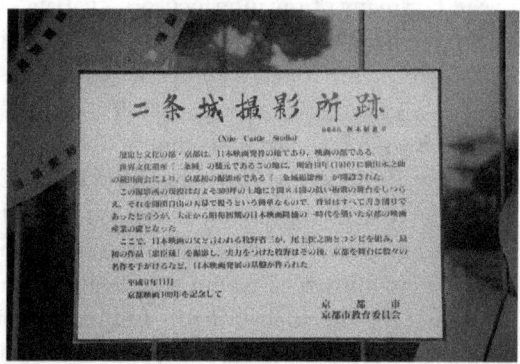

Figure 1.7 A monument near Kyoto's Nijō castle marks the spot of an early film studio (close-up).

WHAT DO WE TALK ABOUT WHEN WE TALK ABOUT CINEMA? 41

Figure 1.8 A sign outside Kyoto's Rissei elementary school commemorates the 'birth of the Japanese cinema'.

Figure 1.9 A sign outside Kyoto's Rissei elementary school commemorates the 'birth of the Japanese cinema' (close-up).

Park from 1904, Inabata was able to arrange to bring the Cinématographe to Japan through his personal contact with the Lumière brothers, having met them in 1877 at the La Martinère technical school in Lyon, where Inabata studied on a prestigious scholarship from 1877 to 1885 (Fooken 2020: 189). By 1896, when the three met again, Inabata was a respected businessman in the textile industry with an aspirational international life. In many ways, Inabata's public persona demonstrated the ideal modern, international Japanese citizen, succeeding in commerce and holding his own with peers around the world. At the beginnings of cinema in Japan, Inabata's story was perhaps the more attractive to a Japanese audience and news readership caught up in the anxieties of competing with an imagined modernised 'West'. A number of participants in this study, including professional film industry personnel, emphasised Inabata's international academic credentials and networking in their accounts of Japan's early cinema history.

Daisuke Miyao notes that the thirty-three Lumière films produced in Japan demonstrate 'how the Orientalist fantasy was contested when it encountered the reality of Japan' (2020: 11). Girel and Gabriel Veyre (1871–1936), another cinematographer sent to Japan by the Lumière Company, appear to have been tasked with capturing everyday life in Japan at the end of the nineteenth century, at least as that everyday life was imagined by Europeans steeped in the aesthetic traditions of Japonisme (Miyao 2020: 11–12). However, the shots that they captured showed Japanese people interacting with the camera and the cinematographers in a way that Miyao argues demonstrates the development of 'a site of negotiation between the French cinematographers and the Japanese people in front of the camera' (2020: 12).

Miyao argues that the subjects of the Japanese Lumière films practised a '"nativized Orientalism," conscious acts of self-exoticization of the non-European people for the Orientalist gaze' (2020, 12). Non-Japanese cameramen emphasised difference, exoticising the representation of Japan in order to increase the attractiveness of their footage for viewers in Europe. However, the negotiation space of the films contains detail that suggests the Japanese participants' agendas as well. For example, Inabata himself agreed to take part in a film showing a Japanese family at dinner, *Repas en famille* (1897), including his daughters Kiku and Mari. During this short film, Inabata looks directly at the camera three times (Miyao 2020: 45) in 'a self-conscious performance of the exotic Other' (Miyao 2020: 46). While Inabata performs a self-orientalised Other, however, he also acts out a specific class performance. Miyao notes that Inabata's kimono and *haori* jacket with family crests, as well as the women's hairstyles, 'are too formal for a daily scene' (2020: 42). In this way, wealthy and worldly participants such as Inabata insisted on an equally fictionalised representation of Japanese people as models of civilisation and deportment. Michael Baskett argues that the dispatching of Japanese cameramen to the Russo-Japanese War in 1904 demonstrates that the 'ideological value' of film technologies for constructing and controlling the national image was well understood in Japan in the early twentieth century (Baskett 2008: 7). I would suggest that this potential was also apparent to viewers and readers of early discourse on cinema, in the popularisation of Inabata's creation myth over Edison's, and in the fierce debates which still rage today as to whether Kobe, Osaka or Kyoto can be considered the birthplace of Japanese cinema.

The introduction of film technologies to Japan was a moment to consider the self, both personal and national, and in relation to other selves outside Japan. This was often a fraught endeavour, as Takeuchi Yoshimi noted, arguing that 'the contradictory need to both catch up with the West by emulating it, and establish a nation-state based on difference, has created fundamental aporia in the modern Japanese experience' (quoted in Gerow 2010a: 31). Takeuchi worried that modernity had become associated so much with the 'West' that the 'Orient' now faced an 'impossible agenda' which could lead to 'definition of the Orient as that which can never be a subject' (quoted in Gerow 2010a: 31). While Gerow cautions that the shock of modernity itself may have occurred before or after the arrival of cinematic apparatus in Japan (Gerow 2010a: 28), the question of Japanese selfhood and subjectivity appears imbricated in discourse on this historical moment. Iwamoto Kenji argues that 'as cinema was born in America, the way of looking is Edison's way of looking' (2006: 8). Yet at the same time, 'cinema was used to cultivate national awareness and form the Japanese national self-image, with emphasis on tradition and history' (Iwamoto 2006: 9).

While bureaucrats, journalists and critics may have worried about what cinema as imported technology meant for a national self, many individual selves pictured onscreen appeared delighted by this first view of themselves from the outside. This state of 'wondrous self-contemplation' is indicated by actor Onoue Matsunosuke's account of seeing himself onscreen for the first time: 'It was as if I were able to watch my own face while I was asleep!' (High 2003: 7). The attraction of watching moving human physicality in close detail in the early years of mass cinema culture blended smoothly into the Imperial state's increasing interest in showing images of aspirational and inspiring 'Japaneseness' onscreen as the nation expanded its borders, occupying Taiwan from 1895 and Korea from 1910.

Audiences, Viewers and Conceptions of Selfhood

Japan's first film critics and scholars did not miss the political and social affordances of commercial cinema. Gonda Yasunosuke's *Minshu goraku no kichō* (*The Foundations of Popular Entertainment*, 1922) presented an account of audiences as members of a new class generated by the growth of capitalism (Fujiki 2014: 78). He criticised other theorists for not engaging with the everyday realities of 'the people', arguing for moviegoing as a learning process through which viewers 'unintentionally trained themselves as social subjects conforming to the current regime' (Fujiki 2014: 80).

As Fujiki notes, Ministry of Education bureaucrats and cultural critics tended to conflate 'audiences' with 'the people'. However, '"the people" is an unavoidably idealized or abstracted concept' (Fujiki 2014: 80). Fujiki cautions that both 'the masses' imagined by the bureaucrats of the 1920s and 'the nation' as imagined in the 1930s 'were all nothing more than ideals, and very far removed from reality' (Fujiki 2014: 92).

Gonda's imagined audience was not in dialogue with the bureaucracy, however, but with film itself, both as text and interface. Gerow notes that Gonda emphasises 'how lower class spectatorship becomes the "subject" of film entertainment, effectively finishing the film as it is viewed in the theatre' in a conceptualisation that could be understood as 'an early form of British cultural or reception studies' (2010b: 37). Gonda's were among the first audience surveys in Japan, positing the viewer as 'the subject of culture' and the film as a text in which spectators could 'insert their everyday emotions and ideas' (Gerow 2010b: 40). He suggested that 'viewers' selves are projected out (*tobidasu*) because of their work with the photoplay to turn the flat into the three-dimensional, an unconscious but difficult task' (Gerow 2010b: 41). The cinema becomes a means by which the viewer can both develop a kind of 'self' and send that self out into the world. In *The Principles and Applications of the Moving Pictures*, Gonda's viewer-self (*jiko*) is 'active' and relatively independent, a point he illustrates with the example of film audiences crying at different moments during a screening, while he imagined that a theatre audience would cry at the same moment (Gonda 1914: 415). While film studios continued to survey audiences intermittently for commercial purposes, however, this conceptualisation of viewer as self soon gave way to the idea of the audience as a group which could be educated in the national ideals of militarising Japan through cinema propaganda.

After the war, studios, newspapers and university groups continued audience surveys. However, the focus was largely on demographic and content issues, and surveys tended to continue the pre-war and wartime understanding of the audience as a mass. Ironically, SCAP GHQ's determination to promote the values of a modern capitalist democracy, including a positive valuation of individuality, nonetheless imagined the Japanese cinema audience as an ill-defined mass whose homogenous ideas could be changed all together in the same direction. Viewers were counted and surveyed rather than interviewed, with some conflicting results.

While the viewer was not yet discussed as a 'self' in audience studies of this period, filmmakers were concerned with the question of self, in the context of the public debates described above. For example, Kurosawa Akira referred to the controversial heroine of his first post-war film,

No Regrets For Our Youth (*Waga seishun ni kui nashi*, 1946), as a woman who maintained such a sense of 'self'. 'I believed then that it was necessary to respect the 'self' for Japan to be reborn' (Kurosawa, quoted in Hirano 1992: 195). Here Kurosawa connects film content to the drive for a new kind of selfhood evident in popular discourses such as those described above. Both Kurosawa and SCAP GHQ posited the film audience as having the potential to be inspired by themes relating to selfhood and the development of a postwar self, but Gonda's discourse of the viewer as a self in encounter with the film text was yet to be picked up again.

With the introduction of television in the 1950s came *jōhō kōdō* (information behaviours) studies, part of a theory of *jōhō shakai* (information society), translated from American communication studies (Takahashi 2016: 59). Drawing from effects theories, uses and gratifications research, and advertising market research, Japanese scholars applied translated questionnaires in common use in American communications studies to Japanese audiences. Uses and gratifications studies became particularly popular in Japan from the 1970s, after prominent mass communications scholars A. S. Edelstein and Elihu Katz presented their work at the International Conference of Psychology in Tokyo. Both the National Association of Commercial Broadcasters in Japan (1976) and the academic community began to conduct empirical research on television viewership inspired by US uses and gratifications studies (Takeuchi 1976; Okada 1976; Hiroi 1977; Tokinouya and Sato 1977; Mizuno 1977; Miyazaki 1981). While the television viewer was understood as an individual in studies that focused on the desires of television consumers, these studies were generally restricted to home viewing and interpreted comparatively in relation to the US (Takahashi 2016: 60). The viewer was simultaneously imagined as apolitical and isolated, as in Tokinouya and Hayashi's claim that 'the levels of gratification gained from interpersonal communication in terms of politics are low in Japan' (1981: 184–5, trans. Takahashi). Toshie Takahashi notes that claims about Japanese collectivism and a desire to prove 'particularities of Japaneseness' dominate this era and body of work on viewers (Takahashi 2016: 61).

Takahashi's own study is one of the first ethnographic accounts of Japanese viewership practice to be published in English (2016). Engaging with television viewers in their own homes through recorded interviews and participant observation, Takahashi uses the practice of television viewing to make a case for the division of society in Japan according to principles of *uchi* (in-group) and *soto* (outsider group) (Takahashi 2016: 110). While Takahashi's argument in some ways harks back to the claims of Japanese uniqueness which she identifies in postwar uses and gratifications studies, her use of these concepts in relation to the new technologies of on-demand television and Internet updates one of the most persistent themes in discourses of self in Japan. *Uchi* and *soto* are spatial metaphors for kinship, but they also provide a useful lens for the study of self-cultivation and self-care. Like Janice Radway's interlocutors' use of reading practices (1984), Takahashi finds that her interlocutors use television viewership and Internet activities to carve out personal space from the demands of the other selves around, whether at home or at work (Takahashi 2016: 171). She also notes that many interlocutors took the invitation to speak about viewership as an opportunity to discuss ideas of Japanese social and cultural norms as opposed to conditions in other parts of the world (Takahashi 2016: 218). My own study participants responded in a very similar way, connecting viewing experiences and memories to wider sociopolitical and historical events and discourses. At the same time, however, the implications of participants' choice to attend public screenings allows us to consider how we can use viewership and fan practices to carve out personal spaces even within public spaces, and to think about our relation to the public through the personal.

(Re)forming the Self through Cinema

There is historical context for the question of reforming the personal through public encounters in postwar Japan. SCAP GHQ censorship officials imagined the postwar Japanese viewer in terms of this kind of malleable selfhood, though their approach to engaging with these selves was articulated in terms of mass publics and group audience response. Beginning the Occupation of Japan on 2 September 1945, the offices of SCAP headed by General Douglas MacArthur identified the cinema as a means to educate Japanese viewers away from pre-war and wartime attitudes (H. Kitamura 2010: 42). On 22 September 1945, Head of the Motion Picture and Theatrical Division of the Civil Information and Education Section (hereafter CIE) David Conde met with film and theatre producers and forty Japanese Bureau of Information officials (Brandon 2006: 18). Reading from a draft document entitled 'Memorandum to the Japanese Empire', written two days earlier, he urged those present to cooperate with the Occupation's goals, particularly in promoting 'fundamental liberties' and 'respect for human rights' (SCAP 1945). Conde advised producers to develop entertainments to educate citizens about democracy, individualism and self-government (Brandon 2006: 18).

While this particular draft was ultimately not sent to the Japanese government, SCAP circulated a 'Memorandum Concerning Elimination of Japanese Government Control of the Motion Picture Industry' on 16 October 1945, directing an end to wartime censorship, 'to permit the industry to reflect the democratic aspirations of the Japanese people' (Allen 1945: 3). However, censorship conducted by the CIE itself began that same month. On 19 November 1945, a list of thirteen themes and topics identified as problematic followed. Number nine targeted media narratives that 'dealt with, or approved of, the subordination or degradation of women' as undesirable, while number twelve warned against stories and images that 'approved the exploitation of children' (H. Kitamura 2010: 36; Brandon 2006: 94). Filmmaker Iwasaki Akira, who was forced to work closely with the censors, recalled that the Occupation personnel 'were convinced that cinema was a most important instrument for effecting the necessary changes to make Japan a peaceful and democratic nation' (1978: 304).

Information Section personnel instructed Japanese filmmakers in the kind of content understood by the Occupiers to be desirable, assessing synopses and screenplays before final film prints were censored or suppressed. The Motion Picture division of the CIE, while not officially recognised as a censoring body, checked synopses, screenplays and filming plans, while the Civil Censorship Detachment (hereafter CCD) examined prints. From 28 January 1946, films required a 'pass' from both the CIE and CCD in order to be released to cinema theatres (Hirano 1992: 40), yet SCAP influence over film content was quite uneven and changed over time. Initially scenarios were examined by Conde himself, despite having no knowledge of the Japanese language (Iwasaki 1978: 308). He was assisted by a number of Japanese-American officers, whom Iwasaki alleges had 'less than perfect command of Japanese' (Iwasaki 1978: 308). Conde was replaced in July 1946 by George Gerke, a member of the Information Division with pre-war experience in the American film industry.

In June 1949, film content control was ceded to Eirin (Film Ethics Regulation Control Committee, Eiga Rinri Kikō). Although officially independent from the Occupation and the Japanese government, the opening paragraphs of Eirin's Code suggest a shared understanding of cinema as a means of influencing audiences, citing the 'great spiritual and moral influences' of the motion pictures as motivating cause for a perceived need to 'prevent any picture being produced which will lower the moral standards of those who see it' (CIE 1949a). As Kirsten Cather notes, Eirin also 'required GHQ approval for the initial set-up of the organization and its regulations' (2014: 98) and the CIE and CCD also inspected the films for the first six months of Eirin's takeover. CIE officers trained Eirin inspectors at the CIE office in the Hattori building in Ginza and the

CCD continued to check pre-production synopses and scripts until the end of 1949 (Cather 2014: 98). Post-production censorship was carried out by the CIE until the end of the Occupation in April 1952.

Overall, impressing new social values on young Japanese minds was a central goal of film contents control between 1945 and 1952, though after the Occupation Eirin's focus shifted towards sexualised imagery (Cather 2014). While Eirin was not a censorship system as such, it became increasingly influential over the 1950s. In 1954 the Prime Minister's Office created a Strategic Committee on Films, Books and Other Media Harmful to Youths (Seishonen ni yugai naru eiga shuppanbutsu nado taisaku senmon iinkai) and the first film to be officially designated 'harmful' was identified two months later (Cather 2014: 108). An age-based film classification system was introduced in 1955, and by 1957 the Eirin seal had become a legal requirement for all films screened publicly in Japan (Grealy, Driscoll and Cather 2020: 12). August 1959 brought revised Eirin regulations which reorganised the original eight sub-categories of Eirin's focus – Nation, Society, Law, Religion, Education, Mores, Sex, and Cruelty and Filth – into five (Cather 2014: 114–15). Cruelty and Filth was eliminated, Law became Law and Justice, and Sex and Mores were reorganised into one single category (Cather 2014: 115). Cather notes that a key change was also made to the Eirin Code preface: 'the moral standards of spectators' became 'the ethical standards of spectators' and the phrase 'films must aim at uplifting the moral outlook of spectators' was deleted entirely (Cather 2014: 115). New regulations were introduced in 1965, and by 1968 the Independent Film Distribution Association (Dokuritsu Eiga Haikyu Kyokai) had been set up to bring independent filmmaking 'into a cooperative and organized union with Eirin' (Cather 2014: 125). While both the systems of control and the institutions which operated these systems changed regularly during the period 1945 to 1968, a unifying feature of all the interventions in film culture discussed above is their foundational premise: that film influences those who watch it to the degree that social attitudes, political affiliations and even lives can be changed by cinema culture.

Cinemagoing in Japan: 1945–1968

The popularity of film grew rapidly from 1945, culminating in a peak admissions count of 1,127,452,000 in 1958 (Motion Picture Producers Association of Japan, 2017). In interviews, many viewers recalled the Occupation era as one without many entertainment options. Koyama san recalled, 'We didn't have much in the way of entertainment, because it was an era without television or video games.' Nodding, she smiled wistfully and remembered, 'In the evening, at the local park, a screen would go up' – here Koyama san drew the modest scale of the screen with one hand, as though bringing the memory up before her eyes – 'so we could have the experience of watching a film.' She smiled broadly. 'That was only around once a year, in my early childhood.' 'Everyone would stand around waiting for it to get dark. As the screen went up, we would all get excited (*wakuwaku shite*).' Koyama san turned to me with sparkling eyes and a big smile, nodding rapidly while mimicking a child's excited expression. Her performance of the happiness of a viewer 'without much in the way of entertainment' anticipating a rare film-screening event emphasised the special occasion that cinema viewing could be for those without much else to divert them.

The cinema was remembered as the major attraction for young children in particular, in comparison to radio broadcasts and reading materials. For example, Takeda san referred to the cinema of his childhood as 'king of entertainments' (*goraku no ōsama*) during our interview, while Hashimoto san recalled begging his elder sister to take him to the theatre again and again. In his final report on the Occupation, General MacArthur noted, 'The prefectural team, SCAP, approached the Japanese people through a variety of channels; these included newspapers, motion pictures, street shows (*kamishibai*), radio programs, courses of instruction . . .' (MacArthur et al. 1994: 203). The list goes on, but only two cited channels are child-oriented, and study participants clearly stated their memories of a childhood preference for the cinema over street shows. In this sense, the cinema provided a young and impressionable audience for SCAP's carefully crafted and censored film content.

This content focused on communicating SCAP's key reform priorities to mass audiences. In October 1945, MacArthur included equal rights for female citizens in five priority reforms ranging from democratisation to demilitarisation. Universal suffrage, female admission to national universities and the elimination of the pre-war adultery law were ratified, and the Land Reform Law of October 1946 allowed female descendants to inherit family property for the first time. By May 1947, support for gender equality had been included in Article 24 of the postwar Constitution, while Article 14 outlawed discrimination on the basis of sex. The legal protection of gender equality was conceived as a means to democratise postwar Japan, and so filmmakers were advised to include gender-equal characters and narratives in cinema productions. The everyday impacts of this aspect of the Occupation censorship process are discussed in further detail in Chapter 5, which deals with gender and the cinema audience.

The Japanese viewer-self was imagined as underdeveloped in relation to its US counterpart. General Douglas MacArthur even suggested that 'the mental level of the average adult Japanese during the Occupation period had been that of a (presumably American) twelve-year-old' (Hirano 1992: 45). This imagined deficient self was to be educated, modernised and improved through engagement with the cinema.

Hiroshi Kitamura notes that as commercial screenings revived in cities after the war, 'filmgoers increasingly took part in group activities to share their excitement and passion in larger communal settings' (H. Kitamura 2010: 174). *Eiga sākuru* (film circles) were formed at work and through unions, while schools and university campuses hosted study groups and clubs (*eiga kenkyūkai* and *eiga kenkyūbu*). Kitagawa Kazuo interprets these activities as attempts to 'resurrect selfhood' during the rapid social change of the postwar era (Kitagawa 2000: 50). My ethnographic findings largely support Kitamura and Kitagawa's assessment of the close relationship of cinema viewing and organised film-related activities to an idea of developing the self. However, ethnographic data can reveal a degree of complexity difficult to discern from historical accounts. In Chapter 6, we explore a number of organised viewer groups, examining their links to commercial production as well as political protest.

As the next chapters will show, my study participants certainly understand their encounters with film as a kind of extending of the self, both into imagined spaces and as a form of self-cultivation and self-improvement. The opportunity to learn about different places and times was a major attraction of the cinema for many. A significant number of my interlocutors stressed the 'feeling' (*kanjō* or *kandō*) aspect of cinema as a means to expand their capacity for ethical or co-feeling with others. Many felt they had indeed been educated or made to think in a different way by cinema. For example, a significant number of participants expressed the desire, as people born during and immediately after the war, to relive the memories and experiences of elder generations through films produced between 1930 and 1950. In this aspect the viewer as self seeks an encounter not only with a film as text but also with the memories and experiences of imagined selves from an earlier time contained therein. Film viewing is not an attempt to resurrect something past, but to stage and restage an encounter with the past.

In this short overview of the theoretical framework, discursive context and scholarly and popular influences on this study in this chapter, I have attempted to situate the ethnographic material to follow within the wider context of studies of the self and the viewer in Japan. In the following chapters, I aim to draw attention to the areas where ethnographic methods can be particularly useful in the study of these issues. Though I began this chapter by reframing Raymond Carver's famous title to ask 'What do we talk about when we talk about cinema?', I am mindful that one of the major utilities of the ethnographic method is that it can incorporate data that manifests outside the realm of language, in the form of feeling. Feeling and sensory awareness are of course key components of the viewing experience. While this chapter has focused largely on discourse, the following chapters weave verbal communications from study participants together with accounts of gestural and non-verbal expression to attempt a more holistic picture of the relation of viewer and cinema as 'that feeling without words':

> I could hear my heart beating. I could hear everyone's heart. I could hear the human noise we sat there making, not one of us moving, not even when the room went dark. (Carver 1981: 62)

CHAPTER 2

The Cinema as a Place to Be

'Cinema' can refer to a single film, a group of texts connected by place, theme, director, actor or time period, or to the film theatre itself. The Japanese terminology is not quite so flexible, as *eigakan* (film theatre) is quite distinct from *eiga* (film). Asking people about their memories of watching films in the postwar era often threw up recollections of particular cinema theatres, as much as memories of film content. Participants in my study often connected the film theatre to specific moments in their lifelong relation to cinema texts and cultures. Reflecting study participants' structural approach to answering my survey and interview questions, I begin this account of film viewing in Western Japan by thinking about the cinema as place, both in the literal geographic sense and as a technology of emplacement, a means of situating oneself in the world.

The experiences related by participants in my study can be loosely organised into two groups, as the memories of those for whom film was the only moving picture entertainment available differ from the memories of those who had access to television as well as cinema. The memories of the generation born between 1930 and 1953, who grew up without television, are generally distinct from those of people born after 1953, who often had personal access to a television by age five to ten. The spread of television was uneven, informed by geographical area, degree of urbanisation and the wealth and class of the household in question. Yet by 1959, sales of television sets had reached 3.5 million, up from 1.5 million in 1958 (Kitaura 2020: 119).

Many study participants in the elder group connected questions about their memories of the cinema to the lack of television in their younger years. Most participants born between 1930 and 1953 prefaced their answer to my first question about their memories of visiting the cinema for the first time, and their impressions of their own lives and the wider social situation in that period, with the reminder that cinema was then the main source of popular entertainment. While study participants in the post-1953 group such as Inoue san remembered being 'brought up by the television', as he described being left to entertain himself, by contrast study participants who grew up in the countryside remembered experiences closer to those recalled by the earlier generation. In this way, as Hideaki Fujiki has observed, opportunities to engage with cinema cultures were unevenly distributed across geographical areas, as well as class and gender divisions, and occupation and age (2019: 290).

Going Out to the Cinema Theatre

While the atmosphere of the more expensive city cinema theatres could be luxurious (Katō 1993), the majority of my study participants, who first visited the cinema between ages four and six, recalled less formal experiences in run-down theatres or public spaces such as suburban shopping areas, or ad hoc screenings in town halls, open gathering places (*hiroba*) or school classrooms and gymnasiums. Cinema theatres in postwar Japan were organised into three tiers: first-tier cinemas were the most expensive and showed new films; the second- and third-tier cinemas mainly showed second-hand reels of not-so-recent films. These theatres were cheaper and popular with children and young families, though many participants complained of the smells surrounding the cheapest seats, and the packed theatres. The cinema was clearly a social space, and a place to be together, yet at the same time it could also be a place to be alone.

This chapter and the next approach the question of cinema as place from a number of directions. Here I explore memories of cinema as geographical place, contrasting the memories of the 1930–53 generation, who recall using the film theatre as a place to rest as well as a convenient distraction, with the attitudes of the post-1953 'television generation' who came to the cinema more deliberately and often with the purpose of engaging with a particular film text.

By covering this range of generational experience, I aim to incorporate the memories of casual viewers as well as film fans into this ethno-history of film viewership in the Kansai region. The casual viewer demographic is often missing from the history of cinema, as film scholarship tends to focus on the memories and value assessments of an elite group of viewers-turned-professional critics, academics, dedicated film fans or industry personnel. Approaching the cinema as a geographical location allows us to incorporate the memories of those who attended the cinema more casually, as well as committed fans.

Consuming cinema content as a means of experiencing other geographical locations was also a recurring theme throughout questionnaire and interview responses, as well as at my participant observation sites. The next chapter will extend the metaphor of cinema as a mode of travelling to consider the cinema as a temporal place, analysing discussions of cinema as a means of connecting to the experiences of previous generations. Repetition and rewatching are considered here as a way of controlling the time of the viewer's own being, while cinema content as memory aid appears to offer a means by which to organise viewers' personal recollections in the later years of their lives.

'It was a time with not much in the way of entertainment'
'Goraku ga sukunai jidai de mo arimashita' *(Kobayashi san 2016)*

For study participants born between 1930 and 1953, as well as those born later in less urbanised areas, the cinema theatre was a place to kill time as much as a means of actively participating in film culture. While certain individual films made strong impressions, many of this older generation recalled the atmosphere and even furnishings of their first visit to the cinema more clearly than details of the film itself. The majority of questionnaire respondents could not confidently remember the title or key details of their first film, but provided the location, descriptions of the cinema theatre and accounts of who they visited the theatre with, conversations they had before and after the screening and some indication of their feelings about the experience. In this chapter, I approach the cinema theatre or alternative viewing space as the geographical location of both the viewer's encounter with a film text and the viewer's encounter with fellow viewers. This is intended to set the scene of the cinematic encounter and to begin from a wide frame of analysis that includes casual viewers who do not identify as fans as well as those who do. Focusing on the cinema theatre as geographical location uncovers how postwar viewers in Western Japan used the cinema as a physical space as much as an artistic or ideological content provider.

In his account of the physical transformations of cinema theatres in postwar Kyoto, Katō Mikiro observes that 'people go to movie theatres to see movies, but that is not the whole story' (1996). Going to the cinema in postwar Japan began with the choice of theatre. Western Japan, including the Kansai region's main cities of Kyoto and Osaka, as well as the more distant Kobe, had a large variety of cinema theatres and public spaces where films were regularly shown. In fact, Kyoto alone had as many as sixty film theatres in the period 1947–56 (Katō 1996). The choices on offer ranged from the modern and well-designed film theatres advertising heating or cooling technologies (depending on the season) to the more basic second- and third-tier theatres located in less stylish parts of town or in the suburbs. Takeda san, born in Tokyo in 1943, recalled, 'As I had no money, I went to the second- and third-tier cinemas, the ones in the run-down areas (*basue*), and those in the suburbs.'

Further still from the new postwar theatres of the city centres were the more ad hoc arrangements experienced by many growing up in the countryside, including the travelling cinemas which projected older movies onto sheets hung in town halls, public parks and schoolrooms (see Figure 2.1). While the up-to-date theatres described by Katō in Kyoto city centre (1996) may have boasted cutting-edge facilities, from new films to up-to-date projectors and air conditioning, the majority of study participants indicated that these theatres were reserved for special treats or one-off events. Family trips to the film theatre involving children as young as four were generally limited to the second- and third-tier theatres, while the only survey respondent whose first cinema encounter occurred in an upmarket city centre cinema was also the oldest, aged nineteen on her first visit.

Attempts to modernise film theatres were charted by local newspapers, which individual theatres used to communicate with their audiences about improvements and new rules. For example, in 1947 the Asahi Kaikan in Kyoto announced in a local newspaper that from May of the same year the 'stuffing system' (*tsumekomi shiki*) that had filled popular screenings to standing capacity would be replaced by a 'capacity limit, one showing' system (Katō 1996). Due to audience dissatisfaction, this was replaced the next year with a substitution system whereby a patron leaving before the end of the screening gave the empty seat to an arriving patron, who could

Figure 2.1 An outdoor screening on the bank of the Kamogawa river near the Delta, home to the Shimogamo studios.

remain in the theatre for the beginning of the second screening of the same film. Participants in my study recalled that such systems created a '*manin*' or packed atmosphere, which was not necessarily disagreeable but could appear threatening or dangerous to certain viewers, particularly those who felt outnumbered in relation to their age or gender. Smiling, interviewee Kobayashi san recalled, 'The theatres were always packed and we often watched films standing up.' In 1947 the Yasaka Grand (which was the only first-run theatre in Kyoto until 1948) introduced the first seat reservation system in Kyoto, which allowed viewers to sit together with their companions. In the cheaper second- and third-run cinemas, viewers were packed in with no regard to who had arrived together. This may be one reason why many women reported feeling unsafe in dark film theatres in their younger years, as Chapter 5 explores in more detail.

The time and expense of travel from the suburbs to the cities was not great, but could dissuade a young family from heading for the city centre theatres for anything other than a special occasion. Of those living within the city centre, all but the wealthiest would be further dissuaded from the more elegant theatres by the difference in entrance fees. In the early postwar years, first- tier cinemas in Kyoto charged 25 or 30 yen, in comparison to the 20-yen tickets available at the second-tier cinemas. The majority of study participants remembered visiting the cheaper Cineplex-style buildings where a number of small third-tier venues were crowded together inside a single structure. Particularly for boys, these theatres presented an opportunity to get creative about viewership, as many male study participants recalled paying entrance fees for one film, only to slip past the ticket desk into a different screening. Young male viewers would repeat this trick multiple times, sometimes buying tickets for later screenings, then doubling back to enter the current screening without paying for that film.

By the 1960s the cost of cinema tickets had increased, and although wages had also grown due to Prime Minister Ikeda Hayato's Income Doubling Plan of 1960, there was still some disparity between the cost of cinema tickets and other ways of spending time. For example, one questionnaire respondent recalled paying 1,500 yen for a ticket to see *Dr Zhivago* (David Lean, 1965) at a time when he regularly paid 50 yen for a bowl of noodles. As an imported film, *Dr Zhivago* would most likely have been shown at a newer and more elegant theatre, while run-down local cinemas in entertainment districts were rebranding themselves as adult film theatres in order to survive (Ueda 2020: 131). In this way, the availability of cinema theatres became more polarised as the postwar period went on.

Uses of the Cinema Theatre Space

Gender, age, class and geographical location informed how participants in my study remembered engaging with the cinema as place during the postwar era. While young male children appear to have been freer in their viewership habits than female children and young women, married women and women with children also seem to have been relatively unhindered in their cinemagoing behaviours in the early postwar era. Several female study participants who had worked mainly in the home during the period 1945–68 related dropping into the cinema during their daily errand routines. A number recalled that in the early years after the war, the cost of a cheap cinema theatre ticket was low enough that many housewives could afford to drop in and out regularly, using the cinema almost like the television would later be used, in that there was no perceived need or desire to watch a screening programme through to the end.

Several female study participants continued this practice into the period that I conducted my study, from 2014 to 2018. For example, while running a week-long questionnaire survey at the Kyoto Bunka Hakubutsukan (Kyoto Culture Museum, hereafter Bunpaku) film theatre described in the Introduction, I was approached by Nakamura san, a lady in her nineties. Nakamura san left a daytime screening midway through the film and sat down with me in the lobby, chatting while she completed a questionnaire. I asked whether she had disliked the film, a famous 1950s melodrama, or whether she had seen it before. On the contrary, she replied that she had liked the film very much, but had dropped into the theatre as a way to kill time between finishing an errand and meeting her husband for lunch. She said that she had become accustomed to popping into the cinema theatre for a short break during the early years of her marriage, when she spent her afternoons shopping for dinner ingredients while her husband was at work. She would sit for around an hour in the cinema before meeting a friend or returning to her household duties.

Like many questionnaire survey respondents, Nakamura san expressed gratitude for the existence of the Bunpaku screening programme. While others focused their expressions of appreciation on the calibre of the films featured, the affordability of the tickets or the innovative programme themes, however, she was particularly pleased with the screening structure, which repeated the same film four times in one week, twice per day on two days scheduled three weekdays apart. A particular film was shown twice on Tuesday and repeated twice again on Friday, another on Wednesday and Saturday, and a third on Thursday and Sunday (Monday was a holiday). This allowed her to drop into the first part of a film without any intention of staying to the end, and if she enjoyed the story or found herself intrigued by the plot, she would return later in the week and watch the rest. I observed the same pattern during three years of participant observation at the Bunpaku theatre, noting that many patrons dropped in or out halfway through a film and returned to the same film at a later screening.

This suggests that the affordances of the cinema theatre as a geographical location, and as a space without significant financial or temporal barriers, shapes the ways that viewers engage with and think about cinema. Nakamura san recalled the cinema theatres of her early married years as easily accessible, in that there was no expectation to arrive at the beginning of the screening, and in that the cost of entry did not prohibit staying only a short time or paying twice to return to see the ending of the same film. As Chapter 5 details, not all study participants remembered the cinema as freely accessible to them, particularly participants who were girls and younger women in the period under study. However, in this particular case Nakamura san's feeling of an easy closeness to postwar cinema culture was communicated as interlinked with ease of access to cinema theatres and the perceived minimal requirements on her to meet a screening schedule.

Getting into the Cinema: Access, Barriers and Incentives

Younger study participants recalled a more unsure relation to cinema access, as while children were not prohibited from attending certain films at most theatres, some did regulate entry by age. In the early postwar years, such regulation seems to have been very much dependent on the area in which the cinema theatre was located. While Imai san, born in Shiga prefecture in 1940, remembered children being forbidden to enter certain cinemas alone in 1945, in Tokyo Takeda san remembered his film fan mother bringing him to a screening of *The Red Shoes* (Michael Powell and Emeric Pressburger, 1948, released in Japan in 1949). Not understanding the setting of this British film as the world of classical ballet, the six-year-old Takeda san mistook the theatrical make-up of the main characters for monster masks, and remembered being terrified. He did not mention the suicide of the main character at the end of the film, perhaps because he was too young to understand the suggestive camerawork. That a parent would take a young child to a film with such narrative themes suggests that the notion of shielding children from extreme imagery or narratives was not particularly widespread in early postwar cinema culture in Western Japan. (In fact, a children's rhyme composed in 1922 shares the Japanese title of Powell and Pressburger's film, *Akai kutsu*, and tells the story of a young girl abducted from Japan by a foreigner, so it appears that sharing terrifying tales with children was not uncommon in a variety of popular media.) Two further interviewees related retrospective surprise at the content of the films they were allowed, and even encouraged, to watch by parents. At the same time, teachers and government officials appear to have been more concerned about the impact of cinema on children's attention spans and potential for criminality, echoing the moral panics around the influence of the film *Zigomar* (Victorin Jassett, 1911) on children in the early 1920s (Gerow 2010a: 54).

As discussed in Chapter 1, the first age-based restrictions on cinema viewing were imposed in 1955 by Japan's movie regulator, the Film Classification and Rating Organization (Eiga Rinri Kikō), known as Eirin. Films were designated 'geared towards adults' (*seijin muke*) and limited to audiences over eighteen. Kristen Cather argues that the influence of SCAP GHQ and the US Hays Code extended into the post-Occupation era (2014: 100), particularly where issues of sexualised content and young viewers were concerned. From 1955, films that were considered appropriate for young viewers were marked as 'recommended' (*suisen*) for youths (Cather 2014: 108.) A Committee on Children's Film Viewing (Seishonen eiga iinkai) was formed of film industry representatives, child psychologists and representatives from mothers' organisations. However, as Cather notes, compliance with these restrictions was patchy, and rural areas in particular were considered to be 'not fully participating', as was the foreign film industry (Cather 2014: 107).

While successive moral panics focused on the impact of cinema technology or the corrupting influence of certain narratives and characters, in the hygiene-aware postwar era, the space of the cinema theatre itself was often discussed as a physical threat to young and vulnerable viewers. Public discourse on the issue of poor ventilation raised by a Department of Public Health survey and published in the *Kyoto Shinbun* newspaper in May 1952 (Katō 1996) highlighted the problem not only as a widely recognised one but also as a shared experience, building a sense of commonality between sufferers.

Many study participants recalled the unhygienic or unsafe atmospheres of the all-night (*ōru naito*) screenings of the 1960s and 1970s, which theatres developed to try to win back audiences as attendance dropped after 1958. Kishida san, born in Amagasaki in 1952, shared his memories of the smoky atmosphere of the run-down theatres with a lively grin, marvelling at the levels of discomfort endured in comparison to today's luxurious cinema theatre experience. Recalling how he would stretch out and slump down in his seat with his feet up on the back of the seat in front, smoking, at all-night shows in cheap theatres, Kishida san acted out this posture during our interview. With a big smile and conspiratorial expression, he slid right down in his chair, lifting a leg to gesture at putting his feet up on the back of the seat in front, and holding an imaginary cigarette. Laughing and casting his eyes to the floor, he said, 'That kind of . . . bad stuff (*yoroshikunai koto*) [laughs out loud], well, it was normal (*atarimae*), it wasn't rare back then.' Kishida san's performance of viewing behaviours which are no longer allowed in contemporary cinema theatres shared some similarities with the speakers whose gestures and expressions were analysed by Peter Stromberg and discussed in the Introduction. Stromberg notes that speakers who revealed their intention to answer an interview question in an unanticipated way tended to amplify their gestures to both explain an unexpected attitude or position and to 'recruit his listener to his perspective' (2021: 430). Kishida san introduced an unexpected element into his nostalgic narrative about going to the cinema in the postwar period by bringing up the issue of endurance as part of the viewing experience and by demonstrating behaviours that may seem antisocial or disruptive to other audience members. By 'generating solidarity through eye contact' (Stromberg 2021: 430) and exploiting some physical features of his own body, such as his long, thin legs, to enhance the comedic aspect of the performance of stretching out in the cinema, Kishida san depicted his youthful viewing behaviours as humorous and nostalgic, and successfully communicated the sense of a young man caught up in his love for cinema, unaware of the other people sharing the theatre space. He also communicated the physical challenge of watching a long 'all-night' programme, which often repeated the same films multiple times.

Physical endurance is still a core element of cinema culture for many in Kishida san's generation. At the Kinugasa film-screening club where I conducted participant observation, I was amazed at the abilities of eighty- and ninety-year-old club members to sit still for over seven hours, often in chilly or humid conditions, to watch two or three films in succession. The majority of the films screened were easily available at DVD rental stores or online, and could have been watched in the comfort of club members' own homes at a more leisurely pace, yet significant numbers gathered each month to sit together on uncomfortable folding chairs for hours. Watching the films together appears to have been an incentive for many members to return regularly to the screening club, as was the lively discussion that followed the screenings. This discussion often opened with shared complaints about the heat or cold in the room, as well as age-related grumbling about arthritis and poor hearing. Sharing complaints about personal discomfort appeared to bond the viewing group in advance of the discussion session, perhaps emboldening many members to voice personal feelings about the film within the shared camaraderie of the viewing group. While the majority of regular members had grown up in the early postwar years, a number of slightly younger viewers, around sixty years old or more, voiced a combination of envy and imagined sympathetic nostalgia for this period of viewership that offered the opportunity to bond with strangers over the cinema environment.

Moving Indoors with 'The generation raised watching television' *'Terebi o mite sodachimashita no sedai'* (Inoue san, born 1958)

Many of the younger viewers stated that they were often motivated to join viewing groups and retrospective screening programmes managed by older film fans by a sense of having missed the peak period of cinema as community entertainment. Participants in my study belonging to this generation often had an older relative to thank for their initial interest in cinema, though the habit of taking young children to the cinema theatre seems to have declined with the spread of television. For example, Inoue san's father, born in 1930, was a fan of Hollywood films, bringing home *Eiga no tomo* (*Film Friend*) magazine regularly to read about his favourite stars and directors. Unlike earlier generations, however, Inoue san was not brought to the cinema by his father, or by any older family member. Instead, he stayed at home with the television while the rest of the family went out to work, watching the films broadcast on TV in the early 1960s.

The first general television broadcast took place in Japan in 1953. On 1 February 1953 NHK (Nippon Hoso Kyokai or Japan Broadcasting Corporation) started broadcasting, followed by Nihon Terebi on 28 February 1953. As film studios began to see television as a competitor, major studios including Tōei, Shōchiku, Tōhō, Daiei and Shintōhō stopped issuing their films to television stations from October 1956, followed by Nikkatsu in 1958. By 1958, NHK had 1.98 million subscribers and the 'living room era' (*ocha no ma jidai*) had begun (Fujiki 2019: 337). Shintōhō films returned to television after the company collapsed in 1961, and in 1964 television broadcast revenue overtook cinema box-office revenues as total television subscribers reached 17.13 million (Fujiki 2019: 337). Films began to return to television as the power relationship between the two sides was readdressed (Kitaura 2020: 119).

Tōei, Shōchiku, Tōhō and Daiei began to invest in private television stations, and film companies began producing 16mm films specifically for television. In 1957 Tōei set up Nihon kyōiku terebi (NET, of Japan Education Television) for education films, and in 1958 began

Tōei terebi purodakushon (Tōei Television Production) (Fujiki 2019: 373). From January 1961 to March 1968, television producer Ushihara Junichi commissioned television films from directors like Shindō Kaneto, Ōshima Nagisa and Hani Susumu for a series called *Nonfikushon gekiba* (Nonfiction Theatre). Hideaki Fujiki points to this series as an example of how cinema and television were interlinked (Fujiki 2019: 373), forming a media ecology or media mix which reflected the 'multi-platform' nature of cinema from its beginning to the present day (Fujiki 2019: 100). By 1964 there were 170 television agencies and television had 90 per cent coverage (Fujiki 2019: 337). A 1967 study by NHK suggested that general viewers spent 3 hours 50 minutes per day watching television, while stay-at-home housewives recorded an average of 4 hours 10 minutes per day (Fujiki 2019: 362).

Television was where Inoue san discovered *chanbara*, the stagey subgenre of period film (*jidaigeki*) devoted to set-piece fight scenes. He recalled the biggest stimulus for his budding passion for film as the TV special *Kinoshita Keisuke Hour*, which was broadcast from 27 October 1964 until 3 October 1974 on TBS (Tokyo Broadcasting System) on Tuesdays at 9pm (in its final year the programme moved to Wednesdays at 10pm, and the name *Kinoshita Keisuke Hour* was used from 1967 onwards). Inoue san recognised the director's artistic flair, but it was the intimacy of the television that really drew him into Kinoshita's world. 'As for films, well, going to the cinema required money. On the other hand, every house had a TV, and there were so many programmes to choose from. TV was more familiar (*midika*), and I always had the sense that the film theatre was something more for grown-ups.' The familiarity of the television set, as opposed to an imagined unknown 'grown-up' film theatre, appealed to Inoue san. This familiar feeling framed his introduction to Kinoshita's work: 'He made great dramas, and when I was a child, I got a sense of closeness (*najimi*) from watching his work.' Around the time he entered middle school in 1971, Inoue san got serious about his cinema hobby, and by high school he was even helping to run a film circle.

At first, Inoue san's account of being 'raised by television' seems to indicate that this generation were less involved with cinema viewership and culture than their elders. It is also interesting to note that many parents appear to have become less interested in taking their children to the cinema as more households bought television sets. The mass saturation of television is often blamed for the decline of the Japanese studio system, as audience numbers fell swiftly each year from a peak of 1,127,452,000 in 1958 (Motion Picture Producers Association of Japan, 2017). At the same time, the purchase of television sets increased as households invested in order to watch the wedding of Crown Prince Akihito and Shōda Michiko in 1959, and later the 1964 Tokyo Olympics. However, it does not follow that this generation of children were uninterested in classical Japanese cinema. On the contrary, many were introduced to famous postwar films through the television, and came to feel a sense of ownership or closeness towards these films, directors and stars based on the framing experience of television viewership. Inoue san was sure that he was not alone here, and in fact he recalled reading that television viewership went up by around 30 per cent each time a classic film was shown.

Though this generation was less likely to visit the cinema at a young age, or with family members, they were nonetheless surrounded by the material culture of cinema. Inoue san remembered his father's film magazines, and taking note of the posters and advertisements for films 'directed at adults' displayed on his route home from school. When study participants of this generation discovered the cinema, they often associated it with their elder family members' regular cinemagoing habits in earlier years. In this way, developing a familiarity with pre-war and wartime films as well as postwar classics became a way to build a connection to earlier generations of family members. As the next chapter details, this mode of engaging with cinema can be understood in terms of the development of 'prosthetic memory' (Landsberg 2004) through cinema viewership. By extending the viewer's sense of personal memory into an earlier era in which the viewer was very young, or perhaps not yet born, a feeling of becoming closer to a nationally significant historical moment can develop, and at the same time, a feeling of drawing closer to family members who personally experienced that moment.

In the historical context of postwar Japan, where elder generations often refrained from sharing their memories with their children due to social taboos or postwar shame about wartime actions, the cinema presented a means for the postwar generations to access narratives about wartime and Imperial Japan. Study participants born in the 1940s and 1950s exhibited a certain fearlessness in discussing the events and ideologies leading up to and during the war, freely using words such as 'war responsibility' (*sensō no sekinin*) and 'blame' in the discussion sessions after the Kinugasa screenings. On the other hand, the eldest group member, born in 1923, never contributed to these particular topics during my observations, despite being a vocal presence in discussions of other issues. In fact, she often intervened to close off discussions about wartime and war memory, reminding attendees that they had gathered to talk about cinema.

While many of the Kinugasa screening club members believed that they could recall something of the end of the war, we can think of Inoue san's post-1953 generation of film fans as a group participating in a kind of nostalgia for Japan as it was (imagined) before they were born. Inoue san grew up during the early years of Prime Minister Ikeda's income doubling plan, and by the time he entered high school the nation was well on its way to the economic boom years that would culminate in the bubble economy of the 1990s. As the country grew wealthier, parents worked longer hours, and older people began to look back with a certain fondness on the early years of the postwar period. All participants in my study described the early postwar period as a time of great poverty and struggle in Japan. However, many also claimed that the era was characterised by a particular honesty, a drive to work hard and a kindness shown to neighbours and fellow strugglers. In an informal group conversation, Yamashita san, Otsuka san and Kimura san, all women born between 1943 and 1946, agreed that the wartime generation had been stronger than any succeeding generations. They laughingly compared their own generation, predicting, 'We won't live so long, we're not that tough!' 'Even though they had hardship and illness, many of the wartime generation are living well past 100.' 'When I get that old, I don't think I'll want to keep living – I'll only miss food and hot spring baths!' Study participants expressed respect (*sonkei*) and admiration for the suffering that the wartime generation had endured. While older participants such as Yamashita san, Otsuka san and Kimura san jokingly regretted the passing of this tough generation, the group born after 1953, including Inoue san, expressed regret that they had never experienced this era at all. Engaging with film texts from the period through the then-new technology of television offered a means to experience a connection to this era and to one's parents and relatives who had lived through it.

As films moved from the geographical space of the cinema to the more private space of the home television set, we can see a shift in the affective impact of viewership, from something social and physical to something experienced as 'close', 'familiar', yet a little lonely. The geographical shift also triggered a temporal shift, as those who remembered being children at home with the television tried to connect to the experiences and values of elder generations by watching films from years gone by. While the next chapter will consider the cinema as a technology through which temporal space can be manipulated, I want to explore some key aspects of cinema understood as geographical space here: the physical location of the film theatre itself, geographical locations as film settings, the idea of the cinema as a window to another world and the experience of cinema as a mode of being in the world.

Hometowns and Cinema Spaces

> I don't know much about the social circumstances around the age I was at kindergarten, but where I lived there was no cinema. I got the feeling that everyone looked forward to the films screened at the district community centre . . . When I was a child, I once saw a tiny cinema in a country town. Later, when I was much older, I saw a picture of the same cinema in *Kinema Junpō* magazine – I was so surprised! I took a trip and visited that cinema. How many times have I had that experience, with the other customers sitting alone inside . . . It was a lonely sight. For some reason I began to think about the Kyōichi Kaikan cinema on Ichijōji street. That was where my own 'film life' (*eiga jinsei*) became really rich. (Anonymous questionnaire respondent 2016)

As reception studies ethnographers such as Annette Kuhn and Toshie Takahashi have noted, interlocutors often respond to a question about media form or content with personal information related to other aspects of the interlocutor's life (Kuhn 2002: 17; Takahashi 2016: 218). Participants in my study often answered my questions about going to the cinema at various points in their lives with an account of where they lived or studied at that time and some details about the character of the place as it related to their awareness of contemporary cinema culture. Like Kuhn's British interviewees, many respondents in my questionnaire survey and interviews drew maps of their hometowns, describing the route from home or school to the film theatre. Particularly in suburban or rural areas, the presence or absence of a film theatre became a device to communicate what kind of place the area was in the early postwar years and how it had changed since, mirroring the 'contrasts between topographies past and present' that Kuhn observed in her own interlocutors' communications (2002: 17).

Kuhn also notes an 'association between proximity and familiarity' in her interlocutors' accounts of attending the cinema in wartime and postwar Britain. She observes a sense of '"going to the pictures" as an extension of home life, a comfortable and unthreatening early venture into the public domain' (2002: 17). In this respect, the accounts given by participants in my study differ, perhaps due to the differences in the political situations between Britain and Japan in the pre-war and postwar eras respectively. Almost every respondent and interviewee who participated in my project made a point of stressing the poverty of postwar Japan, even those born after 1955. Unlike Kuhn's interlocutors, they often drew from film imagery to convey the poverty, discomfort or dangerous associations of the areas in which they lived and encountered the cinema.

Many questionnaire respondents illustrated the poverty and perceived backwardness or isolation of their rural hometowns by citing the lack of a dedicated cinema theatre. One questionnaire respondent born in 1936 answered a question about his first encounter with cinema as follows: 'Throughout elementary school and junior high school, we saw films in the elementary school lecture hall. It wasn't yet the postwar. We lived in the countryside, in a village near the sea.' A common response to the same question included the words *mazushii* or *binbō*, both meaning poor. Most study participants contrasted these first impressions with accounts of change, either in their hometowns or more often after a move to a larger city in the Kansai region, or a temporary move to Tokyo. The rich cinema cultures of the major cities stood in stark contrast to the hometowns of many of the viewers that I interviewed. Imai san recalled that on moving to Kyoto to study at Kyoto University, the number of local cinemas was so great that he began to skip classes to see as many films as possible: 'There was the Gion Kaikan and, eh, what were their names . . . There were so many different cinemas. Old films, there were countless places to see films I hadn't seen before.' Growing up in Ōtsu city in Shiga prefecture from 1941, Imai san had a number of film theatres in his neighbourhood, but in this area children were strictly prohibited from entering the cinema alone. As his father only took him to the cinema on the *obon* (commemoration of ancestors) and New Year holidays, he did not have a strong recollection of his hometown as a 'cinema city'. Moving to Kyoto triggered his passion for cinema, and at the time of our interview he regularly travelled all over Kansai and beyond to participate in film festivals and special screening events.

Long-term residents of Kyoto often described the area as a 'cinema city', echoing Ueda Manabu's observation that the special relationship between entertainment, cinema culture and film production in areas like the Shin-Kyōgoku district have led to the development of distinctive trends in filmmaking and audience demographics in the city (2020: 128). While Kyoto-born participants often illustrated their memory narratives with references to period dramas and classics of *jidaigeki* cinema, those who grew up in neighbouring areas of Kansai used a broad range of film references to bring their depictions of their hometowns to life. For example, Kishida san used the language of genre cinema to describe both his hometown and his neighbours as 'gangster-like' (*yakuzarashii*). Growing up in the Amagasaki area outside Osaka, he observed the activity surrounding the local *yakuza* headquarters as similar to the content of the films he loved to watch from age five. He recalled that the neighbourhood and his family were poor (*mazushii*), but he could visit the cinema freely by scamming the ticket sellers, either buying one ticket which a number of other children would also use to enter the cinema or buying a ticket for later in the week and then doubling back past the ticket desk to go into the current screening. In these accounts, descriptions of the location of the cinema expanded into accounts of the study participant's early life and memories. A question about the first visit to the cinema became an opportunity to describe the atmosphere of a particular regional area in postwar Japan, many of which are now unrecognisable.

Home and cinema were tied together in many participants' memories in a way that suggests talking about cinema as a means of giving an account of one's origins as well as earliest memories. For example, Koyama san described the Kōshien area of Hyōgo prefecture in which she grew up from 1944 with reference to a morning television drama based in the same town, *Beppin san* (Nakigawa Yoshiro, 2016–17). As a child, she had enjoyed walking to her local cinema after noticing a new film poster on the billboards along her route from home to school. She drew a map of these three spaces in a personal letter that she sent to me after completing a questionnaire. Later in an interview, she speculated that the Kōshien cinema likely no longer existed, as she knew that her childhood home was also gone. She had not visited the area for many years, but the destruction of her home rendered the destruction of the cinema equally likely in her mind. In such accounts, references to cinema communicated what an area had meant to a speaker, and associations to film genres and content coloured depictions of home in a way that made them imaginable to a listener from a different generation and place. Cinema is used as both a place marker and as an indication of atmosphere in communications that seek to give an account of the speaker in terms intelligible to the listener.

Living Cinema: Home as Film Location

Place is central not only to memories of the cinema theatre but also to the construction of films and to filmmaking itself. As described in Chapter 1, Western Japan, and in particular the Kansai region and Kyoto, is imagined as the 'cradle of Japanese cinema' (Kaffen 2020: 286) for many reasons, chief among them the arrival of the Lumière Cinématographe there and the use of Kansai-based studios and locations to represent various areas and periods of Japanese history. Local newspapers would encourage the people of Kansai to get involved in the film industry, publishing the planned locations of major filming events, and fans could often visit sets, observe actors at work and even volunteer as extras (Katō 1996). Several participants in my study recalled reading about location shoots or seeing information about them on the television news. One interviewee shared pictures of her ceramicist father appearing in the background of *jidaigeki* period drama film sets to add historical flavour (see Figure 2.2). A number of elderly people in the neighbourhood around the Shimogamo shrine area in the Kamogawa Delta in Kyoto recalled being 'borrowed' from the local kindergarten as small children to populate the background of scenes that required children playing during filming at the studio in the area. (Shōchiku operated a Kyoto studio in Shimogama Miyazaki-cho from 1923 until 1950, when a fire damaged the premises and Shōchiku moved to the Uzumasa area. The Shimogama studio was renamed Kyoto Film Studio and operated until 1975.) Otsuka san, who later married an assistant director at Tōhō studio, recalled that she and her school friends would often run down to a filming location and try to catch the eye of a cameraman. Kimura san remembered that every time she visited the Tōei studio area at Uzumasa in Kyoto as an elementary school child in the 1950s, she would be asked to work as a background actor for a day of filming. Otsuka san teased, 'That's because you're so beautiful!' Kimura san would later marry the son of a famous textile producer in Kyoto, whose cousin worked for the Tōei studio before becoming an independent film director.

Study participants born in major cities or close to film studios recalled regularly seeing stars in the street, or wandering into areas suddenly transformed into another era for the purposes of location shooting. Many took advantage of the opportunity to see stars at public events and screenings as well as location shoots. Otsuka san recalled racing back to Nagasaki after moving to Kyoto to get married, in an attempt to catch a last-minute public appearance of the young actress Kitahara Mie. She still remembered how disappointed she was to arrive too late. Kimura san, now resident in Kyoto, had grown up in the Zushi area, home to the *taiyōzoku* genre of novels and films displaying the shocking lives of rich young middle-class

Figure 2.2 An interviewee holds a picture of her father, trained in traditional ceramic production, working as a background actor.

teenagers in the late 1950s. She attended the same school as the Ishihara brothers, Shintarō, who would write the *taiyōzoku* novels, and Yūjirō, who would star in their film adaptations. While she remembered nurturing a schoolgirl crush on 'Yū-chan', she strongly disapproved of the pressure that the Ishihara family was said to have put on Kitahara Mie when the two actors married. She recalled, 'In those days, actresses were considered the lowest of women' and had few protections, both economic and social. She was much more star-struck by seeing the retired star Hara Setsuko on her many visits to the Kamakura area, where she recalled that she would meet the 'goddess of the postwar cinema' (Yomota 2000) walking in the street – 'She was very tall!'

While those who lived in areas central to film production spoke of feeling this kind of everyday closeness to the making of Japanese cinema, study participants who grew up in the countryside remembered seeing many everyday things for the first time in the course of observing on-location film shoots. For example, Kawakita san, born in Uji prefecture in 1943, remembered seeing a horse for the first time when a local studio filmed a period drama in her area. Koyama san recalled watching famous actors wandering around the Shōchiku studio in Shimogamo-Miyazaki cho. Even today, film crews are often spotted around the Kansai area. I interviewed Koyama san only a week after a television crew had visited the area near her home in Takaragaike in Kyoto, and the Bunpaku museum ran a course for aspiring filmmakers which allowed them to film on location around Kyoto's famous sites. The cinematisation of the Kansai region continues to this day, with a particular focus on regional specificity.

New Geographies Onscreen: Seeing the World through Cinema

Observing actors and location filming around the Kansai area appears to have cemented a sense of Japanese cinema as a local phenomenon for viewers in the region. In terms of film content, however, many study participants referred to the cinema as a kind of window into another world. A large number of interviewees and questionnaire respondents noted that watching films was a way to see places and historical periods outside the viewer's own personal experience. Many respondents remembered the deep impact that Disney's *The Living Desert* (James Algar, 1953, released in Japan as *Ikite iru sabaku* in 1955) had made on their understanding of the world as children. For Takeda san, this was the film that made him want to make films of his own, which he later did in a promotional capacity for Dentsu advertising company. He recalled his surprise on viewing this *kiroku eiga* (a kind of documentary genre close to observational cinema):

> You have the image of the desert as a dead world (*shi no sekai*), don't you? At first that's how it looked. But then in this dead world there appeared living things, one after the other. Living things that you couldn't see at first, like plants and flowers blooming, all these different kinds of living things began to appear. Film lets you see those things you couldn't glimpse in real life. (Takeda 2016)

For Takeda san, as for many other study participants, cinema viewership became not only a means to understand various places and times in the world but also an opportunity to develop a different way of seeing. The language used to explain this is revealing, as many participants used some version of the conjunction *-te kureru*, indicating a sense that something had been given, or gifted, to them in the process of viewing. In some cases, the giver was another person, such as an older person, often a family member, who brought the speaker to the cinema for the first time (*tsurete kureru* or *tsurete morau*). In many such narratives, however, the cinema itself took the grammatical place of the giver in the sentence, as in Takeda san's statement above. The viewer's relation to the cinema is thus positioned as one of receiver of a gift or certain kind of generosity.

Hashimoto san, born in Gifu prefecture in 1943, also remembered *The Living Desert* as an impactful moment in his personal viewing history and as an opening up of the world. He watched the film in his school hall aged eleven or twelve and recalled it as one of the first colour films he had seen. Like Takeda san, he used the word *bikkuri* to describe his amazement at the world the film revealed. While *The Living Desert* may not have made quite the same impact in anglophone cinema histories, it appears repeatedly in narratives by and about the generation born into the decade around 1945. For example, Haruki Murakami's novel *South of the Border, West of the Sun* uses reference to the film as a foundational motif for the central character:

> 'Did you see that Disney film in elementary school – *The Living Desert*?'
> 'Yeah,' I answered.
> 'Our world's exactly the same. Rain falls and the flowers bloom. No rain, they wither up. Bugs are eaten by lizards, lizards are eaten by birds. But in the end, every one of them dies. They die and dry up. One generation dies, and the next one takes over. That's how it goes. Lots of different ways to live. And lots of different ways to die. But in the end that doesn't make a bit of difference. *All that remains is a desert.*'
> (Murakami 1998 [1992]: 57)

Born in 1951, the main character, Hajime, is a little younger than the majority of my study participants, but like them takes the Disney documentary film as a formative influence on his sense of the world around him, recalling, 'Everybody in my elementary school had been herded off to the movie theatre to watch it' (Murakami 1998 [1992]: 146). References to the film scattered throughout the novel suggest an expansive mode of viewing the world beyond the boundaries of Japan, as well as a sense of the relatively small impact of one human life on the world at large. While this verges into nihilism for several characters in the novel, my study participants recalled viewing the film as a moment in which they realised the existence and persistence of life everywhere, no matter how insignificant that life might be. This realisation is credited with prompting a variety of changes in attitudes, from a desire to understand life during wartime more completely to the wish to see other places and rare sights.

In Hashimoto san's case, the film was connected in his memory to a fondness for travel and discovery. Aged seventy, Hashimoto san had driven his motorbike alone from Kobe to Hokkaido, the northernmost part of Japan, in a round trip lasting almost a month. His strong memory of *The Living Desert* was connected to his sense of himself as a person interested in discovery, travel and adventure. In such accounts of cinema as a window onto another world, self-development and narratives of personal becoming were tied up with ideas of the cinema as educational as well as novel. Through learning to see or think in a different way, the young viewer was also imagined as growing towards an individual self, with particular likes and dislikes, hobbies and vocational goals.

Murakami's use of *The Living Desert* also emphasises the passage of time, noting the rapid changes in condition that time passing in the arid desert environment can bring about. Both Murakami's protagonist Hajime and my study participants regularly marvelled at the rapid changes taking place in everyday life in the first decades after 1945. Noting his parents' hardships during the war on the very first page of the novel, Hajime, which means 'beginning', draws the reader's attention to the fast-changing living environment: 'When I was born though, you'd never have known there'd been a war' (1998 [1992]: 2). The 'small, quiet town' in which Hajime lives may be located in Kansai, given the apparent proximity of Kyoto. Regardless of location, however, the clean, modern, single-family homes in which the characters live represent a standardised mode of postwar living perceived to occlude the recent war and its devastation. The fascination of the narrator and my study participants with the representation of natural life pushing up through the desert suggests a desire to uncover some sensory experience or embodied memory from an earlier time period, as part of an overall worldview that insists on connecting rather than separating the wartime and postwar eras, despite their surface difference.

As Chapter 3 explores in more detail, cinema can be used in this way as a mode of travelling through time as well as place.

World Cinema on Japanese Screens

Many imported films such as *The Living Desert* arrived in Japan some years after their domestic debut, giving a sense of Occupation-era Japan as slightly out of step with the rest of the world. Popular awareness of this phenomenon was heightened by the growing entertainment press, both industry- and gossip-oriented, which anticipated such pre-war and wartime classic film imports as *Gone with the Wind* (Victor Fleming, 1939, released in Japan in September 1952) and *Waterloo Bridge* (Mervyn LeRoy, 1940, released in Japan in March 1949). Takeda san remembered *The Living Desert* as hotly anticipated in Japan, although it was two years behind the US release. In this way, cinema situated Japan as not only culturally out of step with the rest of the developed world but also technologically delayed. The first Japanese colour film was produced in 1951 (Kinoshita Keisuke's *Carmen Comes Home/Karumen kokyō ni kaeru*), whereas colour films had been made in Europe and the US as early as 1902 for home movies, becoming more common in feature films in the 1940s. *Gone with the Wind* and *The Wizard of Oz* (Victor Fleming, 1939) were two of the first major Hollywood imports to make an artistic point of using colour film.

As discussed in Chapter 1, cinema in Japan had long been imagined as an opportunity to demonstrate technological parity with the other nations embracing modernity. The state of Japanese cinema after the war, subject to Occupation censorship and hindered by rationing and scarcity of raw materials, including film stock, was therefore associated with Japan's severely reduced standing in the world after defeat. We often attribute the steep rise in cinema attendance in 1946 to a lack of other entertainment options and the relative cheapness and warmth of the film theatre in a period of hardship. It seems equally likely that viewers flocked to the cinema, then showing almost 60 per cent imported films from Allied countries, to see these other corners of the world which had been hidden or demonised during wartime, and to understand where Japan was situated in the postwar global order. Participants in Kanako Terasawa's doctoral study of female viewers' memories of Hollywood films screened in postwar Japan recalled longing for the neat, modern and often luxurious clothes of American and European female stars (Terasawa 2010: 250). Many also expressed amazement at the beauty and glamour of the costumes of *Gone with the Wind*; as Helen Taylor's study of the reception of the film across time and around the globe indicates, British women experiencing wartime rationing had a similar response (Taylor 1989: 362). In this way, imported cinema both underscored Japan's isolation in the early postwar era and at the same time opened up a space for viewers around the world to experience similar reactions and responses.

After Occupation, as the import laws that had been extremely favourable to the US were renegotiated, a wider range of imported films arrived in Japan. At the same time, the Japanese studio system was producing more domestic films, distributing over five hundred films per year from 1955. Many of the imported films that participants in my study remembered viewing were aimed specifically at children, a demographic not explicitly targeted by postwar Japanese studios until the later 1950s.

As the Japanese studio system began to change shape in the 1960s, Japan's independent and avant-garde film scenes echoed similar movements around the world. The first films shown by the Art Theatre Guild (ATG) cinemas set up by Kawakita Kashiko were European art-house films, and many directors who were later funded by the ATG, such as Ōshima Nagisa, had been marketed by the studios as Japanese equivalents of the Italian neorealist and French *nouvelle vague* filmmakers. Shōchiku even went so far as to present a Shōchiku *nuberu bagu* genre inspired by the popularity of the French *nouvelle vague*. Takeda san remembered visiting the first screening of an Italian film at the Kyoto Art Theatre Guild Cinema, now the Kyoto Cinema on Shijō Karasuma street. He returned faithfully for each screening, particularly excited about the range of films shown. From foreign art-house films to the experimental Japanese directors such as Teshigahara Hiroshi, Takeda san recalled that 'they showed films you couldn't see anywhere else. I was so happy to be able to see those films.'

Many participants in my ethnographic study discussed global cinema as a scene of exchange, where Japanese directors could draw inspiration from their European and American contemporaries and be judged on an equal platform. The performance of Japanese films at international festivals was particularly important to Imai san and Takeda san, who closely followed the prizes awarded to Japanese films and filmmakers at the Venice, Berlin and Cannes film festivals. For participants more concerned with social issues, such as Kishida san and Kobayashi san, the global recognition of filmmakers such as Kurosawa Akira and more recently Koreeda Hirokazu, who draws attention to issues such as child neglect in Japan, was of greater importance. In both cases, however, there was a general tendency to think of cinema as an opportunity to give an account of Japan to the wider world and to learn what ideas the rest of the world held about Japan.

Talking About Cinema as Cultural Exchange

Of course, film imports and exchanges are more than just artistic communications. They also speak to structural aspects of communication and exchange. For many study participants, engaging with cinema became a means of engaging with others, and screening events were sites of engagement. While working at Dentsu advertising agency, Takeda san organised the Dentsu eizō kenkyūkai (Dentsu Visual Image Study Group) for employees to watch films together and exchange ideas. While he remembered being disappointed that none of the directorial staff would agree to join, he was gratified when three local embassies agreed to lend films to show at the study group. Takeda san was able to borrow 16-millimetre prints from the Italian embassy, and films by German Expressionist Fritz Lang: 'We watched Godard's first film together, that was fun. But those were pretty different from our regular business at the company!' Deeper analysis of the space of the film circle or study group is the focus of Chapter 6. However, here I would like to draw attention to the role of film borrowing, import and exchange in the viewer's understanding of Japan's role in the world. By borrowing films from local embassies, Takeda san elevated a simple study group to an international event, and it is interesting to note that the embassies appear to have shared a view of cinema similar to that of SCAP GHQ, which considered film as a tool through which to introduce Japanese viewers to other ideas and ways of being.

As this chapter has indicated, cinema as geographical phenomenon, both as a space in itself and as a technology of emplacement, was articulated by my study participants as a major factor in one of the most basic aspects of being: being in the world. Through cinema, Japanese viewers could form some sense of Japan's place in the world, and their place in Japan, as well as the relation of Western Japan to the capital in the East and of the Kansai region within Western Japan. Observing location shooting and local actors situated participants in my study in proximity to the business of cinema, while the experience of seeing new things, both onscreen and at location shoots, positioned the cinema as a window onto the wider world. In the next chapter, we will explore how cinema was used, understood and discussed in relation to time, in order to think more about the role of cinemagoing and film viewership in organising one's daily life, and in organising one's memories.

CHAPTER 3

Times Past and Passing Time at the Cinema

> For the past to be lived in the present, narration is not the only route, and not necessarily the most affectively engaging: the past is there and now, structuring and animating the very contours of a default relationality, animating the transference, the recruitment and use of the analyst, orchestrating the scene of address . . . [analysis is] an allegory for reception itself. (Butler 2005: 68)

The cinema is a temporal location as well as a geographical one – a means to pass time and to be transported to another time, as well as a physical place to be. This chapter considers the temporal nature of cinema from a range of perspectives. The amount of time spent at the cinema, or watching films at home or at special screening events, can be understood as time out of one's life, when we step away from everyday time to experience the manipulated time of film editing. Stepping into a cinema theatre, or engaging with a film at a private screening event, can also take us into another historical era, as we imaginatively inhabit the period in which the film narrative takes place. This chapter also considers time spent in the cinema as a temporal encounter, both with the film text and with other viewers. Discussions of cinemagoing and film viewership that focus on time communicate a variety of aspects of the speaker's self, from experience of, or interest in, a particular historical moment to more quotidian tasks and habits such as killing time between errands or obligations. Thinking about cinema as a means of time travel and of passing time allows us an insight into the hopes and aspirations, as well as the nuisances and frustrations, experienced by film viewers of a particular place and time.

Engaging with a film text can also present a means to order, control or change one's perception of time. Many participants in my study understood cinema content as a way to connect with or reorganise their memories of times past. The second part of this chapter will explore what film as memory aid can mean for both the 1930–55 generation who grew up during the war and Occupation, and for the later generation born after 1955 who wished to establish some connection to that period.

Understanding Time and the Cinematic Experience

In the Introduction I touched on the question of time in relation to the time commitment involved in viewing film texts for the purpose of academic analysis. While the everyday viewer may not have this kind of academic approach in mind during their encounters with film texts, the time commitment of sitting through a film screening must be acknowledged. This seems like a basic point, but it is one that the field of film studies has often ignored in favour of a focus on the treatment of time in cinema itself (see, for example, Deleuze 1989; Martin-Jones 2006; Sutton 2009). If we understand cinema as 'an expression of experience by experience' (Sobchack 1999: 3), the question of how much of another viewer's embodied experience we can understand follows logically. We can begin by thinking of the historical audience as a group of diverse bodies sharing the experience of sitting together in a dark cinema for a number of hours.

A second key point in considering time in relation to viewership is of course the question of memory. Like Annette Kuhn's study of viewership in pre-war Britain (2002), many of the cinemas and screening events recalled by participants in my study are no longer in existence. In this sense, their memories of early postwar cinemagoing were sealed in the past and reawakened in the encounter of the interview. Yet the majority of study participants continued their lifelong encounters with the cinema itself; in fact, their participation in this study was one example of their continued engagement with film. By participating in this study and attending screenings at the Kyoto Culture Museum (Bunka Hakubutsukan, hereafter Bunpaku), or film clubs such as the Kinugasa monthly screening, participants in my study continued to make new memories of viewership. I therefore position their memories of the early postwar era in relation to their continued engagement with cinema as an ongoing experience rather than a memory sealed in the past.

As discussed in the previous chapters, this study approaches the film-viewing experience through the lens of discourse, focusing on the language and expressions used to communicate memories of film viewing and its perceived impact on the viewer's life narrative. At the same time, I am keen not to lose sight of the embodied experiences central to film viewership in this focus on talking about cinema. This chapter develops the discussion of the cinema theatre as place in Chapter 2 towards an exploration of the experience of occupying that place for a period of time. In bringing study participants' accounts of embodied experiences at the cinema into sharper focus in this chapter, I borrow from Laura Marks' description of 'film viewing as an exchange between two bodies – that of the viewer and that of the film' (2000: 149). Marks argues that we can understand how culture is embedded 'within the body' (2000: 152) by exploring sensory experiences in cinema. Analysing study participants' accounts of their experiences of time, and the passage of time, while engaging with film reveals the many cultural and historical factors that participants experience through their bodies. Marks argues that 'perception is not an infinite return to the buffet table of lived experiences but a walk through the minefield of embodied memory' (2000: 152). In the ethnographic material analysed in this chapter, we can see how study participants used the cinema and its stories to deliberately manipulate their relation to time, and alternately experienced feelings of surprise when ambushed by an embodied memory raised by their sensory experiences at the cinema.

Time, Cinema and Japan

As Chapter 1 outlined, cinema and time are caught up in narratives of technological advancement in the early years of Japanese film history. Tessa Morris-Suzuki argues that 'the dimensions of space and time have been deployed in Japanese debates on nationhood' (1997: 4), and cinema culture has been no exception to this national trend. Eric Cadzyn reminds us that 'in the case of Japan, the history of film and the history of the modern nation share approximately the same span of time, both emerging in the 1890s' (2002: 52). Japanese time, as compared to US time or French time, was measured in the development, importing and adapting of cinema apparatus in the early years, as Japan strove to catch up to perceived advanced nations – note the temporally specific language common to descriptions of this endeavour. By the postwar era, in which participants in my study were spending large amounts of time at the cinema, Japanese filmmakers were praised not only as having fully caught up with but even overtaken their peers around the world. For example, Gilles Deleuze credited Ozu Yasujirō with both inventing and anticipating the pure time-image (Cadzyn 2002: 235), becoming 'the first to develop pure optical and sounds situations . . . the inventor of opsigns and sonsigns' as early as the 1930s (Deleuze 1989: 13).

Deleuze distinguished the direct time-image from the movement-image, as 'a co-existence of distinct durations' in which 'a single event can belong to many levels' (1989: 9). The treatment of time in scholarship on Japanese cinema has tended towards a similarly philosophical line of inquiry, exploring the manipulations and representations of time within a film narrative or in the work of a particular director or generation. In this chapter I take a different approach, thinking instead of time as it is experienced by viewers. Following Janet Staiger's warning against 'limiting the writing of film reception history' by 'assuming the time spent watching the film is the context of the event' (2000: 51), I expand this discussion into the treatment of time in the individual life narratives of participants in my study. Staiger argues:

> Some scholars of reception write as though 'experiencing' the text stops at the end of the show. Even if the audience has been perfectly bourgeois and quiet during the movie, talk happens afterward – and a great deal of it. To analyse the ideological, cultural, and personal effects of film viewing, we must also consider postmovie talk by spectators. (2000: 51)

In the following chapter, I integrate analysis of 'postmovie talk by spectators' with historical background on life in early postwar Japan to consider the effects of film viewing on participants' development of a coherent life narrative and sense of self.

Film is 'a medium and methodology of time and memory' which operates on the passage of time and the practice of commemoration (Campbell 2005: 164). Jan Campbell argues, 'Reading film ethnography in relation to hitherto antithetical discourses of psychoanalysis and cultural studies defines film spectatorship as a phenomenological and retrospective screen memory' (2005: 164). While this study largely avoids psychoanalytic approaches, I am indebted to the phenomenological scholarship of Laura Marks and Vivian Sobchack for my conceptualisation of the relation between time and film viewership. Sobchack's understanding of the cinematic subject as 'always in the act of displacing itself in time, space, and the world' and therefore 'always eluding its own (as well as our) containment' (2004: 150) shapes both my understanding of the ethnographic material analysed here and at the same time my awareness of the limits of that understanding. Thinking of the film as a prompt for the production of a memory narrative, we can better understand the role of talking about cinema in creating a sense of an identity or self that can be understood and shared by others:

> ... memory texts may create, rework, repeat, and re-contextualise the stories people tell each other about the kinds of lives they have led; and these memory-stories can assume a timeless, even a mythic quality which may be enhanced with every re-telling. Such everyday myth-making works at the levels of both personal and collective memory and is key, in the production, through memory, of shared identities. (Kuhn 2002: 11)

Spending Time, Passing Time and Killing Time at the Cinema

The treatment of time itself in Japan has been associated with modernity and development, both national and personal. While timekeeping and time-telling devices were known before the Meiji Restoration of 1868 in Japan, the purchase of time devices increased after 1868 as 'time was becoming an increasingly unified social system' in Japan (Voelcker 2021: 116). Meiji ethics readers for schoolchildren emphasised the importance of punctuality and extracting maximum productivity from spare time using the phrase 'time is money' (*toki wa kane nari*), which had become known in Japan in the nineteenth century (Kuriyama 2002: 217, 222). In 1873 the solar Gregorian calendar replaced Japan's lunar calendar, and in 1887 railway time was standardised in Japan. In 1888 Japan standard time was synchronised with Greenwich Mean Time, 'entering a global system' (Voelcker 2021: 116) of timekeeping and awareness of time; how it was spent and what that might say about those spending or keeping it. Time Day (*Toki no kinenbi*) was established in 1920, along with a series of exhibitions which sought to educate the public in the skills and etiquette of managing time (Voelcker 2021: 117). Hideaki Fujiki argues that cinema changed many everyday people's sense of time around this period by rendering time communal (2019: 113–14).

While the educational opportunities afforded by cinema were championed by governments, Occupation forces, educational boards and teachers, these same groups were also acutely aware of the potential dangers of spending time at the cinema, in the context of well-entrenched discourses which advocated against the spending of time on non-productive pursuits. While the scheduling of film screenings could have some disciplining effect similar to that of train schedules (Fujiki 2019: 113–14), in that cinemagoers were encouraged to pay attention to time in order to know when a screening would take place, the common practice of entering a theatre mid-screening continued until the 1960s, somewhat lessening the effect of scheduling on awareness of timekeeping.

There are some historical differences between the temporal experience of going to the cinema in early postwar Japan and visiting the local multiplex today. Double and even triple bills were common screening structures from the late 1940s to the 1970s, as the vertically integrated studios aimed to ensure financial returns on their products by coupling newer, less famous or unpopular films with franchise productions or those that could be expected to have a guaranteed audience. The popular or franchise film would draw viewers, who would often stay for the second film and perhaps form an engagement with a new star, director or narrative series. Newsreels and short animated features could round out a programme to a number of hours. As discussed in Chapter 1, the 'stuffing system' of packing theatres to capacity left many viewers standing for a number of those hours or for a whole programme. While this environment suggests an element of discomfort, the cinema was nonetheless a convenient place for many people to stop while travelling between work, home or school. For example, one questionnaire respondent born in 1943 remembered going to the cinema regularly from the age of eight because it was not always possible to return home immediately after the school day: 'I didn't have a key for the house, so I was relieved to be able to spend time at the cinema.' We can think of the time spent in the cinema theatre not only as time lost or spent by those deliberately seeking entertainment but also as otherwise dead time to be filled with something more entertaining than simply waiting, with the attendant comfort of protection from the elements and perhaps a place to sit.

Yet cinema retains its reputation as a place to lose or waste time that could otherwise be productively used. Postwar teachers appear to have been aware of the attractions of the cinema as a place to spend time that could instead have been dedicated to studying. Many male participants in my study remembered being scolded by teachers for engaging with cinema materials on the way to or from school. Furthermore, teachers and other adults in the lives of my study participants were often cited as having made the first associations that the participants perceived between the cinema as a place to spend time and the danger of being drawn into temptation. The majority of study participants hesitated to name these temptations directly, but many stories connected the cinema to idle vandalism and loitering, as well as more serious issues. Many participants' stories of being scolded or disciplined by teachers or parents for engaging with film culture by lingering over posters or magazines feature a strong suggestion of sexual attraction. In the stories contributed by male study participants, this generally manifested in digressions about the beauty of a certain actress or speculation about friends or schoolmates being attracted to a particular star. In the historical context of the early postwar years, when popular culture appeared to be sexualising rapidly (Saito 2014; González López 2019), the stories of my study participants gesture to an uncertainty on the part of children and teachers as to where and when popular culture could be safely consumed. Time and place were interlinked in that certain places became dangerous or undesirable at certain times; for example, amusement districts were considered potentially sinister after dark.

Even on a socially sanctioned family trip to the film theatre, the cinema had a way of distorting the regular process of time and the accepted way of using and dealing with time. One questionnaire respondent remembered her first trip to the cinema as an occasion for staying out unusually late, and several recalled that being brought to the cinema by a family member often meant missing their evening meal. Going to the cinema was therefore a way of negotiating time, from staying out late to spending time on entertainment rather than schoolwork. One did not even have to watch a film to spend time engaging with cinema culture. Walking slowly past advertisements and billboards, as many study participants remembered doing, or poring over film magazines, was also a means of spending time in the cinema sphere.

Film Viewing and Prosthetic Memory

A significant majority of participants in my study used speaking about the cinema as a way of situating their experiences in a particular time. As a large number were born between 1940 and 1945, with a concentration around 1943, many have a sense of this turning point in Japanese history as an uncertain memory. Several interviewees mentioned viewing films either made or retrospectively set during the war as a means of confirming hazy memories. Many had heard family stories passed down through generations for so long that they were unsure which memories were really their own, if there can be such a thing. For example, Hashimoto san spoke of confirming his memories of air raids with both his older brother and with film texts depicting similar scenes:

> As I was born in Shōwa 18 [1943], well, after that I listened to my older brother, and I confirmed that these things really happened. For example, of course we were out in the countryside, but we often had air raid warnings, the siren would sound and we'd have to run for the bomb shelter. I remember one time falling over on the way – the bomb shelter was at the house next door. Well, I remember that. And on the nights Nagoya was bombed, I remember my father saying, 'Ah, tonight Nagoya's being bombed again, I guess.' I saw that the front face of the mountain was all red. Of course, I also remember my father telling me all about it, and later when I saw films about it, I thought, 'They really showed that well (*umai*).' (Hashimoto 2016)

While speaking, Hashimoto san acted out the air raid experience, waving a hand over his head to represent airplanes, gesturing to the left to indicate the process of evacuating, and sending his hands, head and shoulders forward and down suddenly to mimic falling over on his way to the shelter, laughing sheepishly at his mistake. This animated performance had the effect of bringing me as the listener into the story, and I became focused on expressing sympathy for his panic and fall, rather than assessing the memory claim itself.

While I remained slightly sceptical of the possibility of someone retaining a memory from such a young age so clearly, Hashimoto san's gestures and expressions throughout the story appeared very sincere. Touching his hand to his heart, he insisted, 'No matter how young, you can remember that kind of strong memory, from 2 or 3 years old.' Smiling, he counted out two and three on his fingers, as though to confirm the timeline of events for himself: 'If I was born in 1943 in March, I would have been . . .' Hashimoto san looked down at his hand and counted on his fingers again: '. . . 19, 20, ah, well then, 2 and a half. But I think that I remember it well.' He laughed a little, then nodded decisively: 'I remember it. Yes.' While his repeated laughter suggested that he was aware of the slight absurdity of this memory claim, Hashimoto san's gestures of sincerity, in the hand placed on his heart, and rigour, in the repeated counting on his fingers to verify ages and dates, gave the strong impression of someone who believed his own memory narrative and was invested in making it believable to a listener. While it is impossible to verify whether someone holds a memory of an event of their youth, it seemed clear to me at least that Hashimoto san did have a strong sense of a memory of wartime and that it was important to his account of himself that this memory be included in his narrative.

Assuming that he would not have clear memories from his early childhood years, I had asked Hashimoto san whether he thought that watching films set during the war helped him to understand the memories of the wartime generation. I was surprised when his answer focused on his own early memories rather than the experiences of his elder family members. He mentioned his father and brother, and recalled them telling him about the events of wartime, but he seemed most keen to weave together his family members' testimonies and the narratives and imagery of certain films, not as a means of reconstructing a past in which he was not present, but as a means of confirming his own perceived early memories. In his answers, Hashimoto san appeared to be identifying himself as a member of the 'wartime generation' (*sensō jidai*), rather than a postwar child. In this way, cinema content could present a means of temporal emplacement for the generations born in the liminal years at the end of the war, who were not quite the war generation but also not quite the *apure* (*après*) or postwar generation.

In the narratives of many interviewees and survey participants in this project, a sense of having war memories emerged from affectively charged recollections of going to the cinema, engaging with film culture and sharing film spaces with others. While the basis of these perceived memories in fact (or otherwise) is hard to prove or disprove, cinema was discussed as evoking a closeness to wartime and to the generations who experienced Japan's wars before 1945. The memories discussed in this chapter are therefore not treated as factual historical accounts. Rather, I explore the role of postwar cinema culture as 'enabler of "prosthetic memory"' (Keene 2010: 2; Landsberg 2004). Alison Landsberg coined the term 'prosthetic memory' to describe 'a new form of public cultural memory' located 'at the interface between a person and a historical narrative about the past at an experiential site such as a movie theatre or a museum' (2004: 2). In such encounters, Landsberg suggests that 'the person does not simply apprehend a historical narrative but takes on a more personal, deeply felt memory of a past event through which he or she did not live' (2004: 2). We can therefore understand the process of engaging with war narratives on film as a means of bringing the cinemagoer closer to an understanding of Japan's war history, in light of the 'enabling modalities' offered by cinema culture (Keene 2010: 10).

Landsberg argues that 'through an act of prosthesis enabled by cinematic identification' the memories of events that we did not personally live through 'become part of our archive of memory' (2003: 155). In the memories shared by my study participants, favourite films and fond recollections of cinemagoing could ease even unpleasant narratives such as war and defeat into the 'archive of memory' kept by those with no direct personal experience of the events in question. While date of birth precluded a number of study participants from directly experiencing events that had formative influence on their lives in postwar Japan, many were also unfamiliar with the war histories of specific areas or regions that they later moved to as adults. Western Japan and the Kansai area, as a region comprised of very different major cities with rural areas in between, has a diverse range of war experiences. While rural agricultural areas such as Gifu were relatively safe from bombing, food scarcity was a major issue. The port areas of Osaka and Kobe were vulnerable to attack, while Kyoto experienced minimal firebombing in comparison to Tokyo yet was bombed in 1945 in the Higashiyama ward (16 January 1945) and Kamigyō ward (26 June 1945) (*Kakusareteita Kūshū*, Kyoto Air Raid Memorial Society 1979: 170–1).

Western Japan and the Kansai region also have distinctive migration patterns, as travel between rural areas and the city is today very convenient. It is perfectly possible to work in Kyoto and live in Kobe or Osaka, as many people do. Many participants in my study moved from one area to another for work or marriage. In such a geographically local move, they nonetheless had to familiarise themselves with the particularities of their new hometowns, including specialised dialect, produce, cooking and hospitality styles. A part of this familiarisation in the postwar period involved making oneself aware of what kind of war experiences were particular to one's new region, as opposed to those distinct to one's hometown. This would involve a kind of time travel, as the histories of the recent past became clear to new arrivals in the area. Cinema content helped to situate many study participants both geographically and temporally in the years after the war, as they explored Western Japan's diverse range of war memories through film viewing.

Like many of my interviewees, Koyama san brought a range of photographs and film materials to our meetings (see Figure 3.1). Unlike others who brought favourite film magazines, star photographs, postcards and programme handbills from films they had seen, however, she also brought large printouts of her favourite film posters, and photographs of her local area taken before she was born. Showing me black-and-white photographs taken in 1942, two years before her birth, she pointed out historical details such as the common practice of writing shop signs from right to left, as opposed to today's fashion for writing from left to right. She mixed together the photographs and film posters, laying them out in her lap, and the two sets of materials together prompted her recollections of the everyday life of wartime and early postwar Japan: 'Ah, you know this one! Everyone loved that star back then. Of course, in those days there were no baths in the houses, but there were plenty of big family homes around. Everyone listened to the radio at home and then talked about it at the bathhouse. It was that kind of thing. I hardly saw it, but later at the Bunpaku I could see it [on film].'

Figure 3.1 Koyama san brought photographs and printed film posters to her interview.

Koyama san wove together the aspirational, in terms of stars and nationwide fame, with the extremely banal in her story of the bathhouse conversations, prompted by her collection of film materials. She contextualised her story after its telling by acknowledging that she had only slight memories of this era: 'I hardly saw it.' Yet her experience of seeing films set in this period at the Bunpaku theatre appeared to give her a feeling of ownership over this memory of historical and national change, at least to the extent that she felt able to educate a foreign researcher about the era. She also brought photographs of everyday postwar life taken outside her hometown of Kōshien, in Osaka city centre and in Kobe. Pointing to a picture of returnee soldiers begging in the street, dressed in the distinctive white clothing of those injured in war, she recalled, 'They were always in Osaka city, and in Sannomiya in Kobe . . . You could see them for around ten years after the war. After the Korean War you didn't really see them anymore though. Of course, they're the people who came back after defeat in the Second World War.' Though Koyama san grew up in a smaller town which did not have returnees begging in the street, her brief experiences visiting the centres of Osaka and Kobe, and her identification with the era itself as a period in living memory, contributed to her desire to incorporate these more iconic aspects of postwar life into her personal story:

> Let's see. Well, around the time of the Korean War, conditions in Japan suddenly improved, as if overnight. In the five years before that, the streets were full of injured soldiers, people who had returned from the war playing accordions and shining shoes . . . I was only a child, and of course I couldn't see how conditions were everywhere, but when I looked at the state of Japan, well, it just seemed so poor . . . When I see those stories from my childhood in films, the memories all come back, and I feel nostalgic. (Koyama san, born 1944)

Producing photographs taken by others of the years immediately before her birth was a means of claiming legitimacy for her role as memory keeper, shoring up Koyama san's effort to impart a sense of a historical period which neither of us had directly experienced. Her possession of and fluency in reading these photographs established the Japanese Koyama san, though born slightly later than the period under discussion, as a legitimate transmitter of the story of the era for a younger, non-Japanese audience such as myself. The photographs became a physical manifestation of the same pattern in our discussions on cinema narratives, serving as confirmation of knowledge about an earlier time as well as a handy illustration, or appeal to a shared visual language, which eased the communication of these half-remembered events or prosthetic memories. In Koyama san's spoken memories, cinema and everyday life were tied together, one explaining and contextualising the other. She saw nothing strange in mixing together photographs from her own life and from the time before her birth, and promotional material for films dealing with similar eras and themes.

Koyama san's father did not go to war, but she recalled strong memories of seeing images of American soldiers riding through Occupied Japan in their Jeeps, giving out chocolate. She was at pains to point out that her memories did not include any sense of bitterness or hatred directed towards the Occupiers from the adults and children around her: 'There was absolutely no sense of having lost, I mean, among the children, and we didn't have any people close to us who had died, so a lot of people felt that they [the American soldiers] were here to give help. Because we were children, there was absolutely so sense of enmity.' Instead, she remembered her mother making new clothes from old scraps based on the designs they had seen in Hollywood movies. While the imagery of the photographs that she brought communicated a visual sense of the hardship of the end of the war, Koyama san's stories about imported films and friendships with Americans borrowed from the uplifting effect of much mainstream cinema to present a prosthetic war memory palatable to a non-Japanese audience. Though Landsberg has primarily imagined prosthetic memory as reaching out across generations and bridging the gap between those who have experienced an event and those who have not, we must also consider its transnational impact, extending across places as well as time to build a memory that works for many sides of a past conflict.

While Landsberg disavows 'anything *inherently* positive or progressive' about prosthetic memory enabled by technologies such as cinema (2003: 157), she does argue for prosthetic memory as able 'to affect people in profound ways – both intellectually and emotionally – in ways that might ultimately change the way they think, and how they act, in the world' (2003: 158). The majority of the participants in my study explicitly connected their present-day personal attitudes and political orientations to the power of cinema to communicate difficult truths and sentiments about Japan's war and Occupation. As Koyama san suggested,

> Japan's history and its postwar recovery can be felt through stories on film. It can be a good way to study, and I think that if children can watch good films that touch their hearts, they can become people capable of being moved emotionally. (Koyama, 2016)

Koyama san clearly associated learning from Japan's past with becoming a person whose heart can be touched by others' suffering, and situated cinema as a technology which could help to develop these feelings. In this way, the prosthetic memories fostered by viewing and discussing cinema narratives about wartime contribute to an account of oneself as a person who accepts the 'collective social responsibility' inherent in the promise of cinema as 'a utopian dream' (Landsberg 2003: 158), wherein bridges across diverse experiences, geographies and times can be built.

Cinema Viewing as Time Travel

In looking for the just-missed past experienced by parents and older siblings in cinema content, many of the participants in this study who were born in the 1940s used the cinema as a means of achieving a kind of time travel. Film content itself had an element of temporal disruption during the Occupation era (1945–52) due to censorship and import laws. As discussed in preceding chapters, the strict censorship carried out by the Civil Information and Education Bureau (CIE) and the Civil Censorship Detachment (CCD) of the General Headquarters of the Supreme Commander of the Allied Powers (SCAP GHQ) included a ban on any mention of the Occupation of Japan. Film characters based on Allied personnel, the depiction of English-language conversation and signs, and explicit discussion of rationing and the black market were discouraged, though many filmmakers managed to slip some or all of these aspects into otherwise censorship-compliant texts, such as Kurosawa Akira's *One Wonderful Sunday* (*Subarashiki nichiyōbi*, 1947), which features English-language signage. Discussing the war onscreen was also tricky, as storylines and dialogue perceived to be sympathetic to Imperial ideologies were excised by censors. Period drama films (*jidaigeki*) were discouraged due to their perceived feudal associations, though leading directors such as Mizoguchi Kenji managed to make some Edo period (1603–1867) dramas under Occupation censorship.

After the end of Occupation in 1952, a rush of films revisited the wartime, Occupation and pre-modern eras, covering themes as diverse as the revival of the popular *47 Loyal Retainers* (*Chūshingura*) tale, wartime events (*The Human Condition/Ningen no jōken*, Kobayashi Masaki, 1959–61), Occupation politics and everyday encounters, including Occupation-related sex work (*Gate of Flesh/Nikutai no mon*, 1964), and the atomic bombings of Hiroshima and Nagasaki and their aftermath (*Children of the Bomb/Genbaku no ko*, Shindō Kaneto, 1952; *Hiroshima*, Sekigawa Hideo, 1953; *Twenty-Four Eyes/Nijūshi no hitomi*, Kinoshita Keisuke, 1954). Much post-Occupation cinema was in this sense already period film, dealing with issues that had occurred almost a decade ago.

In the case of the 'war-retro' genre film, made in the 1950s and 1960s but set during wartime, Isolde Standish has argued that commercial cinema logic rearranges traumatic war memories and events 'into ordered evidence of empirical historical facts through the imposition of teleological sequences of time and an all-knowing omniscient narration style' (2011: 52). I believe we can make a similar argument for the representation of life under Occupation in post-Occupation commercial cinema. For study participants who grew up during the Occupation, post-Occupation films set during the war or Occupation periods presented a means of contextualising and exploring their early childhood memories in a retrospective mode.

For many study participants, postwar film content presented a means to connect to the memories of older generations. This was the case both for those who were children during the postwar era and for those born significantly after the war, such as Inoue san, born in 1958. Gesturing outwards from his chest with his right hand in an indication of overwhelming feelings rushing out, Inoue san discussed his preference for films from his parents' era: 'Through films, I can learn about how society was before I was born, things I didn't know (*jibun ga shiranai, chotto umareru izen gurai no eiga, shakai mo shiremasu*), and because of that, I really love those old films and I watch them with a lot of respect (*sonkei*).' Inoue san associated older films, particularly those featuring war narratives, as a means of understanding the unstated experiences of older generations and of developing a respectful understanding of their lives.

Film was conceptualised by many participants in my study as a bridge between generations of a family. Hashimoto san, whose best friend lost his father in the war, approached war films as a means to understand his older friends' and acquaintances' experiences. Placing his hand on his chest in a gesture of sincerity, he recalled:

> We [*watashitachi*], that is, my companions of the same age, had fathers who had died in the war, and whose friends had died in the war, and of course I felt very sorry for them. I don't know much about the actual experience of war, but those films like *Tower of Lilies* (*Himeyuri no tō*, Imai Tadashi, 1953), where the schoolgirls passed away, where they died, and nuclear films [*genbaku no eiga*] and those kinds of things, of course war and that kind of thing is awful [*dame*], from around primary school I thought that. Today we feel that the government should not be forgiven. Because Japan lost the war, and because of the Peace Constitution, we should be 'A Country with no War'. With all their effort, all across Japan, people make every effort not to become like that era again. And so, I think that we got a good influence from those films. (Hashimoto 2016)

From his high-school years onwards, Hashimoto san felt that he was strongly influenced by the content of pacifist postwar war-retro films such as *Tower of Lilies*, and at the time of our interview expressed vehement support for the pacifist goals of Article 9 of the 1947 Constitution of Japan. As Chapter 6 will detail, many viewers attributed their political ideologies to the content of specific films made in the postwar years. Here I'd like to explore the place of generational and family connections in accounts of such viewership experiences. While Hashimoto san imagined viewing war films as a means of attaining greater understanding of the experiences of the elder generations with whom he grew up, his recollections of such movies and his own emotional response were strongly tied to his own family.

Hashimoto san remembered his elder brothers and sisters teasing him about his emotional reactions to particular war films.

> As there were many siblings in my family, my elder brother and sister often took me to the cinema. I remember one time, I must have been around eight years old (I've checked this with my older sister), and my sister took me to a film with Ishihama Akira playing a character who gets sent to war around high-school age. The soldiers have to get up so early and suffer physically. There was that song, I forget the name . . . [sings] *tan tan tan ta ta tan ta ta tan*. That music appeared when the soldiers marched out, and when I saw it I cried a lot. When we got back home, I remember that my sister told everyone, 'Yo-chan caused me some amount of trouble!' (Hashimoto 2016)

In Hashimoto san's accounts, he emphasised his own emotional reaction to war narratives on film, while contextualising his response as unusual in comparison to his elder relatives' own responses and expectations. His sister joked that his emotional response caused trouble for her, as everyone wondered why the child she was escorting was crying. At the same time, he also described certain films, such as the teachers' union-sponsored *Hiroshima*, as 'crying films' (*nakeru eiga*), suggesting that others in the theatre may have been doing the same. In such accounts of viewing war films, crying or otherwise engaging emotionally with the narrative appeared to be a way of coming closer to the elder generation and their experiences, albeit in a particularly postwar way.

Several study participants recalled feeling a similar sense of emotional pity and admiration for those who suffered through the extreme poverty of the wartime and postwar eras in Japan. As previously mentioned, almost every respondent noted the poverty (*mazushii*) of the era, and several expressed gratitude to the elder generations, including their own parents, for working through this difficult time. Born in 1957 in Kobe, Kobayashi san felt that film was an important tool for learning about this era and continues to be so today. Watching war films and film made during wartime, he argued: 'You can understand the feeling not only of those who died in the war, but also those women who became widows', and that the cumulative effect is of something like a 'national experience' (*kokuminteki keiken*) shown on film. Despite the differences in regional and geographical experience sketched above, Kobayashi san, who lived all his life in Kobe excepting his university years spent in Tokyo, conceptualised the time period of the war and Occupation as a kind of national experience or communal experience (*kyōtsu keiken*). Yet he worried that not many people were going to see the films that depicted this overarching temporal experience:

> After the period of high economic growth, Japan's poverty problem didn't exactly disappear, but things certainly changed. People who had been really poor could now have a middle-class lifestyle. At the same time, as years passed since the end of the war, those experiences quickly faded from film, and were replaced by stuff like violent *yakuza* films . . . It's unfortunate, but there aren't any really excellent people shown on film anymore. (Kobayashi 2016)

Kobayashi san connected his respect for the older generation, whose suffering he felt he understood and contextualised by watching films about the wartime and postwar periods, with a higher standard of filmmaking. The idea of excellence in relation to human qualities is extrapolated to excellence in filmmaking.

Inoue san, who approached war and postwar films as a means of historical understanding, similarly expressed as much respect for the craft of filmmaking displayed in the Occupation era as for the character types depicted struggling through difficult historical circumstances, and for their real-life equivalents. Gesturing outwards from himself with one hand in a rolling circular motion that suggested a reel or repetitive turning, he noted, 'At that time, well, the movie theatres were full of people, and at the same time there were many really wonderful movies. No matter how many times you watch them, films from that time are really interesting.' Looking off into the distance with a dreamy expression, he recalled watching Ōzu Yasujirō's films set in the 1950s: 'When I watch his depictions of that period, well . . .' Onoue san smiled gently and tilted his head to one side. 'I don't know if it depicts the average Japan, well, it's so elegant, and people use such polite language [gesturing outwards repeatedly with his right hand, indicating talking] that I think it's really a little unrealistic, but it's a beautiful image of a Japan of the past.' Moving his hand outwards as though sending a feeling out from the chest area, with a distant expression, he smiled: 'When I see it, I get a sense that my heart feels refreshed (*mo hontōni kokoro ga arawareru yō na kimochi ni natte*).' Inoue san also commented on the low camera angle used in Ōzu's films, and like Kobayashi san he connected his respect for those elder generations living in a different 'social situation' with his admiration for the craft and technical innovations of postwar Japanese cinema.

This conflation was evident in the way a number of participants discussed their memories of watching Kinoshita Keisuke's *Twenty-Four Eyes* (*Nijūshi no hitomi*, 1954), an explicitly anti-war film which schoolteachers often showed to their classes. Almost everyone who went to school in the 1950s was shown this film either in class or on school trips to the cinema. The film's depiction of the suffering of the characters during militarisation and war made a great impact on participants in my study. At the same time, many expressed admiration not only for the ideological content of the film but for the innovations in filmmaking that it showcases. The twelve pupils of the title grew from five-year-old children to adults over the course of the film, which spans more than twenty years. Kinoshita Keisuke cast non-professional child actors living on the island on which the film is set, with one particular proviso. Only families of siblings were cast, so that younger and elder siblings could play the same character at different moments in the character's narrative. Inoue san recalled, 'At first I thought the six-year-olds and the twelve-year-olds were the same people, just a few years apart. When I read that they were siblings, I was so surprised! I thought that idea was really interesting.' In coming closer to the elder generations, and a different period in time through watching postwar films, study participants' statements suggested that they felt they were not only learning about wartime and Occupation experiences but also coming closer to a golden age of cinematic artistry and invention.

In its ability to transport the viewer back to an earlier period of their life, the encounter with cinema appeared to have some time-travel-like qualities for many participants in my study. Several recounted pleasurable feelings of nostalgia when watching films from their younger years. Viewers in the post-1955 generations also spoke of nostalgia in relation to watching film texts made before they were born. In these instances, the idea of nostalgia appeared to be more of an imagined national concept than a personal one. These viewers were not only attempting to understand earlier periods of Japanese history, and the experiences of older generations through cinema, but they also appeared to be searching for some kind of imagined national sentiment in regard to the difficult wartime and postwar years.

The Passage of Time: Ageing along with Cinema Culture

In their continued engagement with cinema, viewers of postwar film texts not only travelled imaginatively back to earlier times in national and personal histories but also practised their own technologies of temporal emplacement. Today, various film theatres, studios and institutions capitalise on continuing popular interest in postwar films, directors and stars. Several study participants made a point of attending not only film retrospectives but also 'talk show' live speaking events with directors, studio personnel and stars active in the postwar era. These participants spoke of the filmmakers and stars they encountered in nostalgic terms, yet at the same time directly addressed the passage of time between their first encounters with the star or director's work and the age of both the study participant and the filmmaker at the time of their meeting. In this way, elements of personal self-presentation that resist or deny the phenomena of ageing and time passing were woven together with acknowledgement of the same phenomena.

Hashimoto san remembered attending a 'lecture' (*kōgikai*) event featuring popular actress Yachigusa Kaoru in the Takarazuka area of Kansai.

> It was a lecture followed by a simple party, so of course I got on my motorbike and rode from Kobe over the Rokkō Mountains to Takarazuka to listen to Yachigusa Kaoru talk. And then I went to the little party afterwards. At that time, she must have been around 15 years older than me, but she was still so beautiful (*taihen kirei*). She was so beautiful that I took a lot of pictures, and when I got home my wife really told me off. 'Why did you take so many pictures?' She was quite worried! Of course, that was ten years ago, so by now Yachigusa Kaoru must really have become an old lady (*obasan ni narimashita*). But what can you do about that, eh? (*kore wa shōganai desu kedo ne*). (Hashimoto 2016)

Hashimoto san's story wove together an acknowledgement of the passing of time, in phrases such as 'that was ten years ago', with elements that resisted conventional ideas of ageing, such as a description of his mountaintop motorbike ride and the actress' age-defying beauty. The observation that a particular actress is 'still beautiful' or an actor 'still cool' (*kakkoi*) pervaded many study participants' reminiscences. As discussed in more detail in the following chapter, Imai san brought several photographs of his meetings with actor Mikuni Rentarō and actress Junko Fuji (also known as Sumiko Fuji) to our interview, noting that the two had hardly aged. By contrast, he showed a later photograph of an ill Mikuni just before his death, pointing out how rapidly his condition and appearance had deteriorated. Like Hashimoto san, he treated this event philosophically, shrugging that ageing comes to us all. In this way, continued engagement with the cinema became a means both to place oneself in the wider context of Japanese history and to come to terms with the process of ageing and with one's generation's popular culture and ideals fading into history.

For some participants in my study, ageing alongside the cinema offered new opportunities in relation to how they spent their time. Koyama san shared that her early interest in cinema had been reignited by her husband's retirement from his demanding bank job. Whereas he had been away from the family home for long hours each day during most of their life together, now that he had retired he wished to be at home and make use of his leisure time and the space his working salary had purchased. Many female study participants had expressed frustration at finding their husbands suddenly underfoot after retirement, even joking that they were envious of the free lifestyles of the women whose husbands had passed away. Koyama san expressed no such feelings, but she did articulate the moment of her husband's retirement as a point where their roles changed significantly. He wished to study Latin and French in the home and she felt that it was better to be out of the way when he did so. She began attending daily screenings at the Bunpaku film theatre and at a local community centre in order to make space and time for his studies. At our first interview, she joked that watching films was like a new job, and she had become the 'salaryman' of the family who commuted every day. She took her job seriously, watching around a hundred films per year. Koyama san spoke of film as something that had enabled her new life, and also as the dedicated object of this new life. She hesitated to compare her film viewing with her husband's more explicitly academic studies, but at the same time insisted on her viewing as a kind of learning experience, and on her relationship to cinema as, 'more than a fan; it's my life'.

Although the group of ladies mentioned above frequently joked about envying their widowed friends, those same friends took a similar attitude to Koyama san in terms of associating cinema with a new temporal phase in their lives. In this case, as many of the deceased partners of these participants had worked in the film industry, their widows took responsibility for representing and explaining their work and the context in which it was produced. This group of women in their mid-seventies had been among the most generous of my study participants and friends, sharing precious film ephemera and academic materials with me over the course of this project. Several maintained collections of their husbands' film-related materials and often passed these on to me at interviews and social meetings. For example, Otsuka san gifted me many copies of the highbrow *Kinema Junpō* film magazines that her husband had collected over the years. The magazines that Otsuka san selected from her husband's collection were always the most cerebral, artistic or industry-oriented, for example, a commemorative edition marking the death of director Ozu Yasujirō, a 'Best Ten' edition listing the top-rated films for the year 1964 and a 'Who's Who' of the industry from the same year. Like Koyama san, these ladies embraced cinema culture as a kind of new job for their later years, casting themselves as custodians of a period they all acknowledged as the 'golden age' of Japanese cinema production, even when they would not particularly identify as fans of specific films, directors or stars. As I prepared to leave Japan, a number of ladies in this group gifted their husbands' entire collections of film ephemera to me, and two even visited me in my new home in the UK in the year after my departure. Engagement with the cinema offered many different ways to mark the passing of time, and opportunities to reinvent the self within that context.

Manipulating Time through Film Viewership

The personal time of the self could also be manipulated through film viewing. During interviews and in my questionnaire project, I was struck by how often viewers referred to watching a film many times. While in today's on-demand media culture we may decide to watch a favourite film multiple times, or watch together with a friend who has not seen the film before, many study participants used repetition in a slightly different way in their own viewership practices. The majority of participants in this study stated preferences for watching films in cinema theatres and on television, while a few used DVD stores, and none watched on streaming services or Internet sites at the time of the study. Few came across a repeated film by accident, rather choosing to bring themselves to the cinema or making appointments to watch films on television after consulting a guide. In this sense, repeated viewing was very much a deliberate choice. Hashimoto san emphasised the repeated travelling to the cinema which watching a film several times would necessitate: 'I loved Arakan [actor Arashi Kanjūrō], so I went to see his films many times.' For many, the habit of returning regularly to watch the same film, actor or franchise repeatedly was formed in childhood and continued to the time of our meeting. In this sense, both the practice and the content were continued instances of repetition, where study participants visited the same theatre every day to view films made in the period in which they grew up and first encountered the cinema.

Several stated a belief that the value of a film text became apparent through repeated viewing. All interviewees, and a majority of questionnaire respondents, used a variation of the phrase 'no matter how many times I watch it, it's still enjoyable' to assess the quality of a film. Bad films were described as films you cannot watch many times. The time spent rewatching a film was not considered wasteful, but rather a way to heighten one's appreciation of the kind of cinema that endures across time.

Inoue san connected this kind of cinema to the particular temporal period of the era after the war, as opposed to the period after 1970: 'However many times you watch those films, and repeat them, they're still interesting.' By contrast, Imai san disliked Kurosawa Akira's films because he could not watch them repeatedly without becoming bored: 'For me, when I watch Mizoguchi Kenji or Ozu Yasujirō's films over and over, I don't get tired of them. No matter how many years have passed, they are like new.' The ability of a film to stand up to repetition was considered by many to be a marker of its quality.

Kishida san connected repeated viewing to a heightened affective response to cinema texts: 'Because people are sensory beings (*kankakuhan ningen*), of course the story is important, but if you watch a film several times, by the end you become quite moved (*kandō*), and so the feeling is . . . Well, I don't mean watching the same film twice in a year, but if you watch something a couple of times over many years, well, you can feel the emotions quite strongly.' Viewers appeared to build strong feelings for particular films and actors by watching the same texts several times. In this way, time was manipulated for emotional stimulation, as the nostalgia factor was heightened by drawing remembrances of many periods into the associations of one film. The viewer connected not only with the past Japan shown in the wartime or postwar film but also with the time setting of the film text itself, a memory of the first time the viewer saw the film, or a text by the same director, or featuring the same actor, and memories of each repeated viewing after that layer to form an emotional engagement.

The separation of place and time between Chapters 2 and 3 is not ideal in that both are intertwined in the memories that study participants shared with me and in their continued viewership practices. By separating the two, I have attempted to explore the question of time in relation to the cinema not as an isolated element, but rather by foregrounding the concern in a way that much film studies scholarship has tended to avoid. In part this omission is logical, as the cinema is often imagined as a place that we go to kill, pass or forget about time. Yet this very manipulation of our personal sense of time, as well as the frequent practice of travelling to another time through the content and narrative of a particular film, fundamentally structures our experience of cinema. As beings in time, the cinema's manipulation of time reflexively structures the selves that we build through viewership.

CHAPTER 4

Stars, Occupiers, Parents and Role Models: Cinema as a Way of Being (Japanese)

> Hara Setsuko was so beautiful, and she had so many male fans. I thought she certainly wasn't like other girls . . . When she died last year, so many men came to the Bunpaku memorial event, they were standing in the aisles, and there were no empty seats scattered about as usual. She really had a lot of male fans. But I always felt, how would you put it, she was a bit above everything. Maybe there were people like that in real life, you know, well, kind of closing their hearts and living out their whole lives alone. I thought, 'Well, I guess there is also that kind of way to live' (*sō iu ikikata mo arun da nā to omoimashita*). (Koyama san 2016)

Many participants in this study explicitly connected watching films in the postwar era to the development of an understanding of how to be in the world. For most, this was a question of variety and possibility. Following the narratives of particular characters and stars, both onscreen and off, presented a variety of lifestyles and opinions. In many cases, the ways of living, and ways of being a person, presented onscreen were narrated as suggesting alternatives to the ways of thinking and behaving that were observable at home. The varieties of 'ways to live' displayed by postwar cinema and its characters and stars ranged from the personal and domestic to the political, and from the adoptable, through the adaptable, to the unacceptable.

Stars as Role Models

Hara Setsuko as a Model of Femininity

Exploring the formative impact of star persona in the lives and personal narratives of participants in my study, I am informed by Richard Dyer's definition of the star persona:

> The star phenomenon consists of everything that is publicly available about stars. A film star's image is not just his or her films, but the promotion of those films and of the star through pin-ups, public appearances, studio handouts and so on, as well

as interviews, biographies and coverage in the press of the star's doings and 'private' life. Further, a star's image is also what people say or write about him or her, as critics or commentators. (Dyer 2004: 2–3)

Participants in my study drew not only from film texts in their construction of role model personae from the popular stars of their youth but also from the press coverage and gossip which they often became aware of later in their cinema encounters.

Hara Setsuko (1920–2015), a wartime child star whose image was rehabilitated in the early postwar era by Kurosawa Akira's humanist *No Regrets for Our Youth* (*Waga seishun ni kui nashi*, 1946), stood out among the popular Japanese stars of the Occupation era for many study participants (see Figure 4.1). Kitamura Kyōhei notes that reactions of audiences for Hara's first postwar film were generally divided by age, with those aged between ten and twenty years old supporting the film's representation of youth, while older viewers were more critical (2017: 123). Readers of the two largest film magazines for the demographic aged ten to twenty, *Eiga fan* (*Film Fan*) and *Shin eiga* (*New Film*), voted Kurosawa's film the best of 1946 (K. Kitamura 2017: 131). Yet audience members aged between mid-teens and early twenties recorded a very different experience of the film from that of older critics (K. Kitamura 2017: 131).

Although Hara was in her mid-twenties during the Occupation, her role in Kurosawa's film required her to portray both the teenage years of the protagonist Yukie and her early adulthood as a working, and later married, woman. Hara modelled onscreen the ideal transition from passionate and active schoolgirl to independent and pro-democratic young woman imagined by the Occupation authorities who censored popular cinema (Conde 1965; MacArthur 1994). Yet even viewers who considered Hara a

Figure 4.1 Signed photograph of Hara Setsuko, from the author's collection.

successful modern woman struggled to see her as a practical role model. Koyama san recalled her youthful response to Hara's star persona using the phrase, 'Well, I guess there is also that kind of way to live' (*sō iu ikikata mo arun da nā to omoimashita*). Hara's 'kind of way to live' would perhaps have been difficult to imagine for young female viewers looking for role models in the Japanese studio system before the Occupation period. The star publicly chided reporters for the gossip and industry presses who quizzed her on her romantic life, insisting on her independence, which led some critics and journalists to brand her 'aloof' (*kokō*) (Kawahara 1947: 30). Male study participants who spoke in her favour noted her aura of separateness, which one survey respondent characterised as 'a different kind of dignity'.

Hara's insistence on privacy was often interpreted as secrecy, either hiding a non-heterosexual orientation (Kanno 2011) or, as some speculated, covering a lifelong love for director Ozu Yasujirō, with whom she worked on some of her most famous films, including the 'Noriko trilogy' comprising *Late Spring* (*Banshun*, 1949), *Early Summer* (*Bakushū*, 1951) and *Tokyo Story* (*Tokyo monogatari*, 1953). Hara retired after the director died in 1963 and became a reclusive figure in the Kamakura area outside Tokyo. While the independent Hara lived out many of the new freedoms female citizens had gained after the ratification of the postwar Constitution in 1947, it would nonetheless have been very difficult to live as she had, fiercely independent and without a recognised family structure. The relentless probing of the gossip and industry presses, as well as a number of unfavourable articles attacking Hara's character (Takada 1949: 31–3), demonstrated that such an independent way of living was not yet considered socially acceptable for young women by many public figures and commentators. Female viewers such as Koyama san seem to have recognised this, despite the SCAP propaganda embedded in popular film texts that encouraged young women to be independent and pursue their heart's desires.

While Hara's independent lifestyle may have appeared new and progressive to Occupation personnel and others in the early postwar years, she was not an entirely unfamiliar figure in the cinematic landscape. Her postwar star persona borrowed heavily from her pre-war work, while erasing her participation in wartime propaganda films by emphasising her strong will and independent mindset. While promoting nationalist sentiments during wartime, Hara was among a number of high-profile Japanese female creatives who counter-intuitively maintained an affiliation with Western nations and cultures, during and after the war. Reference to and performances of mastery of Western culture was later a significant aspect of Hara's appeal for many young women watching her films in the postwar years.

Hara's star persona, championed by the Occupation-era film industry as tailor-made for characters and narratives that would 'permit the industry to reflect the democratic aspirations of the Japanese people' (Allen 1945: 3), was built on the legacy of a different kind of young female independence – that permitted to young women during wartime, when a number of everyday social norms were suspended. In the early postwar period, Hara's perceived Westernisation and independent attitude were the target of a backlash from adult, educated and generally elite male film critics. Yet many young female viewers remained attracted to her, finding in her Western dress and idiosyncratic mannerisms a model for their own behaviours.

One study participant, who chose the English pseudonym Elizabeth and included English- language material as well as Japanese in her questionnaire response, recalled copying Hara's smile in the mirror as a young girl and attempting to mimic her laugh. Elizabeth's use of an anglophone name and selected English phrases in her study participation materials indicated an interest in or sense of affinity with Anglo-European culture. It therefore seemed fitting that Elizabeth would indicate some identification with Hara's public persona, inflected with perceived non-Japanese characteristics. Hara was expressly associated in postwar film discourse with Westernised fashions (Tsukamoto 1947: 44), and fans and critics often speculated that she had Russian or German ancestry. These associations were only heightened by her breakout role in the German–Japanese co-production *The New Earth* (*Atarashiki tsuchi*/ *The Daughter of the Samurai* [*Die Tochter des Samurai*], Itami and Fanck, 1937). Hara's Westernised dress and independent manner may have read to Occupation authorities as exemplary of the new democratic capitalist ideals encouraged in the postwar population, but at the same time she embodied the continuation of certain values central to girls' popular culture of the 1930s and early 1940s, such as a spirit of adventure and familiarity with Anglo-European dress and trends.

Yet while Elizabeth prized Hara's exoticism, she recalled reproducing only those behaviours understood as attractive in a highly traditional gendered sense, such as a graceful smile or laugh. She did not express any desire to copy Hara's iconoclastic approach to marriage and family. In this way, some film fans embraced stars as role models, yet practised a selective approach to the elements of the star's life and character that they adopted. Female fans were drawn to Hara's Westernised appeal, contextualised by a wider history of appreciation for Anglo-European tropes in pre-war girls' culture, but rejected her anti-romantic independent lifestyle.

True to Koyama san's observation above, the majority of participants who praised Hara in interviews and questionnaires over the course of my study were male. Hara was claimed by a number of male critics, directors and fans as the ultimate example of an ideal Japanese femininity. Her star persona was explicitly associated with national and even nationalist characteristics, both during the war, in films such as *The New Earth* in which her character explicitly supported Japan's Imperial expansion, occupation of Manchuria and association with Nazi Germany, and after, when her idealistic and nationalist schoolgirl character in *No Regrets for Our Youth* grew up to oppose Japan's war and Imperialistic totalitarian ideology. Yomota Inuhiko has observed that Hara had been both the 'shrine maiden' (*miko*) of militarism and the 'goddess' (*megami*) of the Occupation forces' democratic enlightenment movement (2000: 154).

In such characterisations of her public persona, Hara's foreign associations were blended with an understanding of her star persona as particularly Japanese, both historically and in reference to Japan-specific identities such as the shrine maiden or Shintō goddess. While Elizabeth's questionnaire response called attention to her interest in or association with non-Japanese cultures in elements such as her chosen pseudonym and use of English, she was also keen to educate me in the Japanese ways of doing certain things. The stamped and self-addressed envelope that had been provided for the return of questionnaires issued at the evening screening at the Kyoto Culture Museum (Bunka Hakubutsukan, hereafter Bunpaku) was returned covered in notes, some in English cursive and others in Japanese. Among them, Elizabeth pointed out that in Japan the stamp should be placed in the top left corner of the envelope and that addresses should be written vertically rather than horizontally. Elizabeth's present-day blending of Japanese and non-Japanese elements in her public presentation echoes the star persona she remembers copying as a child.

Takakura Ken as Male Role Model

Today many stars are nostalgic reminders of an earlier era or models for an idealised mode of ageing or working. In the early postwar era, the same star often provided models of the new gendered behaviours encouraged by SCAP GHQ censors and later adapted by filmmakers reacting against those new norms. Hashimoto san remembered the *yakuza* genre star Takakura Ken (1931–2014) as a particularly popular role model for masculinity in his teenage years. Jokingly adopting a posture similar to that of a *yakuza* poster image, Hashimoto san recalled:

> Takakura Ken had a reputation as a good man, always the hero. Yes. Well, men being men, Takakura Ken was the number one aspirational character (*akogare no ningen*), or personality (*jinbutsu*), I think. Of course, women thought he was a good man, and liked him as well. The heroines of his films always came to like him quite a lot! (Hashimoto 2016)

Inoue san similarly recalled a desire to emulate Takakura, referring laughingly to a feeling that 'bloomed' into a sense that, 'Oh, I want to be like that.' Gesturing outwards from his body as though communicating this sense of a feeling developing, Inoue san adopted a confessional tone as he reflected, 'Well, I don't know if he's good at acting, but I really felt that I wanted to be like that . . . !'

The judgement of women, both onscreen and off, appeared to have made quite an impact on the desirability of Takakura's persona and young male audience members' wish to emulate him. Hashimoto san remembered being envious of a friend whom everyone said looked just like Takakura Ken. Conversely, Inoue san found the appeal of Hara Setsuko to be that 'there could be no one as beautiful as her'. Though he appreciated her acting skill, he maintained that watching Hara gave him the sense that 'her own personality, her human nature, permeates through . . . I don't know if this is true or not, but I think that's the reason she was such a big star, that kind of thing, it's why I like her so much.' Inoue san valued the rare aspects of Hara's star persona, such as her unusual beauty. At the same time, however, he also appreciated the sense that her acting style revealed something of the 'real person' beneath, showing her individual personality quirks. This blending of the uncommon and the everyday in the film star persona and onscreen work appeared to be a key element of many study participants' engagement with film stars.

In the recollections and present-day practices of participants in my study, stars were positioned as models of ways of living. However, equally important to study participants was the selectiveness with which they appropriated or adapted the key behaviours, expressions and lifestyle characteristics modelled by stars. The story of this careful selection and adaptation is as much a part of their communication about their relationship with the star in question as the impact of the star's behaviour on their own. Participants articulated points of perceived difference in their own beliefs, attitudes and aspirations by noting that a star beloved and copied by others was rejected, or considered with ambivalence, by themselves. In this way, discourse on stars and their influence among film fans was nuanced and multi-level, encompassing claims to discernment in adopting and adapting stars as role models, rather than a fan's total acceptance of a star's public performance. In the Kansai area, where location shooting and public promotional activities were common, many participants had the opportunity to meet their idols and determine for themselves to what degree the star would become a role model for their own way of being in the world.

Meeting a Film Star: Everyday Encounters in Postwar Kansai

In both imported and domestic cinema productions, film stars were among the clearest means by which study participants recalled learning about ways of being from watching films. Hideaki Fujiki has traced the development of the star system in 1910s and 1920s Japan, noting that while Japanese stars were initially perceived differently from their Hollywood counterparts, whose star personae were created and maintained by the studio system, popular understanding of domestic stars as personae grew rapidly, and Japanese stars and their home studios were soon using the gossip press to correct audience misperceptions about the star's real life arising from audiences' over-identification of the actor's life and ideologies with those of the particular roles the star had played (2013: 185). The mode of discussion employed by many participants in my study indicated that they were well aware of gaps between the crafted public star persona and the film star as 'real' person. Many recounted perceiving changes in their own awareness of stars growing up, particularly the dawning realisation around age eight to twelve that the characters in fiction films were played by actors, and that some actors were more famous, or famous in different ways, than others.

Japan's thriving postwar entertainment press certainly contributed to popular awareness of stars' offscreen lives and activities, featuring 'at home' interviews with stars as well as accounts of set visits, film criticism and box office information on film texts. In Western Japan, and particularly the Kansai region, the negotiation of the star persona as constructed versus ideas about the star's imagined 'real life' played out in a particularly interesting and varied way. As Chapter 2 detailed, the geographical positioning of the Kansai region, and the area's use as location setting for a variety of genres of film, meant that stars were regularly encountered on the streets of Kyoto and in countryside areas such as Uji, as well as on film lots during scheduled or informal set visits. Business interests and star fandom often intertwined, as Shimada san recalled seeing actors like Yukishiro Keiko (1933–) and Kitaōji Kinya (1943–) taking breaks during filmmaking at her family's café. Fan materials such as home-made scrapbooks (see Figure 4.2) indicate an understanding of the star as product in the blending together of film stills showing stars in character, advertisements for specific films and 'off duty' images of stars sightseeing and appearing together offscreen. Awareness of film stars as working actors is therefore widespread among the postwar generations.

Furthermore, several study participants grew up in areas where the cinema became the local trade export and so encountered various industry personnel including actors on a regular basis. Kimura san remembered growing up with the brothers who would become the leading players in the 1950s *taiyōzoku* (sun tribe) genre that presented the rarified world of Japan's young upper middle-class youth to audiences all over the country. The parents of Ishihara Shintarō, the novelist and scriptwriter credited with inventing the genre, and Ishihara Yujirō, the first male star of the *taiyōzoku*, were family friends, and the brothers attended the same school in the Zushi area that became the setting for their scandalising fictions. While Kimura san watched the films like the other viewers of her generation, she was essentially watching an extreme fictionalisation of her own area and associates. She recalls having a schoolgirl crush on 'Yu-chan', though in this account the starry crushes of audience members for film stars blended with the more prosaic fondness for an older and glamorous family friend. An ethno-history of postwar film viewership can uncover such intense intertwining of film fictions with real life due to the film industry's ties to particular geographical regions. This cross-fertilisation continues in study

Figure 4.2 A fan's scrapbook showing stars Ri Kōran and Hasegawa Kazuo, from the author's collection.

participants' attendance at meet-and-greet events with actors, directors and camera personnel who were active in the postwar era.

Several interviewees recounted meetings with stars, both formal and informal, either at planned events that the speaker had decided to attend or observed spontaneously on the street. Imai san was by far the most committed to pursuing interactions with stars, having devoted his retirement to travelling all over the country for cinema-related events. He was particularly fond of the late Mikuni Rentarō (1923–2013), a popular actor among fans of police and gangster dramas of the late 1960s and early 1970s. Imai san brought to our interview a large number of photographs of Mikuni taken at formal events, often featuring himself. He was keen to emphasise the duration of his encounters with this particular star, drawing my attention to the visible deterioration in the actor's health over the years of their acquaintance. In the interviews and questionnaires provided by other participants, Mikuni's name appeared relatively often, and his star persona was generally treated in the same manner that Annette Kuhn observed that her British interviewees treated domestic stars; slightly familiar, closer than Hollywood stars, and more realistically aspirational, particularly in terms of the fan's ability to copy clothing style and behaviours. Compared to late- 1940s stars such as Hara Setsuko, the stars of 1960s Japanese cinema were often discussed by viewers of the era as more accessible, and closer to everyday life. This may have been due to their appearances on television and to the booming high street clothing market which sold products inspired by cinema idols, both new phenomena in the late 1950s and early 1960s.

Though he stressed the number of times they had met, Imai san's mode of speaking about Mikuni was at once familiar and aspirational. Fifteen years Imai san's senior, Mikuni Rentarō featured in Imai san's discussions of cinema as a kind of senior mentor, or *senpai*. Mikuni's advice and wisdom were frequently recalled, particularly in anecdotes where Mikuni's observations provided Imai san with a new way of thinking about a particular artistic or industry-related issue. Imai san was not generally short of opinions; in fact, at the time of our interview he had made something of a name for himself in both local and national Japanese news with his unique contributions to public debates and discussions at film events and festivals, and his forceful, highly stylised oratorical performances. Over the course of our four-hour interview, however, I observed that asking Imai san for a personal opinion or artistic assessment often produced a retelling of an opinion attributed to Mikuni Rentarō, which Imai san recalled having been told at an earlier time. Opinions and revelations attributed to Mikuni appeared early in our interview, but I was particularly struck by Imai san's response to three questions about which directors, actors and actresses Imai san himself had been particularly interested in while growing up. In each case, Imai san answered the questions by naming filmmakers and stars whom he recalled Mikuni having told him that he admired. In these recollections, Imai san's own opinion hardly featured, and it was implicitly suggested that he followed Mikuni's assessments of other actors' skill and standing as one would an expert or specialist. For example, Imai san stated his admiration for directors such as Uchida Tomu (1898–1970), who knew how to 'draw the best performance' from their stars, a technique he said Mikuni claimed to have personally experienced. The careers of Tanaka Kinuyo (1909–77) and Takamine Hideko (1924–2010), two actresses whom Imai san recalled Mikuni describing with admiration, were cited as stellar examples in response to my questions about Imai san's favourite actresses.

Speaking with Imai san almost gave the impression of channelling an interview with Mikuni Rentarō from beyond the grave. Recollections of opinions and preferences communicated by Mikuni to Imai san dominated our encounter. Despite his clear admiration for Mikuni, Imai san even responded to my question about his favourite actors with a list of the stars Mikuni had rated, to the extent of omitting Mikuni Rentarō himself from the list. This omission suggested that Imai san was responding to my questions with almost exclusive reference to Mikuni's perceived expert opinions rather than his own. Throughout our interview, Imai san turned my request to 'give an account' of himself, in relation to his experiences with cinema, into an opportunity to give an account of the privately shared opinions of a recently deceased star. It seems particularly relevant that he selected a moderately famous but not elite star – Mikuni Rentarō's career did not reach the domestic or international levels of fame attained by Hara Setsuko, Tanaka Kinuyo, Takamine Hideko or Mifune Toshirō (1920–97). Though Imai san mentioned these more famous actors and others, he remained committed to giving voice to the experiences of the deceased Mikuni rather than these higher-profile stars. At the same time, Imai san also produced photographs of himself with other stars of the same era, such as Fuji Junko, later known as Fuji Sumiko (1945–). He showed no particular interest in communicating any information that these stars may have shared with him, however, focusing instead on Fuji's exterior beauty.

Imai san's channelling of the professional opinions of Mikuni Rentarō shared aspects of Kimura san's close affection for Ishihara Yujirō, as well as elements of the more distant admiration for Hara Setsuko communicated by Koyama san and Elizabeth. Mikuni was remembered as physically close, as Imai san shared spaces with him on a number of occasions, but also aspirational and distanced, as the experiences and opinions that

Imai related Mikuni sharing with him were outside his own reach. There was something of a spirit of preservation in Imai san's insistence on maintaining Mikuni's contribution to discussions about Japanese cinema even from beyond the grave. Mikuni's persona was preserved and retrospectively somewhat inflated by Imai san's rhetorical performance of deferring to his expertise. Though Imai san gave an account of Mikuni Rentarō rather than an account of himself, there is a sense in which this substitution nonetheless produced something of an account of Imai san, in his determination to champion the artistic knowledge of a star who was not quite an underdog but certainly not one of the superstars of the postwar screen remembered frequently today. The geographical and temporal proximity to film production of the Kansai region in the postwar era created this kind of original circumstance in which a star could become an extension of the self in the practice of talking about cinema.

Being Japanese in the Global Postwar

While many study participants' relation to Japanese film stars was expressly local, their assessments of Japanese cinema products were situated more globally. None of the participants in my study expressed a general preference for Japanese film texts over non-Japanese, or vice versa, though several noted that at different periods of time international films were perceived as superior to Japanese. Of eighty-seven questionnaire respondents, only a small number expressed a preference for Japanese cinema, while the majority selected the option, 'I watch both Japanese and foreign films'. As discussed in Chapter 3, many wrote of wartime Hollywood and British films screened in postwar Japan as a means of catching up on developments in Allied nations during the period in which wartime censorship banned the screening of such films in Japan. While many countries suffered from food and clothing scarcity and rationing after the Second World War, many participants in my study perceived postwar Japan to have been particularly poor, and so the content of Hollywood and European cinema had an aspirational element.

Koyama san remembered her mother copying clothing designs from the costumes of film stars to update her wardrobe for a newly democratic postwar Japan. In fact, Koyama san attended our interview wearing a dress that her mother had made, and a jacket designed from repurposed tweed. Many study participants cited a lack of up-to-date or fashionable clothing as an example of Japan's extreme poverty in the early postwar years. However, the connection between film star fashions and repurposing old or worn-out clothing to copy those styles echoes the memories that interlocutors shared with Annette Kuhn in her ethno-history of 1930s British cinema-going. Kuhn observed that a number of her interlocutors recalled making clothing, or having clothing made by a family member or friend, in an effort to look as 'smart' as the British and Hollywood stars of 1930s cinema (2002: 107). Drawing from Michel De Certeau's *The Practice of Everyday Life* (1984), Kuhn calls this experience 'making do' (2002: 123). Like Kuhn's interlocutors, participants in my study also related their experiences copying the styles of film stars as a significant part of their everyday lives. In the context of postwar Japan, copying an American or European star was quite a different proposition to styling oneself after a Japanese star, particularly in the case of viewers who copied a star's take on traditional dress and styled their kimono after Takamine Mieko or such stars who were praised in the press for their Japanese fashions.

In accounts of copying a star's clothing, Western Europe and the US were explicitly positioned as richer and more fashion-forward than early postwar Japan. While Kuhn's interlocutors recalled class difference as the major structuring factor that placed the glamorous fashions of cinema out of reach for the everyday person, participants in my study stressed geographical and ethnic differences, as well as Japan having lost the war. In the first years of the Occupation, the perception of Japan as lagging behind the European and anglophone world appeared to be widespread.

A number of Occupation personnel and US citizens visiting Japan reported that films, particularly imported Hollywood features, appeared to have made a significant impression on Japanese audiences' dress and behaviours. Lucy Herndon Crockett, an American resident in Japan, remembered a Japanese woman sharing her impression that in American imported films, 'men's behavior to women is especially refined' and that 'these things are now influencing our social life' (1949: 205). Indeed, Crockett also recalls a Kyoto University student telling her that 'he and his friends learn from the American pictures how to light a cigarette for a girl, hold her coat, open a door for her' (1949: 204), indicating that the content of American cinema influenced the physical behaviours of some young viewers.

Offscreen as well as on, the Occupation period was a time of intensive material cultural exchange, as the large number of American servicemen involved in the Occupation brought with them a mass of material culture unrivalled even by the influx of Anglo-European trends in the interwar period. From luxury goods traded for favours, to the clandestine exchange of materials for black-market sale, the early postwar years saw a flurry of imported trends and materials from the US. From 1945, Peter Armstrong notes that 'traditional patterns of clothing and materials were considered to encapsulate pre-war attitudes and were discredited under the guise of education and modernisation' (2011: 222). In Japan and Germany, imported items 'possessed a spurious attraction by dislocation with the past' (Armstrong 2011: 222).

As the Occupation stabilised, Occupation personnel brought over family members who contributed to this exchange of products, fashions and behaviours (de Matos 2007). For example, the wives of British and Australian servicemen, as well as their more dominant US counterparts, produced pamphlets describing how to perform domestic duties in the American, Australian or British home, intended for use by their domestic 'helpers' who were assigned by their husbands' military employers. These pamphlets found wider distribution after the end of the Occupation, forming the basis for the role of the postwar *sengyō shufu* or professional housewife.

Anglophone women also commented on Japanese adoption of Western dress and issued advice on wearing American, Australian and British clothing. Cinema was often channelled as a global language that could be used to communicate between cultures, as in Australian Maida Williams' (later Coaldrake) account of her own role in the Anglo-European influence on postwar Japanese women's dress:

> Unashamedly intrigued by this foreign woman [Williams], they lifted her skirt to see how the seams were sewn, they smelled her scarf, they studied her hair and head from several angles, and said what they thought in conversation with each other and with her. Fortunately I couldn't understand much, but behaved as I thought a film star would in those circumstances, remembering how much the Japanese girl had absorbed of Western culture from the film, and how keen she was of absorbing a great deal more. (Quoted in Coaldrake 2003: 302)

Williams recalls her response to the Japanese women's physical investigation of her clothing and its arrangement as mimicking a 'film star'. In this aspect, Williams and her curious interlocutors are not too different, as a large number of Japanese viewers also recall copying film stars' clothing and mannerisms in their efforts to adapt to the new circumstances of the Occupation.

While we rarely see depictions of Anglo-European and American servicemen in Japanese entertainment films or magazines before 1952, Anglo-European beauty ideals were dominant in postwar cultural production. Imported materials including American and British films conveyed an image of a wealthy, fashionable world outside Japan, crafting an aspirational image. The first postwar Japanese actress to appear on the cover of a major film magazine was Kishi Keiko for *Kinema Junpō* in 1954: from

1945, Hollywood actresses had dominated the covers of film magazines and fashion magazines alike, though the publications themselves contained detailed information on Japanese cultural productions and events as well as Anglo-European and Hollywood-informed beauty news.

Of course, American and Anglo-European trends had influenced Japanese fashion and beauty ideals in the pre-war 1920s, particularly in popular discourse around the cinema. While discussions of 'Westernisation' in pre-war Japan did acknowledge an element of perceived inferiority to the source cultures, postwar Anglo-European and American influence on Japanese body ideals was particularly loaded in the context of defeat and Occupation. Issues of perceived inferiority in comparison to an idealised West made the task of dressing the body somewhat fraught; while the Anglo-European fashions modelled by film stars were aspirational, ridicule was meted out to those who wore them incorrectly.

Non-Japanese commentators were not the only offenders in this respect. In the booming print media, critics and gossip columnists became the judges of star bodies and fashions. For example, Hara Setsuko and Tanaka Kinuyo, the two biggest stars of the postwar era, were regularly mentioned in articles critiquing the dress of high-profile stars. In the fashion and gossip press surrounding film culture, Tanaka was ridiculed for her 'lack of style' in choosing Western clothing, while Hara was described as 'a Western dress person' (Tsukamoto 1947: 44). Tanaka and Hara were the targets of a similarly critical article in *Eiga Goraku* in April 1948, which argued that they had no '*iroke*' or sex appeal (Matsubara 1948: 13). Critic Matsubara Ichirō connects this to their wearing of Western dress, claiming that actresses who suit Japanese dress, such as Yamada Isuzu and Mito Mitsuko, have 'masses of *iroke*'. In this way, the delicate negotiations between the respective images of a reimagined postwar Japan and an imagined 'West' played out on the star body.

The associations of Anglo-European fashions and beauty, as opposed to Japanese, were not simplistic or binary. Western fashions and hairstyles were alternately modern, business-like and sexualised, while kimono alternately invoked tradition and sex appeal. In contrast to Matsubara's argument about *iroke*, many film texts and star profiles used Japanese kimono as a kind of visual shorthand for character values such as 'traditional', 'modest' and 'virtuous'. For example, in an 'at home' interview for film magazine *Eiga Fan* in 1949, ex-child star Takamine Mieko took interviewers on a tour of her home to demonstrate how her star persona had developed from cute girl star to refined woman (Sanada 1949: 6–7). The large pictures of her tasteful home emphasised her aesthetic qualities, including a portrait of Takamine in kimono, sitting demurely in her tatami mat room.

The interviewer emphasised her beauty, refinement and dress sense in her choice of kimono matching the home furnishings. She was described as a 'longed-for' (*akogare no sutā*) and 'sympathetic' star (*kyōkan o yobaseru sutā*) (Sanada 1949: 6–7), an ideal example of postwar Japanese womanhood. Alongside the boom in Western fashions and physical behaviours, there was a recurrent interest in repositioning Japanese national dress and its associated bodily postures as similarly aspirational and refined.

Catching Up: Postwar Japanese Film Production versus Hollywood

The early Occupation-era sense of Japan as behind or backward compared to the Allied nations also played out in cinema viewership and ideas about film production. As mentioned in Chapter 2, the Occupation-era film import laws strongly favoured the US, and to a lesser degree other Allied nations, and so Hollywood films were among the most prevalent non-Japanese film texts onscreen in the late 1940s. After Japan regained independence in 1952, import laws were altered for greater diversity, and the Japanese studio system entered its peak period of competitive overproduction. From the mid-1950s, Japanese films greatly outnumbered imported films, and at the same time Japan resumed overseas export of Japanese cinema and co-production. The majority of participants in my study spoke of this period in terms of Japanese film production drawing level with its Allied counterparts, and even overtaking certain production centres in terms of popular acclaim, both at home and overseas.

Japanese cinema dominated the international film festival scene in the early postwar era, winning a significant number of awards at the European film festivals of the 1950s, as well as at the US awards ceremonies. The Japanese film industry had the added advantage of exclusive contracts with US film theatres, brokered during the Occupation and its aftermath. The monster genre (*kaijū eiga*) developed at Tōhō studios was distributed in America through United Productions of America (UPA, originally an animation studio). Popular reception was so great that Tōhō was later able to open its own dedicated cinemas in the US, including the Tōhō La Brea in Los Angeles, and another two cinemas in San Francisco and New York. Tōhō established Tōhō International Ltd in Los Angeles in June 1954, just behind Shōchiku, which set up offices in London and Los Angeles in 1953 (Yau Shuk-ting 2010: 137). International appreciation of Japanese film style and content led to the building of actual Japanese cinema theatres overseas, while domestic audiences enjoyed the global recognition of Japanese cinema and participated enthusiastically at the domestic box office.

Japan's rapid economic recovery and widespread social change in the first decade after 1945 was reflected in domestic film production. Whether my interlocutors were aware of the speedy development of Japanese cinema at the time is unclear. Members of the 1930–55 generation certainly articulated an awareness of Hollywood films coming to Japan late; for example, Takeda san made a point of noting the different distribution dates of *The Red Shoes* (Michael Powell and Emeric Pressburger, 1948, released in Japan as *Akai kutsu* in 1949) and *The Living Desert* (James Algar, 1953, released in Japan as *Sabaku wa ikite iru* in 1955) in Japan, compared to their release dates in the UK and US. It seems unlikely that he would have had this knowledge as a child, and perhaps even learned or confirmed the dates for the purpose of our interview. As Chapter 7 will detail, many interviewees prepared extensive materials and notes, suggesting that they undertook a degree of personal research before our meetings, perhaps inspired by their experiences answering the earlier questionnaire. On the other hand, given the number of study participants who recalled engaging with para-cinematic materials such as film magazines, posters and advertisements, it is possible that Japanese audiences were aware of these films far in advance of their import to Japan. In that case, the sense of Japan as temporally behind anglophone and European film culture would have been apparent even to children.

Japanese domestic film production began to keep pace with Hollywood from the mid-1950s, and at the same time post-Occupation changes in import quotas rebalanced the number of domestic and imported productions onscreen in favour of Japan. Overseas co-productions, particularly with Hong Kong, attracted global attention at this time, positioning Japan as a leading creative force in East Asia. By the early 1960s, with the beginning of exhibition activities by the Art Theatre Guild however, discourse on Japanese cinema as underdeveloped compared to the Anglo-European world had resurfaced, as the ATG made a concerted effort to bring critically acclaimed films from Eastern and Western Europe to Japanese audiences, at the same time reproducing an idea of the European cinema environment in their artistic film theatres with strict protocols. Takeda san recalled being motivated to contact European embassies to borrow film reels for the informal film study group at his workplace by what he perceived to be the clear artistic superiority of European cinema. In a circular way, the admiration that participants in my study expressed for Hollywood and European cinema fed back into a sense of the 1950s and 1960s as a peak artistic era for Japanese cinema also, as many cited the success of the films described above at international film festivals as a kind of outside seal of approval for the Japanese film industry. Engaging with cinema in the early postwar period fostered a sense of Japan as catching up to, and eventually matching, the world nations considered to be at a developmental peak. This discourse continued at the time of my study, particularly in terms of the Japanese animation industry. Although study participants expressed an overwhelming preference for live-action classical cinema over animated film, they were nonetheless proud of the international reputation of Studio Ghibli animation studio, and many attended screenings of internationally recognised animated films such as *Your Name* (*Kimi no na wa*, Makoto Shinkai, 2016) and *In This Corner of the World* (*Kono sekai no katatsumi ni*, Katabuchi Sunao, 2017). In this way, encounters with cinema subtly shaped my study participants' sense of what it has meant to be Japanese at different historical junctures.

Growing Up with the Cinema in Postwar Japan

In later life, many study participants used discussion of Japanese cinema to express a changing sense of Japan's place in the world and their changing identities as Japanese citizens. In stories about early cinemagoing, however, participants tended to focus on how the cinema expanded their understanding of their own personal worlds. A repeating pattern in stories of early cinema experiences is the description of surprise, shock, fear or the retrospective knowledge that the participant had witnessed something 'not for children' in the cinema theatre. Annette Kuhn suggested that the memories of certain film fans among her British interlocutors who attended the cinema in the 1930s convey a sense of 'loss of self' at the cinema (2002: 233). By contrast, participants in my study tended to emphasise their engagement with the cinema as a means of extending and growing the self by coming into contact with sights and ideas that they had not previously encountered. This may be explained by the difference in continued engagement with the cinema; while Kuhn's interlocutors generally did not continue to engage with cinema culture throughout the course of her study, except to rewatch old favourite films, participants in my study were all active within contemporary cinema culture as well as nostalgic for the 'golden age' of the 1950s and 1960s. All attended public film screenings, and many attended film circles, clubs, discussion sessions and public lectures about cinema. In this sense, the testimonies described in this book are relevant to study participants' modes of engaging with the cinema at the time of writing, as a means of self-development.

As mentioned previously, several participants indicated retrospective awareness that as children they had watched films containing themes and imagery more appropriate for adult audiences. Kobayashi san expressed amazed surprise at the films he had been allowed to watch in the late 1950s. His mother was a film fan, and brought him to the cinema often when he was of kindergarten age. Recalling her love of cinema, he looked wistfully off to the right: 'My mother was a person who loved cinema. Well . . . Tōhō, Tōei, Shōchiku, she watched all those studio productions.' Smiling at her cleverness, he remembered, 'She got all those special offers for stock holders. She could watch absolutely anything!' Kobayashi san laughingly described his mother as 'a person who did not think at all about what films were aimed at children'. 'How should I say this . . . she did not think that children should watch only children's films.' Nonetheless, he used the conjugation *morau* to express his gratitude towards his mother for bringing him to the cinema theatre (*tsurete itte moratte imashita*), but also expressed an ironic appreciation for the fact that these trips allowed him to see many adult or inappropriate things. 'Well, those kinds of films children wouldn't generally see, including period dramas, war films, horror, romance films: I watched them just like an adult, I had that kind of background.' Kobayashi san recalled these experiences as broadening his personal horizons, showing him aspects of life outside his own experience. He did not appear to feel any sense of a loss of innocence on behalf of his childhood self. Rather, he suggested a feeling of gratitude towards his mother for the gift of introducing him to new things at a young age.

Of course, many themes and narratives went over the heads of their child audiences. Many participants in this study related experiencing surprise on returning later in life to a film they had seen as a child. Watching the same films as adults, they became newly aware of content and style elements that they had misunderstood or ignored entirely as children. Though he recalled his local cinema being quite strict about allowing children into adult films, Imai san remembered watching a film directed at adult audiences while still a child. In the tone of someone chiding themselves retrospectively, he frowned: 'Because I was still young, I couldn't understand it at all. It wasn't at all interesting. After many years, when I had become an adult, I watched it again and thought it was a great film!' Koyama san similarly recalled her lack of understanding of star persona as a child. 'For children, that was just some other thing, we didn't understand it. When I go back now to those films I watched as a child, I think the feelings I experience are very different to those I had when I was young.'

The memories of these interviewees contrast with Kuhn's account of an interlocutor rewatching an old film with her child and discovering it to be disappointing. As mentioned above, Kuhn's study involved cinemagoers who did not remain particularly interested in film in later life. These casual viewers attended the cinema in the pre-war era when entertainment was scarce, but only two joined fan appreciation societies and none were members of cinema clubs at the time of their participation in Kuhn's study. By contrast, participants in my study all regularly engaged with cinema culture in their adult lives and advanced years, and we made contact at a variety of retrospective film theatres and clubs. Participants in my study therefore had regular opportunities to revisit the films of their childhoods. In doing so, many expressed amazement at the way postwar films must have opened their eyes to new worlds as children. In such testimonies, participants simultaneously expressed a sense of cinema having widened their personal worlds in their childhood, and at the same time related an experience of rewatching a particular film as a means of reconnecting with an idea of their childhood self. In this way, cinema viewership was imagined as a means of extending the self in several directions at once.

Interviewees and questionnaire respondents repeatedly used the words 'surprise' (*bikkuri*), 'attraction' (*miryōku*) and 'longing' (*akogare*) in their accounts of going to the cinema as young children. In their retelling, these memories had a retrospective element of understanding exposure to novel sights as personally formative. As discussed in Chapter 2, a large number of participants in this study mentioned the deep impact that Disney's *The Living Desert* had made on their understanding of the world as children. Many articulated surprise at the sights revealed in the documentary, particularly in relation to observing animals they had not previously seen. Takeda san recalled, 'I was so surprised (*bikkuri shimashita*)! At first you couldn't see anything, then living things began to emerge one after the other from this seemingly dead world. The thing about film is, it lets you see things you've never seen before.' This memory appeared to be formative for Takeda san's contemporary viewing practices and even his self-identity: 'Because I like that kind of thing, I became a person who loves documentary film. Documentaries are always full of surprising things, and I like that.' Takeda san connected his first positive experience of being surprised by film content to a lifelong interest in exposing his mind to unimagined things. He also enjoyed introducing others to surprising or novel sights, and co-organised a monthly film circle dedicated to appreciating foreign classics, Japanese avant-garde and contemporary international independent films.

Of course, not all experiences of surprise at the cinema are pleasurable. Takeda san and many others recalled early instances of watching distressing or frightening films. Like Kuhn's interlocutors, participants in my study often recounted their own unpleasurable emotions through the reactions of others. Though in Kuhn's study, 'Anecdotal memories of early cinemagoing are few and far between',' she notes:

> all of them centre on informants' responses to films and behaviour in the cinema. These are always represented as excessive or in some other way inappropriate. In recounting such memories, informants are clearly constructing themselves – like the legendary audience fleeing in terror from a screening of the Lumières' film of an approaching steam engine – as not yet versed in the proper ways of 'reading' films and of conducting oneself in the cinema. (Kuhn 2002: 58)

Takeda san in fact used this exact mode of representation, explaining that he was frightened by the stagey make-up of the characters of *The Red Shoes* because he was 'not normally used to seeing faces like that, when I compared them to the people around me, there were no examples of that kind of face'. He remembered searching for real-life examples of the surprising things he saw onscreen in the faces of those around him. Like Kuhn's interlocutors, whose 'initiation narratives are obviously treasured from family legend rather than direct memories' (2002: 58), Takeda san's story drew from his mother's account of the event, which he retold later. Similarly, Hashimoto san's account of having been made to cry by a surprisingly sad war film in Chapter 3 also rested on the memories of his older family members, who while not present in the cinema, recalled his sister complaining about his behaviour.

In later life, many participants came to seek out the kind of amazement they remembered feeling in their early years of cinemagoing. Takeda san noted his admiration for the Surrealists' early 'virtual reality' films for their sharp 'sense of reality' (*genjitsukan*), which 'gives a real shock to the brain's reactions'. At the time of our interview, he stated a contemporary preference for 'films with surprises', feeling that they strengthened the experience of viewing films. Many study participants expressed gratitude to the cinema for confronting them with difficult emotions and hard social truths. In such accounts, encounter with the cinema became an invitation to expand one's personal horizons, not only by seeing surprising things or feeling surprise itself, but through an invitation to shared sensory experience and co-feeling.

Expanding the Boundaries of Being through Cinema

Inoue san, born in 1958, recalled treasuring the opportunity to experience new things through film, particularly experiences that he imagined to be 'from another world' (*betsu no sekai*) or from another place or time.

He joked that his fondness for Hollywood film was perhaps related to the opportunity it provided to observe non-Japanese actors' physicality and style. He imagined this kind of opportunity as 'outside my own personal experience', though at the same time he compared the non-Japanese actors in which he took an interest to myself and my partner, who was also present and filming the interview. Many participants expressed an interest in encountering non-Japanese people, particularly those who could speak Japanese, and this factor is not insignificant in terms of the kind of people who volunteered to participate in my study. People who expressed an interest in non-Japanese culture, or encountering non-Japanese people, made up the majority of those who volunteered for this study.

At the same time, many expressed a sense of longing or desire for contact with non-Japanese people in a manner that rhetorically situated such encounters outside their range of personal experience. As in Inoue san's articulation above, several participants paradoxically expressed their lack of opportunity for encounter with non-Japanese people during our own encounter, which was itself an instance of international collaboration. This suggested to me that the position of being physically or linguistically cut off from the Anglo-European encounters they saw on film was a felt identity rather than lived actuality for many study participants. The expression of longing for Europe and North America is an established attitude among this generation of film fans, particularly in Western Japan, to the extent that expressions of regret related to a lack of opportunity for encountering people from these regions surface even within such an encounter itself.

If the relative paucity of opportunity for Anglo-European encounters outside the cinema was an imagined rather than literally experienced reality, what did those who longed for Europe and America expect from an international encounter? The answer to this question may share elements with expectations about encountering people and themes from other times or places through cinema, discussed above. In both kinds of encounter, participants expressed their desire not only to know but also to feel what the other was feeling. This kind of co-feeling *(kyōkan)* appeared to be generally understood as a means of learning about the world and its history, and at the same time as a means of growing, improving or extending the self. For Kobayashi san, cinema offered a window into the kinds of extreme emotions provoked by extreme situations or events that he felt he was unlikely to experience himself. Hara Setsuko was a particular favourite because of the extremity of her emotional expression:

> Talking of human emotions (*kidoairaku*), well, you know, happiness, there's also sadness, well, there are lots of famous actors who can convey those kind of emotions.

But anger, anger, well, are there really even two people who are alike? For example, Yoshinaga Sayuri san and those types, their anger is mostly directed at their role in society and social inequality, there's that kind of thing . . . it's not really a scary kind of anger. But scary now, that's Hara Setsuko, it's really instantaneous how quickly she can make a scene really scary, that's what I remember. (Kobayashi 2016)

Hara's emotions were not out of place or inappropriate in Kobayashi san's recollections. Instead, he recalled coming to realise the social import of the themes of her films through experiencing her extreme expressions of emotion. Talking about her performances of anger, he spoke of watching Kurosawa Akira's *The Idiot* (*Hakuchi*, 1954), an adaptation of Fyodor Dostoyevsky's novel in which Hara plays Nastasia, renamed Nasu Taeko. The film is set in snowy Hokkaido, drawing on Japanese perceptions of regional and ethnic difference to explore social hierarchies and inequalities. Kobayashi san remembered feeling these inequalities keenly through Hara's furious performance:

The social situation of lower-class people is really, well, realistically portrayed . . . That kind of difficulty, really all kinds of difficulties, well, that era is really like another country (*chigatta kuni*), that Japan has really been replaced by time, it's impossible to understand what it was like before . . . The critics at the time said the film was a failure, but I don't think so. (Kobayashi 2016)

Kobayashi san connected the strong emotions stirred by the film to his own imaginary of what wartime-era Japan might have been like, with corrupt war criminals oppressing everyday people. This link, which many participants also made, between being carried away by the strong emotions expressed on film and the imagined experience of wartime events was central to his appreciation of postwar cinema.

Kobayashi san was particularly preoccupied with experiencing the feeling of living through Japan's militarisation and wartime periods through cinema. He educated himself in the history of the era and was well versed in the political and international developments and agendas that led to Japan's Imperial expansion effort and entry into the Second World War. Yet his interest was focused most intensely on the experiences and ideas of everyday people living unremarkable lives during this period: 'Well, "war" doesn't have just one general meaning, you could say. We had the Second World War, and then in Japan we had the Sino-Japanese war, the Asia Pacific war, and those were really national experiences (*kokuminnteki keiken*).' He looked to cinema for a way to understand the hopes, dreams and fears of people undergoing these historical experiences. He believed that by feeling the suffering of everyday people in Imperial Japan, today's

Japanese citizens could be persuaded of the value of everlasting pacifism: 'Of course, it's not an easy thing to talk about, but the construction of Japanese people's consciousness, and also social consciousness, and the human view of life are really connected to cinema, I think.'

A significant number of participants shared Kobayashi san's view of cinema as a means of both educating oneself and feeling historical moments, with a view to improving or expanding one's personal ethics in relation to war, social inequality and trauma. Kishida san understood cinema as a social justice motivator and exposer of state violence. Watching documentaries on the Minamata water-poisoning incident, and fiction films portraying the treatment of *buraku* people in Japan, he felt a strong sense of the urgency of social injustice. Takeda san was also concerned with the political situation of postwar Japan, and often saw parallels in fiction film with contemporary social issues. Watching Mizoguchi Kenji's *Ugetsu* (*Ugetsu monogatari*, 1954), for example, he discerned a critique of contemporary militarism in the film's historical narrative.

Though the questionnaire distributed in the first stage of this study was designed to invite open responses, one slightly more leading question was included on the reverse side. Participants were asked to select one response from a range of five, rated from 'Strongly Disagree' to 'Strongly Agree', in answer to the question, 'Do you feel that watching a film has ever changed your way of thinking?' This question was inspired by the strategies, including censorship, pursued by SCAP GHQ that suggested that key political and bureaucratic actors may have believed that Japanese viewers could be influenced to change their attitudes to such issues as feudalism and gender inequality through watching films (Conde 1945; Conde 1965; MacArthur 1994). The majority of respondents answered 'Agree' or 'Strongly Agree' and a number provided an example of such an instance in the box below the question. During interviews, as well as in participant observation and in personal conversations, participants freely returned to this question, strongly maintaining that cinema had changed their ways of thinking about the world and their place in it.

Kishida san believed that film could change one's way of thinking through feeling: 'Well, when you get a strong feeling (*kanji*), your own, well, your thinking becomes elevated by the film, it changes . . . when I watch a film like that I think "So there is also that way of thinking" (*sona kangae mo arun da rō*).' From Koyama san's memory of a feeling that she could understand a new possible way of living by watching Hara Setsuko, to Kishida san's recollection of experiencing a new 'way of thinking', it is clear that growing up with the cinema in postwar Japan had a significant impact on participants' understandings of how to be; how to be an adult, how to be Japanese in the postwar context and how to be a global citizen in the world. The next chapter explores the gendered implications and limitations of transmitting models for living through cinema culture. In Chapter 6, we trace the history of amateur film clubs and gatherings in the Kansai region to explore how these budding awarenesses became organised, often political, movements.

CHAPTER 5

Gender Trouble at the Cinema

We can think of the cinema as gendered in a number of ways: as a gendered physical space, as gendered in its appeal or content and as gendered in its modes of production, to name just a few. As the preceding chapters have suggested, the question of gender arose often in my ethnographic study during interviews, questionnaire surveys and participant observation. Gender in Japanese cinema history has been explored in relation to particular film genres (Standish 2005; Zahlten 2017) and Hollywood imports (H. Kitamura 2004; Terasawa 2010; Kitamura and Sasagawa 2017), and as a factor in the crafting of star persona (Fujiki 2013). A smaller number of studies have queried the gender demographics of the Japanese cinema audience at particular historical moments (Laird 2012; Hori 2018; Fujiki 2019). This chapter takes an ethnographic approach to the examination of gender-related factors troubling Japanese cinema in the period 1945 to 1968, beginning from the expectations about cinema's role in changing public attitudes to gender documented by the General Headquarters of the Supreme Commander for the Allied Powers (SCAP GHQ) during the Occupation of Japan (1945–52). During this period, audiences responded to censored cinema content, and the provision of cinema theatres, in a number of unpredictable ways that countered SCAP expectations. Applying a similar logic to the common narrative that a lack of interest in the cinema on the part of female viewers led to shrinking audience numbers after 1958, the second part of this chapter explores various gendered factors in cinema access and enjoyment in the late 1950s and 1960s that complicate this picture.

In the early years after defeat, when film was imagined as a means to change viewers' attitudes towards Occupation-mandated social reforms, the cinema was enlisted in the push towards democracy and gender equality, at least as far as those states were imagined in 1945. Female audiences were imagined as the recipients of narratives and performances showcasing proactive women availing themselves of the new rights for female citizens included in the 1947 Constitution of Japan. Yet as the cinema audience began to decline after 1958, film critics in the popular press blamed women for turning their backs on the cinema. While some writers opined that women had defected to television, others blamed the very independence that Occupation-era censored cinema had aimed to foster for creating a situation in which women were choosing to spend their newly disposable incomes on other leisure pursuits (Uryū 1967). At the same time, a boom in *yakuza* (gangster) narratives brought increased violence to stories focused on male characters, and many sexualised and soft-porn films of the 'pink' genre further privileged the heterosexual masculine perspective (see Figure 5.1). Critics and scholars have suggested that this violent sexualised cinema content had little to offer many female film fans (Standish 2005; Zahlten 2017).

This chapter takes a new approach to the question of gender as a motivating element in cinema audience demographics and experience, by asking members of that audience about their memories of the era. Beginning

Figure 5.1 The Senbon Nikkatsu cinema theatre on Senbon street, now a 'pink' cinema theatre.

with the censored cinema of the early Occupation, which we could interpret as pro-female, in design if not always in practice, this chapter explores the gaps, omissions and contradictions in our understanding of the Japanese cinema audience as a gendered demographic. By exploring issues of access, relation to film content and the role of cinema in the everyday lives of men, women, boys and girls, we can better understand various aspects in which the cinema appealed or did not appeal to viewers of all genders, as well as a number of structural and situational factors fostering or restricting engagement with the cinema and its stories.

While marketing and perceived common-sense wisdom have often encouraged us to think of a particular audience demographic as gendered in certain ways, attention to everyday factors such as how children could enter the cinema, and at what times work and chores had to be done, reveals how easily the best-laid plans of industry personnel, censors and advertising agents can come undone. Genre designations such as the 'women's film' should not lead us to easy assumptions about the demographics of the audience for such films, just as an elaborate censorship process does not give us any guarantee that the censoring body's aims were successful. The ethno-historical approach can provide useful nuance for our understanding of audience opinions and behaviours, conflicted and counter-intuitive as they often are.

Gender and the Occupation Audience

During the Allied Occupation of Japan, female audiences, particularly children and teenaged girls, were a demographic of great interest within the intended market for censored cinema content, designed to support the democratic re-education of the Japanese populace (Allen 1945). The 1947 Constitution of Japan introduced a new status for female citizens in everyday life through the provision of divorce and inheritance for women, and the recognition of equal rights, at least within marriage. Early postwar cinema characters and narratives modelled these new rights. Yet an ethno-historical approach gives a conflicted picture of the cinema audience who viewed these narratives, revealing that an easy inference of mass female viewership from female-oriented film content, marketing and censorship is not supported by the memories of female viewers of the era.

Guided by the large number of young female characters in early postwar Japanese film texts, as well as by Allied Occupation communications outlining the importance of reaching female media consumers (see Tsuchiya 2002; Conde 1965), I began this study with the expectation that a significant majority of those volunteering to participate would be female.

As the Introduction detailed, however, I found that women were more reluctant than men to speak with authority on this era of cinema viewership, as female study participants reported restricted access to the cinema theatres of their youth. Investigating the factors that kept female viewers away from the cinema allows us to explore the potential impact of a disproportionately small female audience on Occupation-era attempts to use the cinema for re-education purposes.

In the initial stages of the study, I found that women who expressed interest in the project were reluctant to adopt the expert witness stance favoured by male study participants. This contradicted my expectations, which were based on previous studies of the content of popular cinema texts of the early postwar era (Coates 2016). Furthermore, studio bosses, marketing and directives published by SCAP GHQ often specified the monetary and ideological imperatives of targeting female audiences (Wada-Marciano 2008: 80). In order to explore the relation of female audiences to Japanese cinema in the postwar era, I began to ask study participants about their memories of accessing cinema theatres, uncovering significant differences between male and female participants. There appeared to be a disparity between SCAP's focus on the re-educational value of the cinema for female citizens and the gender of the Occupation-era audience.

Understanding the Relationship between Female Audiences and Cinema Culture

While early studies of popular culture in Japan considered the participation of women in mass entertainment cultures, the audience for cinema was imagined by many scholars as predominantly male at the beginning of the twentieth century (Fujiki 2019: 41). As militarism increased in pace throughout the 1930s, the public were reimagined as *kokumin*, or national subjects, which as Hideaki Fujiki has observed, tended to marginalise women within discourses on popular culture (2019: 361). During wartime, many male bureaucrats and critics focused on the role of women as homemakers, and film critics such as Oka Kunio wrote of women's perceived 'stereotypical feelings' (*ruikei tekina kankaku*), which restricted their appreciation to entertainment films rather than highbrow cinema culture (Fujiki 2019: 187). Fujiki notes the misogynistic basis of such stereotyping of women, and the frequency with which terms such as 'lowbrow sentiment', 'American films' and 'individualism' were used in relation to female audiences (2019: 187). For example, in 1939 Oka claimed in the magazine *Japanese Film* (*Nihon eiga*) that women were only interested in entertainment films (*goraku taii no eiga shika*) and that women as consumers had a subjectivity formed only by their desires (*yokubō shutai*) (Oka 1943: 89; Fujiki 2019: 131). Oka wrote of women's perceived 'vulgar feelings' (*teizoku kanjō*) as the reason for their love of American films, which propagated ideologies counter to wartime goals (Tatsumura 1943: 89; Fujiki 2019: 131).

As wartime ended and the Occupation of Japan (1945–52) began, women and young female citizens were repositioned in public discourse by Occupation authorities keen to posit new rights for women as part of a democratic agenda for postwar Japan. A number of elements in early postwar cinema culture, from film content to advertising, have been taken together with Occupation personnel discourse to imply a significant female audience for cinema in Japan over the period 1945 to 1960, as Colleen Laird has noted (2012: 116). Using interviewees' memories, data from industry reports and sources from Japanese fan magazines and period publications, this chapter seeks to add nuance to our picture of who the early postwar audience was, why and how they appeared in the cinema theatre and how they engaged with ideologically framed film texts.

Extant historical scholarship reveals the role of cinema in the everyday lives of girls and women. Many girls' schools placed restrictions on visits to cinema theatres (Bae 2008: 359), suggesting that schoolgirl viewers may have wished to attend the cinema regularly (perhaps more regularly than teachers and parents would have liked). As Chapter 4 discussed, a significant number of study participants of both genders remembered agitating to be taken to the cinema by parents and older siblings. Cinema was clearly an object of fascination for young would-be viewers of both genders, though how teachers and parents attempted to control children's access to cinema appears to have been differently gendered in many cases. At the same time, as Kanako Terasawa argues, 'by prohibiting cinema attendance and making, to some extent, the cinema an object of the adult world, as well as "another world", the attraction of the cinema theatre was enhanced' (2010: 173). While my study is focused specifically on the Kansai region and the surrounding area of Western Japan, it should be noted that many of my findings in this chapter echo and support those of Terasawa's study of female viewership of Hollywood cinema in postwar Tokyo.

Girls were clearly interested in the cinema, judging by discussions of cinema-related topics in magazines marketed to young female readers, often including articles written by female teenagers (Bae 2008). Discourse on the cinema as both place and mode of entertainment or education reflected many pressing issues in everyday life. For example, in transcripts of two round-table discussions on the subject of girl–boy relations published in the September 1951 issue of *Girls' Friend* (*Shōjo no tomo*) magazine, the six middle- and high-school-age girls and six boys featured mentioned the cinema in relation to their changing social lives. Many of the girls spoke negatively of the practice of going to the cinema alone with a boy ('Shōjo bakari' 1951: 74–5). Yet as Catherine Yoonah Bae notes, it was 'the activity of going to the movies (as a one-on-one date with a boy, and doing so secretively) rather than the particular content of the movie itself that garnered disapproval' from other teenaged round-table participants (2008: 350). In their memories, where to go to participate in cinema culture, and whom to go with, presented a major obstacle for a number of participants in my study.

As discussed in detail in Chapter 1, postwar cinema content was developed under strict information dissemination and censorship guidelines. Underpinning the censorship of cinema and other popular entertainments, legal articles, SCAP directives and GHQ memos clearly identified 'women' and 'children' as the intended audience for media narratives that could educate viewers about the new rights and freedoms available to these groups. For example, SCAP Record '000.076 Women's Affairs' includes the transcript of a speech given by E. Lee at a number of social education conferences in many prefectures in Japan which identifies the 'relationships that are changing with democracy', including relationships between children and their parents, teachers and pupils, and romantic partners (1946–9: 1). The speaker counsels against gender segregation at all levels of society and specifically identifies the need for 'mixed young people's clubs' and the socialisation of children in a gender-equal manner (1946–9: 1).

Occupation authorities emphasised the need for women, children and students, as well as adult men, to educate themselves about what gender equality could mean for female citizens (Mayo 1984: 282). A CIE proposal for 'instituting gender democracy' suggested that politically informed film content could complement the political education conducted through community organisations, clubs and education programmes (Koikari 2002: 35). In the early postwar era and into the 1950s, as many Japanese citizens 'embraced the overwhelmingly popular rhetoric of democracy' (Seraphim 2006: 45), women and girls were encouraged to participate confidently in public democratic life by taking a variety of public stages, including those of the beauty contest (Aoyama 2008: 289) and even the film studio, as competitions for new film stars such as the New Faces search gained popularity. Yet Occupation authorities and cinema industry personnel alike appear to have largely relied on the general popularity of film to bring female viewers to the pro-democracy postwar cinema.

There is some indication that individual producers and distributors attempted to ensure that female citizens participated in postwar cinema culture. The Central Motion Picture Exchange (hereafter CMPE), which managed the distribution of US films, targeted features explicitly at female audiences. For example, a postwar remake of *Little Women* (LeRoy 1949) featured promotional events including 'four-sisters contests' which girls with four sisters could attend for free (H. Kitamura 2010: 102). Yet female viewers remained in the minority at many cinema theatres.

Prior to the Occupation, wartime surveys also show the general female audience to have been on average significantly less than 50 per cent of the total (Hori 2018: 88). Studies of particular theatres show some outlying data, particularly around the central Tokyo district. For example, a poll taken in the Shibuya and Ginza districts of Tokyo in late 1941 recorded a turnout of 41.1 per cent female viewers, but this was considered 'an absolute predominance' (*danzen yūsei*) at the time (*Eiga junpō* 1941: 54). In light of these figures, Hikari Hori argues that 'it is safe to assume that women viewers were in the minority', and moreover, 'immediate postwar statistics do show that more men saw movies than women in the late 1940s and early 1950s' (2018: 88). Furthermore, survey takers found that female viewers were generally students and working women, both with disposable incomes (Hori 2002: 55).

An audience survey from 1946 estimates the nationwide audience between the age of ten and twenty years old at 10 per cent, viewers between twenty and thirty years old at 70 per cent, viewers in their thirties at 12 per cent, and viewers in their forties at only 3 per cent (*Eiga geijutsu nenkan* 1947: 118). While I have not been able to find comprehensive figures for the gender demographics of the audience during the Occupation period, taking the later 1950s gender demographics discussed below together with wartime surveys, as well as anecdotal evidence from my ethnographic study, it seems reasonable to suggest that female viewers were in the minority throughout the Occupation, and that girls below the age of twenty, a major target of SCAP social reform, may have been even less than 5 per cent of the general commercial film theatre audience in the 1940s.

Female viewers, and particularly younger girls, were disproportionately under-represented in cinema audiences compared to their numbers in the general postwar population. In 1945 the population was 47.1 per cent male and 52.9 per cent female, with four million more female citizens than male; by 1950, female citizens outnumbered men by one million, or 51 per cent to 49 per cent, a demographic trend that continues today (Ministry of Internal Affairs and Communications 2017). People under nineteen years of age made up 47.6 per cent of the total population of Japan in 1945, with girls at 23.7 per cent, falling slightly to 45.7 per cent in 1950, with girls at 22.5 per cent.

Girls and young women attended the cinema in significantly smaller numbers than male viewers, particularly when we consider their representation in the Occupation-era population as a whole. This pattern is borne out by nationwide studies of fan activities: for example, annual surveys conducted by the film magazine *Film Friend* (*Eiga no tomo*) registered the gender of respondents as two-thirds male (H. Kitamura 2010: 165). Female viewers did participate in writing to fan columns, and a number of the magazine's advertisements were for female-oriented products such as lipstick (H. Kitamura 2010: 165). Yet editorial staff suggested that the lesser participation of female film fans indicated the continuation of 'traditional' social norms (*Eiga no tomo* 1951: 37), including the muting of female voices in the public sphere, particularly those of the young, less independent and less well off.

It seems odd that neither the Occupation authorities who oversaw gender-egalitarian film content targeted at female viewers, nor the studio personnel that actively marketed films to girls and young women with an eye on the studio's economic future, nor even the advertising agencies employing film stars in order to target female consumers, appear to have ascertained how many girls and women were actually in the cinema audience. From a commercial perspective, perhaps studios considered younger viewers a negligible audience demographic, as they did not control the spending of household income on cinema tickets. Yet a number of interviewees recalled being offered reduced prices or free entry at certain cinema theatres for being under the age of seven or ten, and so it would appear that individual theatre management personnel recognised the value of recruiting children, who would often bring a full-fee-paying adult or older child with them. The memories of the era related by viewers below suggest that a number of factors prevented female viewers from attending the cinema in the same numbers as male viewers. Taking such a grassroots view of Occupation communications complicates the top-down narratives preserved in SCAP documentation and the reports and memoirs of Occupation personnel (for example, MacArthur 1994) to demonstrate the limits of SCAP influence, and reminds us to assess such narratives as statements of intent rather than concrete achievement.

Organising the Audience: Cinema Theatres as Structuring Devices

As described in Chapter 2, cinema theatres in early postwar Japan were organised into three tiers. First-tier cinemas were the most expensive and showed the most recent films, while second- and third-tier cinemas showed older films, often in shabbier surroundings and using older prints and equipment. While Tokyo's first-run cinemas had the exclusive right to showing new films, this system was less practical in Western Japan and the Kansai region where there were fewer first-tier cinema theatres. Nonetheless, the second- and third-run theatres were cheaper and more informal, and so these theatres were popular with children and young families.

Female study participants in particular reported often feeling uncomfortable and unsafe in packed theatres in their younger years. While the *ojōsan* (young ladies) of wealthy families had no difficulty accessing elite cinemas, girls from poorer backgrounds struggled to afford the safer first-tier cinemas, yet hesitated to enter the rowdy and dirty second- and third-tier theatres. The question of class is generally a tricky one in today's Japan, with the largest number of the population identifying as middle class. By noting parents' occupations, family levels of education and other factors such as connections to nobility and the royal family, however, I was able to ascertain that around one quarter of my study participants were from elite backgrounds. Access to ready funds appears to have been a more significant factor in cinema attendance than class, as female study participants from elite families recalled attending second- and third-tier cinema theatres. Interviewees from elite families had some vague memories of discussions about the impact of lower-tier cinemagoing on one's reputation, but many remembered being too young to take these issues very seriously. On the other hand, older study participants who were in their twenties during the Occupation recalled a sense of real physical danger at some downmarket theatres, another finding supported by Terasawa's research on Tokyo female audiences (2010: 166).

The availability and willingness of an elder friend or relative to bring them to the cinema further limited many study participants' access to the film theatre, as Koyama san recalled that 'in those days girls couldn't go to the cinema alone'. Siblings and relatives featured most frequently as cinemagoing companions in my study: as demonstrated above, going to the cinema alone with a boy could open the girl viewer to criticism from other girls as well as adult family members and teachers (Bae 2008). In the elegant first-tier cinemas, audience members could sit with friends and family, untroubled by the *man'in* (packed) atmosphere of the cheaper theatres, as an anonymous questionnaire respondent recalled. Yet these safer spaces were more expensive. In the early postwar years, superior cinemas in Kyoto charged twenty-five or thirty yen, in comparison to the cheaper tickets available at the second-tier cinemas. Young female viewers were generally restricted by cost and opportunity to the second- and third-tier cinemas, and female study participants recalled being instructed by parents and teachers to view these spaces as dirty and dangerous. By contrast, male study respondents generally remembered the smoky, noisy atmosphere of the cinema theatre as exciting and even glamorous, providing an opportunity to watch older male teenagers and men smoking through double-bill programmes. The very physical organisation of the cinema theatre therefore contributed to female study participants' sense of being disproportionately restricted in their cinemagoing compared to male study participants.

While the elegant first-tier cinemas of the Occupation era advertised theatre-cooling techniques, including enormous blocks of ice with flowers frozen inside, the majority of female interviewees and questionnaire respondents recalled the dirt and stench of the second- and third-tier theatres. As discussed in Chapter 1, newspapers and film critics drew attention to issues like poor ventilation inside cinema theatres in the popular press (*Kinema Junpō* 1952: 54). Many participants in my study emphasised the change in cinema culture from the Occupation era to the present. For example, an anonymous questionnaire respondent born in 1943, who began attending the cinema in 1948 at the age of five, wrote, 'In those days the film theatres weren't so beautiful (*utsukushikunai*). Now they look like hotels!' At the time, critics complained that many postwar cinemas were like warehouses, that screenings often started late or were halted due to lack of film prints, and had broken chairs (*Kinema Junpō* 1952: 54), suggesting that run-down cinemas were a feature of film culture across Japan at the time. While female study participants tended to record their appreciation of the comfortable and clean cinemas of today, a number of male study participants expressed regret that it is no longer possible to eat, drink and smoke in the cinema theatre.

A significant number of female interviewees and questionnaire respondents also mentioned the unpleasant smell of the cheap seats near the toilets. Yamashita-san, born in 1946, recalled, 'The smell was terrible!' (*nioi ga kusai!*). For children and younger viewers, these were the most affordable seats in the most affordable theatres, though the stench could give the movie-viewing experience a sense of sufferance. Female study participants noted these distractions more often than male participants, suggesting a discourse of female viewers being more sensitive to these considerations, if not an actual practice of such issues further dissuading girls and women from attending.

Even when explicitly encouraged to go to the cinema, female viewers met various obstacles to spending time freely there. Cinemagoing was frequently used as an incentivised babysitting exercise, according to the memories of many of my study participants. Of those who recalled being asked to take very young children to the cinema, many female study participants remembered being forced to leave the theatre or becoming distracted from the film onscreen by the behaviours and demands of younger siblings. A significant number of younger viewers, both male and female, recalled forcing an older sister to leave the cinema theatre or miss key moments of a film by crying, shouting or otherwise behaving in a manner requiring intervention. For example, Hashimoto san remembered his elder sister complaining that he caused her 'some amount of trouble' by crying in the cinema during a screening of *Boyhood* (*Shōnenki*, Kinoshita Keisuke, 1951). Only one male respondent remembered bringing a younger child to the cinema, whereas the rest remembered being brought to the theatre by elder sisters or mothers. When *Kinema Junpō* authors complained of children running around in the theatres during screenings (*Kinema Junpō* 1952: 54), anecdotal evidence suggests it was generally mothers, sisters and female relatives who were running after these children.

In contrast to the rarity of a visit to a first-tier cinema theatre, several interviewees remembered frequently visiting the cheaper Cineplex-style buildings where a number of small third-tier venues were crowded together inside a single structure. These buildings offered more freedom of access, as buying one ticket would often allow a viewer to stay through multiple screenings. A number of male participants in my study recalled entering the cinema without paying by claiming to have an urgent message for a friend inside the theatre. In contrast, female study participants' memories of accessing the cinema as children and teenagers in the early postwar era tended to feature warnings against visiting certain areas of town at certain times and reminders to remain with friends or family members, prohibiting the free entry enjoyed by their male peers. While the CIE's David Conde had argued for 'the mission given to film to democratize Japan' (1965: 251) and Occupation personnel identified the cinema as a key tool for the re-education of the Japanese populace, a significant imbalance in the gender of the postwar cinema audience, as well as differing ideals of acceptable cinema-going behaviours for male and female viewers, raises questions about the efficacy of using the cinema to educate female citizens.

Imported Cinema and Impressionable Audiences

SCAP controlled the import of foreign films to Japan, with a heavy bias for American Hollywood productions, according to the 'one-distributor-per-country rule' announced in December 1946 (Terasawa 2010: 55). In that year, thirty-nine American films, five foreign films of non-American origin (imported before the war) and sixty-seven Japanese films were screened in cinemas. The CMPE was inaugurated in May 1947 as a private enterprise to import and distribute Hollywood films. By 1950, foreign imports had risen to 185, 133 of which were American (Terasawa 2010: 55). A new quota system was introduced in the same year to cap foreign imports based on the number of films from a particular country shown over the previous ten years. Many imports specifically targeted women and young viewers, as female audiences were considered to be more interested in Hollywood cinema, and schoolchildren were imagined as a new generation with fewer ties to wartime ideology and greater potential to become ideal postwar democratic capitalist citizens. Hollywood romantic dramas and melodramas, humanist narratives about schoolchildren, educational documentary films and animated films were aimed at these demographics. Narratives that centred on female heroines taking their destinies into their own hands proliferated on the Japanese screen during the Occupation in a large number of imported American and European films.

Yet the reception of film content designed to empower young female viewers was not always consistent with the re-education processes imagined by SCAP GHQ. Consideration of the varied modes of reading texts is crucial to understanding the limits of SCAP-approved cinema content for reforming everyday attitudes. The responses of young female viewers to film content selected for its democratic and gender-equal qualities could be significantly different from that imagined by censors and studio personnel. For example, Yamashita san and Otsuka san recalled their memories of Disney's *Cinderella* (Geronimi et al., 1950), which premiered in Japan on 7 March 1952, as less than favourable. The two visited the cinema separately to see the film, aged six and nine respectively. Both recalled a negative initial response to the film, which they elaborated upon during our conversation by mocking the narrative and its characters, encouraging each other in escalating their attacks on the film and its perceived morals. In this respect the recollections analysed here must be understood as living memories rather than objective record.

In Japanese advertising since 1952, Laura Miller notes, 'Cinderella is used to denote individual agency to overcome obstacles or to achieve one's dreams' (2008: 394). This is consistent with the Occupation policy of supporting the importation or creation of film texts that model democratic tropes such as independence, aspiration and agency. While a *Kinema Junpō* survey in 1957 appeared to suggest a preference among women for such 'Cinderella stories' (1957: 45–9), by contrast, Yamashita san and Otsuka san remembered understanding Cinderella as a 'selfish' (*wagamama*) heroine making a silly fuss about a party. They questioned her decision to prioritise independence and romance over family, asking, 'Why couldn't she just stay at home?' Cinderella's insistence that all single women had been invited to the ball may have been supposed to represent democratic reasoning, while her subsequent romance with Prince Charming emphasised women's rights to the independent pursuit of romantic love, as protected by the new Constitution. Both women did recall a childhood perception of new ideas of romance as the subject of much discussion, increasing as they entered their teenage years, and both subsequently made love matches in their early twenties. Furthermore, they recalled that local gossip disapproved of husbands and in-laws restricting young brides, and sympathised with young women oppressed by their families. These recollections, though mediated by the passage of time, would suggest some awareness of democratic treatment of women in romantic partnerships, if not gender-equal treatment exactly. In this sense, the values modelled by independent heroines like Cinderella were recalled as part of the discursive language of their childhood and teenage years. Yet Yamashita san and Otsuka san recalled their impressions of the heroine as needlessly forceful and dramatic, and joked that such passionate defence of one's independence and romantic happiness read very differently in Japan than they imagined it would in the United States. Both consciously and unconsciously, female viewers were influenced by cinema content, but not always in the prescriptive manner imagined by Occupation officials, industry personnel and advertising strategists.

For the older demographic of film viewers, genres such as the *josei eiga* or *onna no eiga*, often translated as 'women's films', as well as the *hahamono* 'mother films' and the *tsumamono* 'wife films', suggest a commercial attempt to attract female audiences. Where these films were shown in first-tier theatres or areas considered safe, the economic considerations outlined above also applied to women visiting alone, while a number of my study participants recalled going to the cinema with female friends in their early twenties. Couples of dating age also attended cinemas together, as did the occasional married couple in my survey. These memories support Shōchiku studio head Kido Shiro's famous assertion that, 'Women never go to the cinema alone. They will always bring either a friend or a lover' (quoted in Wada-Marciano 2008: 80).

In fact, the majority of female participants in my study recalled being brought to the cinema by parents, older siblings or dates, rather than instigating the trip themselves. Yet the establishment of the cinema as central to modern dating behaviours suggests that cinema culture did play a part in fostering the new postwar ideal of the romantic couple as an equal partnership. In Kurosawa Akira's *One Wonderful Sunday* (*Subarashiki nichiyōbi*, 1947), a character even mentions the cinema as a 'cheap date' and an opportunity for young men and women to share some time together, away from the demands of work and family. Not one of my study participants willingly brought up the topic of romantic interactions during film screenings, and I was wary of addressing the issue. Annette Kuhn notes that in her study of 1930s cinema attendance in Britain, only one male interlocutor addressed the topic uninvited (2001: 138). It is certainly an awkward question to bring up during a filmed interview. Yet analysing archival material that discusses couples' behaviours in the cinema, it seems likely that attending the cinema with a partner significantly changed the viewing experience. A 1950 article on 'The state of couples in the movie theater' related that couples in the cinema often responded physically when a scene with 'sex appeal' (*sei teki appiiru*) appeared onscreen. Such scenes are described as including 'dialogue containing the words "I love (*ai*) you," "I like (*suki*) you," "marriage," "body," and "pregnancy,"' or scenes including 'a kiss or some other physical resolution' (Fukuoka 1950: 165). Fukuoka reports observing couples kissing or interacting physically with one another during these scenes, while other audience members called out commentary.

Attending the cinema with a partner appears to have presented some viewing distractions, and at times shaped the viewing experience around the preferences of a companion rather than one's own. This trend continued up to the time of my own study; during participant observation at a number of retrospective film screenings and cinema events, I frequently observed elderly couples leaving early at the insistence of the male partner. Conversely, a number of elderly women who attended retrospective screenings regularly expressed their enjoyment of a new freedom to choose their own viewing content, time and place. In many cases this coincided with a change in gender roles at home, as the retired partners wished to use the domestic space for their own pursuits, and their wives left the home during the day to make space. In our first interview, Koyama san expressed this arrangement as a reversal of her previous role, noting that while her husband remained at home, she was the 'salaryman', and going to the cinema was like her job. This freedom contrasted with her memories of the early postwar years, when women accompanied by partners or children experienced any number of distractions in their cinema viewing, while younger girls perceived significant barriers to attending the cinema alone in relation to personal safety and socially acceptable gendered behaviour.

Audience Decline and Gendered Viewing Practices

With the end of the Occupation in 1952, SCAP pressure to apply popular cinema to change social attitudes disappeared. In fact, SCAP censorship had begun to tail off in the second half of the Occupation, culminating in June 1949, when the Motion Picture Code of Ethics Committee (Eirin) took over. By then, elements of studio infrastructure introduced to meet the practical demands of SCAP reforms had become standard, such as the hiring of large numbers of new female actors to meet SCAP's demand for female leading roles. Having invested in the telling of stories thought to appeal to female audiences, the major studios became the main drivers of concerns around female audience numbers after 1952. Yet the Sunday Audience Survey conducted by the Six Domestic Film Company Production Materials Survey Group (Hōga rokusha seisaku shiryo chōsa kai no nichiyō kankyaku chōsa), which sampled the audience demographics on selected Sundays at cinemas around the country, indicates that the total postwar female audience peaked in 1956 with a turnout of 37.4 per cent (Uryū 1967: 89).

Barriers to attending the cinema as a female viewer increased during the late 1950s and 1960s for many participants in my study. For example, Koyama san experienced a lone trip to a cinema in Kobe in the 1960s as dampening her childhood enthusiasm for cinema. Growing up during the Occupation in Kōshien, she had enjoyed walking to her local cinema with her elder sisters, drawn by the film posters on the billboards along their route home from school. Though 'in those days, girls couldn't go to the cinema alone' (*hitori de eigakan ni josei ga iku yō na jidai de wa nakatta*), she could enter the cinema for free as an elementary school student. Laughing, she recalled, 'Because I was an elementary student I didn't need to pay the entrance fee', and so her two elder sisters would take her with them frequently when they walked the short distance under the train tracks to the local cinema. She was often able to watch a favourite film two or three times in this way. Yet visiting Kobe as a young married woman in the mid-1960s, she found the local cinema intimidating, recalling that 'it took some courage' to go in (*yūki ga hitsuyō*). The theatre was full of older men, and she felt uncomfortable being there alone. Eventually she stopped going to the cinema, picking up the habit again in later years when her husband's retirement encouraged her to take up a hobby outside the home.

Koyama san's experience is echoed by a number of female writers quoted by Alexander Zahlten (2017: 68). Arguing for a confluence of genre theme and screening space as unattractive to many female viewers, Zahlten notes that 'the screening spaces that Pink Film infiltrated were increasingly, and increasingly hermetically, marked male' by the mid-1960s (2017: 68). Author Kurahashi Yumiko is quoted describing the 'cheap' smells of the 'middle-aged' men and students that fill the theatre, while critic Yajima Midori wonders at the fascinated responses of theatres filled 'mostly with men' to amateurish pink genre films (2017: 68). In these women's responses, we can see not only the echoes of Koyama san's discomfort but also reference to the displeasing sensory reminders of lack of luxury that irritated the girls and women quoted in the first half of this chapter.

By the late 1960s, female editors at *Seijin eiga* reported that it was nearly impossible to enter a pink-film theatre as a woman without being molested (Zahlten 2017: 68). As a significant number of theatres and film features were now 'pink', this had implications for the landscape of cinemagoing in Japan more broadly. Hideaki Fujiki argues that a series of coinciding factors, including the reduction of programme pictures, the increase in pink film production and the majority male demographic of the cinema audience, combined to make it more difficult for women to enter cinema theatres from the second half of the 1960s (2019: 385). As women audiences decreased from even their extant minority proportion of the early Occupation-era cinema viewership demographic, the overall audience for the cinema was also in sharp decline.

In 1967, critic Uryū Tadao noted the absence of women in mainstream film theatres in *Kinema Junpō*. In fact, the female audience had been missing for almost a decade before the publication of Uryū's article drawing attention to the issue. Tōei studio films drew a slightly larger female audience, but Uryū notes that this was unusual (1967: 88). Uryū acknowledged the 'great social constraints' that faced women, but argued that it would be difficult to imagine what an ideal percentage of female audiences would be, due to the difficulty of factoring in these social constraints in numerical surveys of the cinema audience (1967: 89). Yet the number of female viewers kept falling into the 1960s, dropping below 30 per cent for the first week of surveys in 1964, an all-time low (Uryū 1967: 89). The ratio crept up above 30 per cent again in 1965, reaching 33.8 per cent in 1966. However, as the overall number of viewers continued to decline, the actual number of women going to the cinema decreased even as the ratio of women in the cinema increased slightly.

It is notable that Uryū made no attempt to describe the 'great social constraints' keeping women from the cinema or to suggest a solution. He speculated that an increase in 'male-oriented films' (*dansei muki eiga*) and erotic and violent content might cause an ordinary woman to feel 'shyness, shame and fear' in the cinema (1967: 89). Yet environmental factors such as the location of cinema theatres and the spaces women inhabited in the1960s should also be considered as factors in the decline of female audience numbers. Women's presence in the workforce dropped from 55 per cent to 46 per cent between 1960 and 1975 (Fujiki 2019: 361), suggesting that a decline in the numbers of women commuting to public workplaces may have resulted in smaller numbers of women filling the hours after work with visits to the cinema. As larger numbers of women stayed at home, those homes were also increasingly built in relatively self-sufficient suburban areas, lessening the female footfall around city centre cinemas during weekdays. Going to the cinema became a hobby rather than a part of everyday life in the 1960s (Fujiki 2019: 374), and not only for women. The imagined audiences for this particular hobby became the target of film companies, rather than the general public (Fujiki 2019: 374). As women and children were thought to be the larger consumers of television, including television films, cinema theatres screened more sexual and violent content for the imagined alternative demographic of film hobbyists (Fujiki 2019: 374).

Pointing out that the largest number of television viewers in the 1950s and 1960s were girls aged twelve to seventeen, Uryū noted that by 1967 female viewers were generally more than 50 per cent of the television audience. At 1pm on a weekday, girls and women even made up 70 per cent of the television audience (Uryū 1967: 90). The inclusion of television viewing figures and mention of alternative entertainment pursuits in an article titled 'Cinema's recovery begins with women's mobilization' suggests that women's viewing behaviours were to blame for the sorry state of cinema attendance. Uryū concluded that 'the television is a larger and stronger draw on audiences, and so the countermeasure that the Japanese film world must take is to find out how to secure (*tsunagitomeru*) [the patronage of] women to the film theatre' (Uryū 1967: 90). Women were encouraged to return to the cinema to save Japanese filmmaking:

> If cinema becomes only male-focused, the scope of the subject is limited. We have closed our eyes to the poverty of Japanese cinema, as male-focused films are becoming a mass production of inferior goods (*soseiranzō*). The quality of Japanese cinema will drop, and not only women but also men will begin to limit their watching of Japanese cinema. (Uryū 1967: 90)

Uryū appeared to be appealing to women to participate in cinema culture in order to safeguard the artistry of the medium for its largely male audience base. Furthermore, Uryū argued that the television content that drew female audiences in such large numbers was 'contemptible' (*bubetsu*), suggesting that the female demographic captivated by the new medium had been corrupted by consuming bad-quality viewing material (Uryū 1967:

90). While women were called upon to reinvigorate the Japanese cinema, at the same time many female viewers were positioned as a lost cause – lost to television and lost to contemptible content.

Imagined Audiences and Remembered Experience

The disproportionate difficulties that female viewers remembered facing in entering cinemas in certain areas and at certain times, along with the distractions posed by caring for others within the space of the cinema itself, seems to have impeded the free consumption of cinema narratives for many women. As these narratives were often censored with a female audience in mind during the Occupation, and produced by studios that at least voiced an intention to appeal to women for financial reasons, the barriers that girls and women faced in entering the cinema directly undermined attempts to engage female viewers. The independent female citizen may have been a prominent character in films of the postwar era, but she does not appear to have been in the cinema theatre in the numbers that her fictional representations, or SCAP documentation, may lead us to assume. By paying attention to who can be in certain spaces and under what conditions, we can better understand the structural forces governing access to film and, subsequently, shaping gender ideologies.

Furthermore, we must allow for the possibility of audiences reading against the grain, channelling the hidden histories of particular images, characters or tropes and revisiting their own readings with new interpretations over the years to come. Based on ethnographic evidence, it would appear that 'the mission given to film to democratize Japan' (Conde 1965: 251) fell short in some significant ways in reaching young female citizens during Occupation. The mission given to female viewers by critics such as Uryū Tadao, to 'mobilize' in support of Japanese cinema, likewise overlooks a number of significant factors which rendered many female audience members' experiences quite different to those of the writers who documented postwar film culture in Japan. By documenting the voices of those whose experiences, memories and opinions are not given space in *Kinema Junpō*, we can achieve a more sensitive understanding of the many roles cinema played in the everyday lives of everyday people. In the next chapter, we will see how political organising around the cinema attempted to make change in those everyday lives.

CHAPTER 6

Organised Audiences and Committed Fans: Cinema, Viewership, Activism

From the memories of younger children taken to the cinema by older family members to the casual viewers who used the cinema as a place to stop or rest, the preceding chapters have explored the recollections of incidental participants in cinema culture as well as more dedicated fans of film. Chapter 6 turns to the dedicated cinemagoer with an account of historic film-related grassroots organisations in postwar Kansai. Beginning with the activities of the Kyoto kiroku eiga o miru kai (Kyoto documentary film viewing group, 1955–62), an amateur film-appreciation group that evolved into a film production unit, this chapter traces the increasingly political activities of film clubs and circles in Kyoto. As we move into the 1960s, the second part of this chapter considers the relation of the kinds of selves developed through film viewership to the activism of the decade. Exploring how viewers found models for activist conduct, and also spaces and reasons to abstain from activism, in the very same cinema, we can see how cinema is used as a flexible signifier in discourse, particularly in relation to giving an account of one's personal politics.

Organised Film Viewing and Political Activism

During participant observation at a monthly film-screening event in northwest Kyoto called the Kinugasa eiga kai (Kinugasa Film Club), the three organisers introduced me to Asai Eiichi (1933–), co-leader of the previous incarnation of the club and producer of the film *Nishijin* (*Nishijin*, 1961). Perhaps understandably, discussion around the club's mission tended to look back to previous decades, when the forerunners of the organisation had driven direct interventions into local exhibition practices and reception. Their desire to situate the contemporary Kinugasa eiga kai as a kind of descendent organisation from Asai's group suggested the importance of a sense of lineage for this organised audience group, and highlights the role of younger, later or descendent audience groups in remediating (and perhaps glorifying) the activities of their forebears. While Chapter 7 explores the phenomenon of such citizen-organised groups as a significant part of the 'crafting' of cinema culture in postwar Japan, this chapter links film clubs, circles and regular screening groups, and the Kinugasa eiga kai in particular, to a mode of talking about cinema that touches on political identity and ideology.

Many postwar clubs and circles were not expressly political, but nonetheless regularly scheduled sessions in which members 'often connected local problems to larger issues facing the working class and the Japanese nation as a whole' (Bronson 2016: 124). Andrew Gordon identifies three basic roles for circles in this era: 'recreation and self-cultivation', the development of 'democratic citizenry' and the creation of 'a national political movement' (2009: 98). While we might think of film circles and clubs as recreational then, the format of the organised film-viewing circle itself, which tended to emphasise group discussion as well as group viewing, could nudge the group towards consideration of wider issues, including political and social issues, and so create political awareness leading to political engagement through the relatively apolitical practice of meeting to watch films together. The format of the event itself is key here:

> Circles brought into question the idea that people should be organized hierarchically and led from above by farsighted elites. Intellectually, circle activism challenged the privileged position of a vanguard – intellectuals, politicians, bureaucrats – as the only source of socially useful meaning. Organizationally, circle activism presented an alternative to the hierarchical, centrally directed model of the established left, forging instead a more egalitarian form of human organization and interaction – what literary critic Ara Masato referred to as 'horizontal connections' (*yoko no tsunagari*). Such intellectual and organizational innovations made the circle movement an ideal model for later, more overtly political civic groups. (Avenell 2010: 23)

While the circles and clubs for film viewing discussed in this chapter were not explicitly political at the point of their formation, their activities often spilled over into activism and deliberate political engagement.

Many clubs and circles, including film-viewing groups, began as workplace organisations. Simon Avenell argues that while 'the agents of the left were among the most active organizers of cultural circles', nonetheless 'workplace cultural circles never lived up to their revolutionary potential' (2010: 45–6). As workplace circles began to decline in popularity in the 1960s, independent groups, sometimes politically affiliated and sometimes not, became the more common cultural circle format (Avenell 2010: 46). In the case of film circles in particular, many originated in educational establishments including schools and universities, which also became hotbeds of political activism in the 1960s. Labour unions began to expand workplace circles (*shokuchi sākuru*), within which there was often a regional organised film circle (Uryū [1958] 1994: 747).

Reflecting on the development of film circles within the film world, as well as in schools, universities and workplaces around the country, critic Uryū Tadao noted that film study groups, clubs and circles had been popular since the late 1920s and into the 1930s ([1958] 1994: 747). After the war, he argued, film-viewing organisations took a new political turn and focused on educating the public about democracy. Recalling his own experience of high school film circles in the wartime years, Uryū argued that the postwar reform of the school system introduced high school film circles to political issues through a focus on the 'social elements of film' (Uryū [1958] 1994: 747). 'In the early years of the postwar, the emphasis on political and social elements of the film circle was strong . . . American films were borrowed and shown, and taught viewers about democracy' (Uryū [1958] 1994: 747). Against a socio-political background of severe poverty and rapid social change, film circles were sites of education as well as entertainment.

The Tokyo Film Circle Convention (Tokyo eiga sākuru kyōgikai, shortened to Tokyo eisakyō) was formed in 1948 and used circle activity to encourage the creation of democratic films. They also aimed to support the activities of democratic cultural groups and to 'protect' Japanese culture (Uryū [1958] 1994: 748). The labour union circles, film theatre friendship groups (*eigakan no tomo no kai*) and study groups within the Tokyo eisakyō all clearly prioritised social and political concerns among their aims. This focus on raising public awareness of social and political issues was not confined to Tokyo, but appeared in the manifestos and advertising materials of clubs, circles and other film organisations in Kyoto and Osaka, as well as other areas.

In the early years of the postwar, Uryū argued, the emphasis on political and social elements within film clubs and circles was strong (*kyōretsu*) (Uryū [1958] 1994: 747). The Tōhō strikes (1946–9), which were led by the studio unions, are often associated with the beginnings of a boom in film club and circle activities which expanded across the country from 1949 (Uryū [1958] 1994: 748). As the Korean War broke out from 25 June 1950 and the anti-war film *Listen to the Voices from the Deep* (*Kike wadatsumi no koe*, Sekigawa Hideo, 1950) was released, more film clubs and circles were formed around the mass movements (*taishū dōin*) of the period (Uryū [1958] 1994: 749). Against the background of the Red Purge, the formation of politically informed film-viewing organisations for citizens continued to gather speed in 1952 and 1953 (Uryū [1958] 1994: 749).

Finally, a shift in focus from political concerns to economic concerns in the mid-1950s increased the number of organised film clubs, circles and events even further (Uryū [1958] 1994: 749). In the mid-1950s, viewer-led film organisations and self-organised screenings became a topic of conversation among critics such as Uryū, informing not only how cinema was viewed but how film culture was discussed. By 1955, 300,000 people across Japan were members of a film-viewing circle (Fujiki 2019: 387; Nakai 1958: 60).

Creating a Film-viewing Organisation: The Kyoto kiroku eiga o miru kai

The Kinugasa film club, in which I conducted participant observation and recruited many study participants from 2016 to 2018, was the most recent incarnation of a film-viewing organisation that traced its roots back to the early 1950s. As noted above, the current organisers of the Kinugasa eiga kai made a significant point of this lineage, as well as the political activities which had grown out of earlier versions of the organisation. Introducing me to Asai san, the co-organiser of the first incarnation of the group, the present-day organisers were keen to share the legacies of this earlier version of their film club, and to stress the deeply embedded history of their activities. While Chapter 7 explores the activities of the Kinugasa eiga kai in 2016–18, this chapter details the political activism of its antecedent, the Kyoto kiroku eiga o miru kai, in order to investigate the relation of cinema culture to political organisation and activism in the early postwar era.

In 1953 Asai Eiichi was twenty years old. At an old coffee shop near Kawaramachi in central Kyoto, he met and formed a friendship with Fujiki Shoji, a forty-one-year-old theatre group organiser whose theatre circle had just ousted him from the organisation (possibly for being too politically focused) (Morishita 2009). Fujiki wanted to continue the artistic and political organising he had been developing within the theatre group and Asai wanted an education in documentary film. Together they formed the Kyoto kiroku eiga o miru kai, which ran from April 1955 to March 1962 (Asai 1961a: 21). Satō Yō notes the film-viewing group's historical precedents in such organised groups as the the Kyoto engeki kurabu (Kyoto theatre club) and the Kyoto katei shohi kumiai (Kyoto family consumer cooperative) (2013: 41). Based on these models, Asai and Fujiki 'created a cooperative type of film society that is different from the enlightenment type of film society' (Satō 2013: 41). These 'cooperative type' clubs and societies focused on 'liberating the senses' and raising awareness of both aesthetic and political elements of cinema culture (Satō 2013: 41), in contrast to the 'enlightenment type' of organisation, which had tended to focus on education.

Monthly screenings were held at the Yasaka Hall in Kyoto, Gion Kaikan, Kyoto Prefectural University of Medicine and other city locations. In a conversation in late 2016, Asai san recollected that the primary motivating factor in the club's initial programming choices was to enable people to 'see films that can't be seen within the frame of commercial cinema' (*shōgyō eiga no waku*). Documentary films by the Scottish John Grierson and American Robert Flaherty were screened at the group's meetings, Japanese directors were invited to discuss their own films and solo exhibitions would often be arranged, showing work by Matsumoto Toshio, Wada Tsutomu and Tsuchimoto Noriaki. At the same time, however, Asai san recalled the early years of the club as 'an era of politics' (*seiji no jidai*) when popular interest in investigative journalism and social issues was growing.

The club's activities soon expanded to include the bulk buying of film-screening tickets for distribution among the membership. This had the effect of packing out commercial theatres for selected screenings and so the operation quickly became somewhat political. As Fujiki and Asai san had leftist political leanings and an interest in grassroots organising, members were channelled towards leftist films, particularly those focused on labour issues. In this way, the film club became a commercial tool, supporting the public screening of films with political themes in agreement with the outlook of the organisers. This was not unusual – many film-viewing groups deliberately mobilised their membership to support particular projects, directors or studios. In fact, the film clubs and circles organised around studios and commercial publications were developed to do just that, providing the studio or publishing house with a base of ticket buyers who could be directed towards certain screenings to financially support the business and its projects. Fujiki notes that this was a common mode of encouraging attendance at a film circle (2019: 387).

While watching political documentaries from all over the world, the group remained aware of problems at home. The Kyoto kiroku eiga o miru kai membership began to plan for the production of a documentary film driven by a growing awareness of labour issues and the treatment of workers in the local area. A sub-group of members formed a production unit within the Kyoto kiroku eiga o miru kai and collaboratively produced *Nishijin*, which won the short documentary award at the Venice Film Festival in 1961. Following the producers' bankruptcy and a fire at the offices, however, the film circle folded and was reborn as Shi dokyumentari shinema (Shidofu) in in June 1964. The core members of Shidofu would go on to create the Kinugasa eiga kai, where I conducted participant observation from 2016 to 2018.

As Janet Staiger observes, 'historical circumstances sometimes create "interpretative communities" or cultural groups such as fans who produce their own conventionalized modes of reception' (2000: 23). In this case, the historical circumstances of the area of Nishijin in north-west Kyoto gave rise to an active and politically engaged mode of reception that culminated in an attempt at production. Jackie Stacey has argued that such group exchanges 'condense and make more tangible the collaborative, and yet always enigmatic, production of a sense of self' (2013: 51). In the next section of this chapter, we can see how the work of organising a film-viewing group turned film production unit in the process of creating *Nishijin* could also create a politically engaged and socially conscious sense of self, both for the members of the Kyoto kiroku eiga o miru kai and for the organisers of the successor viewing clubs which repeatedly invoked the original's activities to historicise and legitimise their own pursuits.

Nishijin *as Political Activism*

The experience of the rebellion makes a we out of the I and him or her – the experience of the rebellion lets us know 'I was not alone!' (Ichida 2020: 44)

Kyoto kiroku eiga o miru kai's self-produced film critiqued the working conditions of weavers in the Nishijin area of Kyoto, from which the finished film takes its name. However, we can also understand the project as a critique of the late-1950s and early-1960s consumer society of Income Doubling-era Japan as the condition under which the exploitation of the weavers continued. Nishijin weavers made a highly specialised and expensive brocade used in the production of luxury kimono. *Nishijin-ori*, a kind of *sakizome* (cloth dyed before weaving), is thought to be one of Japan's oldest craft products, dating back 1,200 years. In 1976 the weaving process was designated a National Traditional Craft (Nishijin Textile Industry Association 2020). 'Nishijin' is now a registered trademark of the Nishijin Industrial Association.

The Committee on Labour Relations, which consisted of business and labour representatives, had been debating the status and rights of cottage weavers known as *chinbata* during the 1950s. While manufacturers had argued that *chinbata* were self-employed, as they tended to work in their own residences (Hareven 2002: 60), in 1957 the Committee ruled that *chinbata* were in fact entitled to legal protection on maximum hours and minimum wages. Yet the manufacturers resisted. Tamara Hareven quotes a production manager in one of the Nishijin firms, who compared the weavers' labour to that of housewives, asking, 'Does a housewife stop her work after eight hours, if her tasks are not finished?' (Mr Hiraoka, quoted in Hareven 2002: 61). The dismissive attitude and pejorative feminising of the weavers' work implied here illustrates the widening gap between the weavers and the manufacturers' associations in the wake of the 1957 ruling.

Weavers complained of an 'exploitative and paternalistic relationship between the manufacturer and the weaver' (Hareven 2002: 100). The manufacturer, occupying the role of *oyakata*, or independent labour contractor, situated the weaver as *kokata*, or dependent worker. This hierarchy had developed in the factories and textile industries of Meiji Japan (1868–1926), where employers would make lump-sum contracts with *oyakata*, who would find workers willing to do the job, supervise the work, manage production deadlines and pay the workers. As the Japanese terms indicate, 'the *oyakata-kokata* bond was a peculiar combination of father-child relationship and exploitation' (Annavajhula 1989: 17). Hareven's weaver interviewees echoed this assessment, complaining of 'a hierarchical line between the manufacturer [*oyakata*] and the weaver [*kokata*] in Nishijin' which extended to slowing or quickening the pace of the weavers' work according to budgets and deadlines (Konishi, quoted in Hareven 2002: 100).

While some weavers who responded to a 1962 survey of weaving households in Nishijin expressed their preference for working at home, others complained that 'the cottage weavers' sense of solidarity is very low' (Mr Matsushita, quoted in Hareven 2002: 98) and that the situation was not conducive to Nishijin weavers unionising to protect their new rights. Whether they worked at home or in factories, however, the working conditions were very harsh, and these skilled workers struggled in poor conditions to make elaborate woven and embroidered materials for expensive kimono and accoutrements.

Asai san recalled becoming aware of the occupational injuries suffered by the weavers that were treated at Horikawa hospital, in part because the hospital had both film club members and members of the Communist Party within its workforce. The combined symptoms of the weavers were collectivised as 'Horikawa disease', after the name of the hospital which treated the workers, located close to Nishijin in the north-west area of Kyoto. Not coincidentally, pre-war Horikawa had also been one of the larger *buraku* districts in Kyoto, home to a discriminated minority caste. Asai san remembered the discussion of the late 1950s focusing on this health issue as exemplary of a wider social problem (*shakai mondai*) evident in late-1950s Japan, as the discourses of equality and human rights that had characterised the early postwar years gave way to an acknowledgement that Japan was still very unequal. Labour rights, poverty, illness and class division combined to make the story of the weavers highly appealing to the leftist politics of many of the members of the Kyoto kiroku eiga o miru kai. The core membership decided to make a film to bring Horikawa disease and the suffering of the weavers to public attention.

Kyoto kiroku eiga o miru kai emphasised the qualitative change of group members' consciousness as its primary goal, rather than financial gain, political influence or increasing membership (Satō 2013: 42). In these aspects, the Kyoto kiroku eiga o miru kai was similar to the audio-visual education movement, in terms of assembling a screening programme of documentary film for public education. Fujiki and Asai received support from local educators, and the film circle was seen by some as something of an extension of education practices (Satō 2013: 42). Yet Satō argues that the success of the group's activities depended on the personalities of Fujiki and Asai, as well as Kyoto city's particular affinity for politicised arts groups (2013: 42).

Against the social, historical and political background described by Asai, the 3 August 1958 screening of Luis Buñuel's *Los Olvidados* (*The Forgotten Ones*, 1950), accompanied by a lecture from Hanada Kiyoteru (also known as Hanada Seiki), may have inspired the group to think about the representation of underclasses and oppressed groups (Satō 2013: 49). Satō quotes member Takahashi Akira, who claimed that the meeting had inspired him to think more deeply about social issues (Satō 2013: 50). At the same time, club members who were employed at Horikawa hospital and many local doctors, nurses and hospital administrators urged the group to think about developing a film about the workers' condition (Wada Marciano 2014: 379).

Political agendas, artistic aspirations and the production of Nishijin *(1961)*

Director Matsumoto Toshio, who was approached by Asai san to direct the film circle's project, remembered that 'they were left-wing, but still not what you call a political organization. I think they were the first to try to cultivate new spectators and make the kind of films they wanted to see on their own' (Gerow 2015). Making a film upon request from a non-professional group was not unusual in the 1950s (Wada Marciano 2014: 379) and labour unions regularly commissioned films. Matsumoto recalled, 'Documentaries up until then were mostly made with the backing of a labor union or Communist Party organization. If you thought of doing something different from that, you had to create a completely different support structure because there was no foundation for making such films or showing them' (Gerow 2015).

While Matsumoto was known to the Kyoto kiroku eiga o miru kai due to the regular speaking and exhibition opportunities that the group offered to Japanese directors, he also had some extant connections to Nishijin, having worked at the Shin Riken company, which specialised in science documentaries and industrial promotion films, from 1955 to 1959 (Raine 2012: 144). The Shin Riken company had produced a two-minute short news film on the working conditions in Nishijin, which was broadcast on 8 October 1958, highlighting the suffering of those who produced the 'beautiful kimono worn by the *maiko* of Gion' (Morishita 2009). Matsumoto's third film, a documentary called *Children Calling Spring* (*Haru o yobu kora*, 1959), had also focused on issues of labour exploitation in its account of the 'back-breaking jobs' which the children undertook (Gerow 2015). The director recalled that 'in those days, a good documentary was defined as something that, first of all, had a poignant subject, and then was socially or politically controversial' (Gerow 2015). Yet his own approach was already developing along different lines, as he wondered 'whether there wasn't a need for documentary to assume a subjectivity that could make visible what was invisible. In that sense, I felt that documentary and the avant-garde have to be connected within a moment of mutual negation' (Gerow 2015). If the Kyoto kiroku eiga o miru kai had hoped that the Nishijin weavers would receive a similar treatment to the *Children Calling Spring*, they were to be disappointed.

Matsumoto and Asai san have recorded slightly different memories of the project planning. While Matsumoto recalled bringing the subject of the Nishijin weavers to the group (Gerow 2015), Asai san presented the topic as emerging from the contacts, experiences and political interests of the Kyoto kiroku eiga o miru kai members. Nonetheless, producer and director agreed to focus on the subject of the weaving industry in Nishijin, bringing on board poet Sekine Hiroshi (1920–94) as a co-writer, Miyoshi Akira (1933–2013) as composer and cinematographer Miyajima Yoshio (1909–98). Asai remembered that Miyajima, who had led the Tōhō studio strikes discussed earlier in this chapter, agreed to co-operate without compensation. Nishijin textile companies were approached to sponsor the film, and Kyoto kiroku eiga o miru kai members sold micro-shares of 80 yen (approximately $5 in today's US dollars) to local people to help fund the film (Wada Marciano 2014: 379). A filmmaking association was founded from within the Kyoto kiroku eiga o miru kai membership, with some members directly participating in the production. Morishita infers from contemporary newspaper reports that expenses totalled around 2.5 million yen, with an estimated deficit of 700,000 yen (2009).

While Matsumoto recalled that he 'got their approval to address Kyoto's Nishijin', his goals, at least as he remembered them in a 2015 interview with Aaron Gerow, appear to differ slightly from the political consciousness-raising aims expressed by Asai san. Matsumoto remembered having 'the aim of giving form to something more deeply submerged within the situation, something warped and hard to express. I wasn't trying to depict the place called Nishijin or show people weaving, but to give shape to the thick, silent, unvoiced voices lurking beneath Nishijin' (Gerow 2015). By contrast, Asai san remembered wanting to film in colour in order to show the beauty of the weavers' work. Due to the tight budget, Asai san's wishes could not be accommodated and the filming was completed in black and white. In the end, Asai san surmised, 'Perhaps it's better for "Matsumoto Toshio's avant-garde" that it should have been black and white.' That the end result was to further Matsumoto's career is not disputed by the production team nor by Matsumoto himself. 'Opinion was divided over the results, but the fact it won the Silver Lion at the Venice International Documentary Film Festival helped clear the way for my next steps' (Matsumoto, quoted in Gerow 2015).

Tensions between the political aims of the Kiroku eiga o miru kai, the commercial requirements of the production team, the artistic desires of Asai san and the avant-garde sensibilities of Matsumoto are echoed in the jarring effect of the film's style and soundtrack. Matsumoto sought to create 'the form of a cine poem that persistently piled up exacting images' (Matsumoto, quoted in Gerow 2015). In contrast to the deeply local origins of the film's planning (Morishita 2009; 'Nishijin' seisaku jōei kyōkai handbill 1961), Yuriko Furuhata observes that Nishijin 'refuses to provide any establishing shots' (2013: 34). Layering close-up shots of weavers' bodies and fast-moving machinery, 'Matsumoto deliberately works against the expectation of a recognizable and lucid image' (Furuhata 2013: 35). The question of the workers' physical health is briefly addressed with shots of moxibustion treatments, their stress and dissatisfaction with scenes showing weavers praying, and the poverty of the area in footage of children playing with rusty nails in the dirt. However, overall the emphasis of the twenty-five-minute film appears to be firmly on the aesthetic rather than the explicitly political.

The film previewed in Tokyo on 27 June and in Kyoto on 12 July 1961. The limited release was met with a significant volume of print criticism, both positive and negative. *Nishijin* was given a special feature in the

September issue of *Kiroku Eiga* (*Documentary Film*), the pre-eminent Japanese journal of the time for documentary cinema, in the same year. The Nishijin Textile Association strongly objected to the film, particularly to the depiction of the weavers suffering in poor conditions under their watch. The scenes which most offended the Association might have been those of an Association meeting, filmed from above in order to render the board members truly absurd, with bald heads and combover hairstyles. In this scene, the soundtrack features a jumble of edited and remixed voices, repeatedly sticking on one or two ridiculous phrases that underscore the emptiness of the values of this managerial class, in stark contrast to the honest labour of the suffering weavers.

Nishijin was to bankrupt its producers, bringing the Kyoto kiroku eiga o miru kai to collapse under the weight of recriminations and sending Asai san fleeing debt, moving to Osaka. The high cost of production and marketing overran the production group's funds and despite the Venice award the film was not a commercial success. Furthermore, Nishijin's textile industry personnel applied significant pressure to the filmmaking association to re-edit the film with added footage, releasing a sanitised parallel version, *Orimono no machi, Nishijin* (*The Weaving Town of Nishijin*, 1961) (Wada Marciano 2014: 380). Finally, a fire at the offices wiped out the remaining film club's membership cards and members' dues, and the film circle folded. The memory did not seem too bitter during our interview in 2016, however, as Asai san related the story of the production of *Nishijin* from the lobby café of a hotel facing Nijō castle. 'After the commercial failure of *Nishijin*,' he remembered, 'the Kyoto kiroku eiga o miru kai had become famous in every sense, and so it disbanded.' The film-viewing group was reborn in June 1964 as Shi Dokyumentari Shinema, or Shidofu for short. Asai san briefly joined this successor group, keen to share his passion for avant-garde film, which remained undimmed by the disaster of *Nishijin*'s production. However, the members of Shidofu were looking for films with a strong journalistic sense and so Asai san moved on to the Gendai geijutsu no kai (Contemporary Art Society). Young members of Shidofu would go on to create the Kingasa eiga kai in their retirement years.

Kitagawa Kenzō has argued that these diverse 'cultural movements' after the war were both 'conscious [and] subconscious' attempts by the Japanese public to 'resurrect their selfhoods and search for direction' in times of large-scale change (2000: 175). Morishita notes that the stated goal of Kyoto kiroku eiga o miru kai was to observe recordings of everyday life and this is clearly connected to the attempt to resurrect a leftist Japanese selfhood and find a new direction for the movement. In fact, Morishita records that a junior high school teacher who watched the film at the time argued that 'Nishijin is a microcosm of Japan itself'. In this way, we can understand the film circle's effort to make a documentary film themselves as an attempt to record something of the members' political concerns for postwar Japan, as symbolised by the weavers' struggles. The second part of this chapter opens out from this microsite that demonstrates the political concerns and activities of organised audience groups in 1950s and 1960s Kansai to consider more general political attitudes developed through, fostered by and communicated in discussions of cinema culture. In the following section, I explore memories of cinema culture of the politically charged 1960s, in which study participants use the cinema as communication device to both form and articulate a sense of a politically identified self.

Japanese Cinema and the 1960s

As discussed in previous chapters, attendance at the cinema was falling sharply in the 1960s, from a peak of 1,127,452,000 in 1958 to 313,398,000 in 1968 (Motion Picture Producers' Association of Japan). The number of cinema theatres was also decreasing, from a peak of 7,457 in 1960 to 3,814 in 1968 (Motion Picture Producers' Association of Japan). The majority of the films available in theatres were made in Japan; in 1968, 494 Japanese films were screened and 249 imported films. At the same time, the average admission fee increased every year, reaching 262 yen in 1968, up from 236 the previous year, compared to 72 yen in 1960 (Motion Picture Producers' Association of Japan).

Management personnel within Japan's major studios had initially hoped that the political mood of the 1960s could present a solution to the downturn in cinema attendance. At Shōchiku and Nikkatsu, radical and politically outspoken young directors such as Ōshima Nagisa, Imamura Shōhei and Suzuki Seijun were quickly promoted and grouped together for marketing purposes as Japan's own nouvelle vague (*nuberu bāgu*). While there was a degree of cross-influence between Japanese filmmakers of the era and their French counterparts, the young directors objected to the hijacking of their dissenting voices for the studios' commercial purposes, and by 1968 Ōshima, Imamura, Suzuki and many contemporaries had left the studios or been fired, moving into television, documentary and independent filmmaking.

As Oguma Eiji suggests, the larger number of those involved in the political demonstrations and activism of the 1960s divided their time between politics, music and theatre (Oguma 2009: 93). I would suggest that the activities of this group also included cinema attendance, not only at those cinemas directly connected to political theatre such as the Art Theatre Guild's Sasori-za in Shinjuku but also at the declining number of mainstream film theatres showing the work of politicised filmmakers such as Ōshima alongside genre films and pure entertainment features. The memories of the cinema audience can shed light on the role of cinema-going, as well as film content, in forming the political imaginaries of this group of partially involved and sometimes even disinterested occasional participants in 1960s politics and activism.

In interviews and questionnaire surveys, I repeatedly encountered discussions about 1960s activism and what these memories, as well as the movement itself, meant for the personal histories of study participants. I group the discourses roughly into three distinct areas of sentiment expressed by three relatively distinct groups of research participants. The first group, just under one-third of the total number of research participants, found some reflection of their feelings and aspirations for the political movements of the 1960s in the popular cinema of the time. These participants recalled casting popular film stars and characters as role models for their activist conduct and outlook. The second group, by far the largest number of participants, remembered the activist movements of the 1960s as disruptive to their enjoyment of popular entertainments such as the cinema and appreciated the film theatre as a space away from everyday concerns, including politics. In the most extreme cases, members of this group even situated 1960s activism as directly impeding their own creative ambitions to make films and remembered the political activities of the era as detrimental to their career aspirations. Similarly, the last group did not participate at all in political activism in the 1960s, but recalled the era with a wistful sense of longing. These research participants were generally the youngest in the study and often cited their young age or their geographical location as the main reason for their non-involvement in political activism. Instead they imagined the cinema as communicating the mood of the era from a distance, allowing them a vicarious experience of activities they remember having wished to join. In these ways, cinema as a discursive object is used reflexively by fans and audience members to describe, explain or justify feelings, political attitudes and memories unique to personal circumstance and character.

The majority of participants in my study explicitly connected their film-viewing experiences to their memories of contemporary political issues. As most were born in the early 1940s, the most frequently discussed political reference point was the end of Japan's Fifteen Years War and the Second World War, followed by the American-led Allied Occupation of Japan (1945–52). Most of the survey participants who were children in this era were still actively engaged in contextualising and understanding their memories of the period through cinema at the time of our interviews. The same generation were teenagers and students during the political protest movements of the 1960s and their memories and opinions of these movements were similarly framed in relation to cinema, as well as explicitly connected to issues of war and Occupation. These highly politicised viewers actively sought out political meanings and inferences in popular film texts, yet their own expression of their feelings about, and involvement in, 1960s activism was often conflicted. Some film fans wished to be closer to the political action, while others strove to avoid it. All used the cinema as both space and discursive mode to associate or distance themselves from 1960s activism.

Cinematic Role Models for the 1960s

Born in 1943, Hashimoto san was twenty-five in 1968. He participated in the earlier protests against the renewal of the Japan–US Security Treaty (Anpo) and the Japan–Korea Treaty (1965), as well as the anti-Vietnam War protests that followed, and in 1968 demonstrations around the country. While film scholars today may think of the independent and left-associated filmmakers such as Ōshima and Matsumoto in relation to protest movements and cinema, Hashimoto san drew his inspiration from a different genre – the *yakuza* film. He recalled the heroes of the genre as displaying a particular characteristic that he expressed as 'Gaman ni gaman' – continuing to endure with self-control. Acting out Takakura's posture on a popular poster that he recalled having seen at a festival, which showed the character's back tattoo, Hashimoto san turned his back to me and gestured to the tattooed area: 'At that time, there were the student demonstrations where students could be caught by police.' Hashimoto san clasped his left arm above the elbow with his right hand to indicate being caught, his serious expression emphasising the implications: 'If you were caught, that affected your chance of finding employment. But even though students were afraid, it was imperative to stop the war in Vietnam, and to go to demos. Because of this, we took the *yakuza* motto "Gaman ni gaman".' Hashimoto san held his left wrist with his right hand in his lap and acted out a series of formal decisive bows, as though playing an onscreen *yakuza* character: 'Because in the end, of course . . .' he smiled. 'Well . . . Takakura Ken modelled this "it has to be done" feeling.' Hashimoto san pointed in front of himself, then mimed slashing downwards with a sword. Placing his hand on his heart in an expression of personal response to such cinema imagery, he recalled, 'That was, well, we felt that we were the same,

I think. That's why I think Takakura was really a big hit.' Hashimoto san continued to rub his left arm with his right, as though expressing unease or personal discomfort, as he discussed the feeling that students needed to stand up for what was right in this period. In this respect Takakura Ken and other stars of the *yakuza* genre were the model for his engagement with demonstrations and protest culture. *Yakuza* heroes embodied the spirit of never saying 'It can't be done' (*yaranai to ikenai*) for Hashimoto san and his fellow activists. Hashimoto san recalled, 'We tried to imagine we were the same.'

Yakuza genre films dominated the Japanese studio system as audience attendance declined from its peak in 1958. Tōei studio marketed itself as the home of the *yakuza* genre film from the 1960s, though Daiei studio also invested in the equally popular female *yakuza* series, beginning with the *Woman Gambler* series (*Onna tobakushi*, 1967–71) which ran to twelve instalments. In 1968 an anonymous critic reported in *Kinema Junpō* (*The Movie Times*) that cinema theatre managers 'deplored the *yakuza* film, on the grounds that female and teenage fans were few' (Anon. 1968: 83). Yet female-led films such as the *Red Peony Gambler* series (*Hibotan bakuto*, 1968–72) opened up *yakuza* film to a wider audience from 1968, becoming particularly popular with male and female students alike (Iijima 1969: 70). The first instalment screened as a double bill with *Soldier Gokudo* (*Heitai Gokudo*, Saeki Kiyoshi, 1968) in Tokyo on 14 September 1968, selling an unprecedented 30,200 tickets in the first week and 70 per cent of that total in the following week (Anon. 1968: 83). In one sense then, the ubiquity of the *yakuza* genre film in the 1960s ensured that audiences, politically minded or otherwise, had significant exposure to *yakuza* lifestyles and ideologies as they were imagined by cinema producers.

In 1968 film critic Akiyama Kiyoshi argued that '*yakuza* films express the consciousness of our present times' (Akiyama 1968: 64). More than simply reflecting the feelings of the era, however, he suggested that the genre was able to 'somehow give comfort to the viewer's heart' (Akiyama 1968: 64). Study participants such as Hashimoto san recalled the affect of Takakura and other *yakuza* stars as hopeful, demonstrating both the possibility of being able to endure physical challenges, injustice and violence and at the same time the positive results that such endurance could yield in dismantling inequalities and holding corrupt powers to account.

Critics at the time also suggested that the appeal of the *yakuza* genre film for students and young activists may have been similar to the appeal of activism itself, in that both appeared to offer an opportunity to organise collectively and socialise within a group structure. For example, film critic Hojo Nobuhiko argued that supporters of the *yakuza* genre film within the cinema audience might have felt themselves to be included in the 'camaraderie' of the ensemble cast for the finite period they spent in the cinema (Hojo 1970: 50). Yet Hashimoto san's identification of Takakura as a particularly significant role model for himself and his activist friends is an interesting counter to such dominant understandings of the importance of the *yakuza* genre for student activists. While fellow students, film critics and scholars of the era often focused on the group aspect of the *yakuza gumi* (group), emphasising the collective nature of political activism, Takakura's most famous *yakuza* characters were principled loners who despised both the police and prison guards and the organised ranks of the *yakuza* hierarchy. In the popular *Abashiri Prison* series (*Abashiri bangaichi*, 1965–8), for example, Takakura's character repeatedly avoids group alliances, preferring to make single lateral bonds with men of his own age to challenge the *yakuza* hierarchy rather than join the ranks of the brotherhood. It should be noted that by the start of the *Abashiri bangaichi* series, Takakura had appeared in more than one hundred films and had a well-developed and nuanced public image not entirely reflected in his role within this single series. Furthermore, Takakura was claimed as a role model by both left-wing and right-wing critics, fans and audience members. As Hashimoto san identified as politically left wing, his adoration of a *yakuza* idol might be surprising given the popular association of the *yakuza* with the political right wing. However, Takakura's nuanced public persona appears to have been sufficiently flexible to allow for both right- and left-identifying viewers to seek political resonance in his onscreen characters.

If Takakura's *yakuza* characters offered the opposite of the group camaraderie identified as attractive to viewers by critics such as Hojo, his image appealed in other significant ways. Isolde Standish has suggested that the 'powerful masculinity' performed by Takakura and other young male characters of the *Abashiri Prison* series provided both aspiration and outlet for contemporary male audiences in their performance of a type of masculinity 'predicated on physical strength and stoicism' (2000: 160). Standish argues that Takakura's protagonist 'closes the gap between the ideological image of masculinity and social experience, thus offering a vicarious solution to the eternal consequences lived by most men' (2000: 161). It is possible that Takakura offered a model for young viewers that did not champion collective activism, but rather demonstrated a way to maintain an ideologically constructed and valorised independent masculinity in spite of the social demands of the activist era.

Audiences such as Hashimoto san looked to *yakuza* film stars not only for a model for how to conceptualise their behaviour as activists but also for a more generalised value system in the 1960s. Writing for *Kinema Junpō* in 1970, Hojo Nobuhiko argued that *yakuza* film not only reflected 'the very human desire to live a proper life' (*seijitsuna ningentekina kanbō*), but that 'people often look to such fiction to tie themselves to something and build a life' (1970: 50). In 2016 Hashimoto san and his friends continued to insist on the importance of showing the political protests of the 1960s onscreen, in both retrospective film programmes and in new film texts. This group agreed on the potential of cinema to foster political change and often expressed anti-war and anti-nuclear sentiment, in particular in relation to key films by directors like Kinoshita Keisuke, Shindō Kaneto and Kobayashi Masaki. Many study participants expressed the wish that these films could be shown to younger Japanese viewers as a means of ensuring the continuation of political attitudes, including challenging government decision-making perceived to endanger everyday people.

On the other hand, when members of this group participated in a retrospective screening of Ōshima Nagisa's *Death by Hanging* (*Koshikei*, 1968) followed by *The Ceremony* (*Gishiki*, 1971), they declared themselves bored. The screening organiser for that month who had selected the films expressed feeling regret at her choices as early as thirty minutes into the first film: 'I felt, "Enough already!"' (*mo ii yo!*). She recalled the films having made a great impression on her in her activist youth, when she saw *Death by Hanging* screened on a white sheet hung up in the local park. In the wealthy corner of north-west Kyoto that hosted the monthly film screening and discussion, however, she expressed dismay at Ōshima's didactic tone and wondered at how his films had inspired her as a young woman.

Cinema as Escape, Demos as Disruption

While a number of participants in the study reported drawing political inspiration from popular cinema, film viewership and creative production was conversely a means for some to escape or excuse themselves from political movements. For example, both Hashimoto san and Takeda san's accounts of cinemagoing in their teenage and later student years included complaints about the 1960s student movement as an inconvenience. Like Imamura Shōhei's protagonist in *The Insect Woman* (*Nippon konchūki*, 1964), political demonstrations inconvenienced their personal mobility. Takeda san, also born in 1943, remained concerned with the political situation of postwar Japan and often noted parallels in fiction film with contemporary social issues. Watching Mizoguchi Kenji's *Ugetsu* (*Ugetsu monogatari*, 1954), for example, he discerned a critique of contemporary militarism in the film's historical narrative. However, his personal cinema-related experiences positioned him in opposition to the student movements, rather than inspiring him to join in demonstrations.

Having failed the entrance exam to his parents' choice of university in Tokyo, Takeda san moved to Kyoto and studied to enter the university several years after graduating from high school. As a relatively mature undergraduate student, he devoted most of his time to the amateur filmmaking club within the university. After a year as a junior member, he graduated to a level of membership that allowed him to plan and make his own short film. In the same year, however, the student film club closed due to insufficient funds and their room at the university campus was occupied by the student movement. He graduated in April 1968 and entered company life, steering clear of the student movement in particular and activism more generally.

Takeda san associated the student movement with the disruption of his planned film and subsequently his career. Instead of becoming a filmmaker, he joined a famous advertising company, working in the production section making internal information films for private companies. While he sympathised with the political attitudes of leftist auteurs, he continued to view grassroots activism and protest as a nuisance rather than an effective political strategy. He felt he suffered further misfortune a few years later when the film-viewing group he had joined was forced to close in 1970 after only three years. '[The group] continued from 1967 to 1970, but as the 70s were still the era of Zenkyōtō, it also broke down mid-way', he remembered. At a loss, he set up a film-viewing club within the advertising company instead, and was surprised to find that the dedicated attendees were the members of the labour union: 'In the end, the directors didn't come at all!'

While blaming the student movement, and Zenkyōtō specifically, for obstructing his filmmaking plans, Takeda san nonetheless continued to think about film and film-related organising from a politicised perspective. Perhaps due to his experience with the labour union at his company, when he tried again to establish a film-viewing club after retiring he insisted on a horizontal organisational structure without hierarchy. While Takeda san's memories of filmmaking in the 1960s were rhetorically organised as a device to distance himself from the student movement, his broadly leftist politics were evident in his conception of the ideal group structure as a horizontal one.

Expanding the Self through 1960s Cinema Culture

While we might understand Takeda san's relationship to 1960s activism, mediated through cinema discourse, as ambivalent, the third distinct group perceptible among participants in the study regarded the era with a sense of longing (*akogare*). Over 10 per cent of questionnaire survey respondents noted that their first experience of going to the cinema involved seeing newsreel footage of public protests, from the Anpo demonstrations of 1960 onwards. These respondents were generally the youngest in the study, born between 1945 and 1955. The average age of a first cinema visit was six years old, and a number of respondents in this category recall visiting the film theatre from the age of four or five, learning about Anpo and the student movement from newsreel films. One interviewee from this cohort, Matsuda san, explained that he treasured the opportunity to experience new things through film, particularly things 'outside my own personal experience' (*jibun no jitaiken to wa dekinai*). Among the younger group of study participants, this was a common attitude towards the political movements of the older generation. People born in the 1950s often expressed regret that they had been too young in the 1960s to participate in the activism and protest movements that shaped the decade. Of course, many of these study participants had been children or young teenagers and observed the demonstrations and public protests around them, even if they did not directly participate. For those living outside the urban centres where much protest activity was focused, television, newspapers and radio, as well as conversations at home and at school, brought key moments and issues from the protest movements into their everyday lives. In these ways, members of the generations who identified as 'left out' of the 1960s political movement nonetheless had strong memories of the protests.

If the relative lack of opportunity for involvement in 1960s political activities outside the cinema was an imagined rather than literally experienced reality, what did those who longed for this era expect from a cinematic encounter? The answer to this question may be rooted in participants' expectations about encountering people and themes from other times or places through cinema. In both kinds of encounter, participants expressed their desire not only to know but also to feel what the other is feeling. This kind of co-feeling appeared to be generally understood as a means of learning about the world and its history, and at the same time as a means of growing, improving or extending the self.

For Kobayashi san, another research participant born in 1955, cinema offered a window into the kinds of extreme emotions provoked by unusual situations or events that he felt he was unlikely to experience himself. He was particularly interested in cinema that focuses on Japanese perceptions of regional and ethnic difference as a means to explore social hierarchies and inequalities. In Kurosawa Akira's films, for example, Kobayashi san noted, 'The social situation of lower-class people is really, well, realistically portrayed.' This realism gave him a sense of transcending time and place: 'That Japan has really been replaced by time, it's impossible to understand what it was like before.' Yet his interest was focused most intensely on the experiences and ideas of everyday people living unremarkable lives during periods of social and political turmoil. He looked to cinema for a way to understand the hopes, dreams and fears of people undergoing historical experiences. By feeling the suffering of everyday people in previous decades, Kobayashi san argued that today's Japanese citizens could be persuaded of the value of everlasting pacifism: 'Of course, it's not an easy thing to talk about, but the construction of Japanese people's consciousness, and also social consciousness, and the human view of life are really connected to cinema, I think.'

A significant number of study participants shared Kobayashi san's view of cinema as a means of both educating oneself and feeling historical moments, with a view to improving or expanding one's personal ethics in relation to war and social inequality in particular. Kishida san, born in 1956, similarly understood cinema as a social justice motivator and exposer of state violence. Watching documentaries on the Minamata water-poisoning incident and fiction films portraying the treatment of *burakumin* in Japan, he felt a strong sense of the urgency of social injustice. Many participants in this study associated film viewing with developing modes of co-feeling, whether with other viewers or with film protagonists. At the same time, many participants placed a high value on the role film played in expanding their consciousness, making them aware of new possibilities. Film viewers who value community, equality and the search for new and better future models of sociality may have been predisposed to think about their relation to cinema as connected to leftist politics, whether they participated in, avoided or felt left out of the protests and activities of 1960s Japan.

The ethnographic material collected in this study suggests that while most participants reported cinema playing a significant role in their changing attitudes towards 1960s activism and its legacies, those attitudes themselves are not consistent across generation, class and other differentials. Personal aspiration and aspirations for Japanese society more broadly conflicted in many participants' accounts of the era and their feelings about activism. While participants like Hashimoto san insisted on the relevance of cinematic images of 1960s protest cultures today, others like Takeda san remembered only disruption to their personal cinema-related aspirations. Cinema audience response to 1960s political movements onscreen was ambivalent, yet discussions about thinking and feeling the 1960s through cinema continued. This chapter has attempted to introduce the nuances and personalised memories of the time, in order to understand the significance of these events not only on the political scale but also on the personal level, and how this shapes our perceptions of history and politics.

Framing these memories around the Kinugasa eiga kai, and particularly the activist filmmaking project of its predecessor the Kyoto kiroku eiga o miru kai, reveals the persistence of structural or organisational memory in film fans' relationships to the political culture of the 1960s. It is noteworthy that the very public failure of the Kyoto kiroku eiga o miru kai's efforts does not seem to have dampened the political enthusiasms of a number of the members of its successor group, the Kinugasa eiga kai. And yet, the same members willingly offer memories that would seem to contradict their ongoing political commitments, today largely focused on pacifism and social justice. Talking about cinema and memories of filmgoing can give us an emotive insight into the political culture of a period and provide a discursive object through which film fans can relate their recollections and feelings of the era. In the next and final chapter, we will look at how talking about cinema and commemorating film eras of the past can be understood as a creative pursuit that generates a sense of self in the process of giving an account of oneself through communications about cinema culture.

CHAPTER 7

Crafting the Self through Cinema Culture

This book has proposed an understanding of film-related memory as a mode of 'giving an account of oneself', arguing that talking about film offers people a way to negotiate their individual subjectivities and experiences as viewers, within the normative social frameworks modelled by classical cinema narratives and by the behaviours and reactions expected within a cinema theatre or other viewing space. At the same time, performing a passionate relationship with a film text, creator or moment in cinema history allows the speaker a mode of distinguishing themselves as an individual subject. The spoken and written communications that make up the ethnographic materials analysed in this work can be understood as at once performances of compliance with social norms and at the same time as claims for recognition of an individual self with particular tastes, preferences and memories.

Beginning with a close reading of Dorinne Kondo's phrase 'crafting selves' (1990), which refers both to the construction of a sense of self or identity and to decorative and creative work undertaken by many of her study participants, this chapter considers the role of the work of making or creating in the shaping of a sense of self through engagement with cinema culture. The creative activities of many study participants included designing and hosting their own events, organising screenings, running discussion sessions and creating media content, as well as more personal self-documentation like the hand-drawn maps and diagrams that participants shared with me. By exploring the role of making and crafting in the communication practices of my study participants, this final chapter argues for the study of discourses and communication practices, including the creation and collection of film ephemera, as an essential element in our understanding of film history.

This chapter explores how the self is crafted through narratives about a relationship to cinema, investigating how the physical materials that my study participants collected, archived, created and donated can be understood. Almost all participants in my study created pre-prepared notes and printed life narratives, which many consulted during interviews. Interviewees often gifted copies of memos, notes or timelines of their lives, or copies of photographs and posters, prompting me to think about how viewers integrate the stories of their lives into cinema discourse. In many cases, the narration of the self was literally crafted in the hand-drawn maps and diagrams that participants shared with me, and in the social activities, media appearances and dedicated speaking events that key participants organised to share their stories about cinema.

Crafting Selves: Subjectivity and Creativity

As noted above, Kondo's use of the word 'craft' does double duty in her extended ethnographic study of a family-run workplace in 1970s Tokyo (1990). Kondo's study participants were all involved in some kind of craft or another, from the sweets created at the family factory to the performers at the local culture festival (*bunkasai*) who specialised in 'Japanese music, poetry, and dance, and exhibitions of paintings, flower arrangements, and crafts' (1990: 59). At the same time, Kondo is interested in the creation of a sense of self, asking, 'How did the people I knew craft themselves and their lives within shifting fields of power and meaning, and how did they do so in particular situations and within a particular historical and cultural context?' (1990: 10). This book has approached a similar set of concerns, and this chapter brings together an exploration of the practices of crafting and creating with an investigation of how participants' senses of self were formed through their narrations of their relationships to postwar Japanese cinema. Like Kondo, I am interested in how my study participants crafted, or created, their senses of self and how they arranged their lives both practically and ideologically in relation to cinema culture. While the elderly participants in my own study were largely removed from the 'shifting fields of power and meaning' of the daily workplace to which Kondo pays attention, they were engaged in a later life project of understanding the 'particular historical and cultural context' of the Occupation of Japan (1945–52) which had shaped their young lives and the political movements of the 1960s which for most had marked the end of youth.

The 'crafting' or making explored in this chapter takes three forms: objects and materials created or collected by study participants for themselves and shared with me as part of our encounter; materials, largely documents and maps, created by study participants for the purposes of explaining or describing something specifically to me in the context of our interviews; and the works, activities or events created by my study participants for a wider public. I will first explore the two more private forms of crafting shared between my research participants and myself, before providing some brief historical context for the public-facing materials and activities analysed in the second part of this chapter.

I have noted above a key difference between Kondo's ethnography and my own ethno-history, in that while Kondo's primary fieldsite is a workplace, all the participants in my own study had retired from official working life. However, the role of working and performance in the workplace as 'a way to craft ideal selves' (Kondo 1990: 106) continued to inform the creative activities and outputs of many participants in my study. In some of the works discussed below, I think that we can see a desire to continue, if not working, at least the sensation of 'working joyfully, throwing our full energy into work' that Kondo identified as key to the formation and development of a self in relation to others, where 'Happiness means the connection of self to other selves' (Kondo 1990: 106).

Furthermore, the activity of participating in this study itself should be understood as creative and generative, in that participation involved the production and sharing of narratives about the self. Annette Kuhn argues, 'When informants tell stories about their youthful filmgoing, they are producing memories in specific ways in a particular context, the research encounter' (2002: 9). This 'producing' is a work of crafting or making, and so the creation of memory narratives at the heart of the interviews and surveys that make up this study are in themselves works of effort and design, created in order to communicate:

> Thus memory texts may create, rework, repeat, and re-contextualise the stories people tell each other about the kinds of lives they have led . . . Such everyday myth-making works at the levels of both personal and collective memory and is key, in the production, through memory, of shared identities. (Kuhn 2002: 11)

Kuhn draws our attention to the ongoing nature of the production, reiteration and redesigning of memory texts, from spoken narratives to hand-drawn maps and written materials. Similarly, Kondo insists on a continuous process of people 'constructing new arrangements of meaning and power as they craft their lives' (1990: 225) and many of the claims, narrative directions and performances discussed below should be understood within this shifting and responsive mode.

Narrating the self through stories about engagement with cinema culture brings both the self and a history of that cinema culture and its contexts and meanings into being. In *Giving an Account of Oneself*, Judith Butler notes that in the later works of Michel Foucault, 'The subject forms itself in relation to a set of codes, prescriptions, or norms, and does so in ways that not only (a) reveal self-constitution to be a kind of *poiesis* but (b) establish self-making as part of the broader operation or critique' (2005: 17). This understanding of self-constitution as *poiesis* emphasises the generative quality of the undertaking, in that *poiesis* 'produces or leads (a thing) into being' (Whitehead 2003: 5). By creating both a narrative about the self and a material work, social activity or public event through which to communicate that narrative, participants in my study crafted material engagements with that selfhood.

Creative and Collection Practices among Study Participants

As discussed in the Introduction, during the survey period of my research project I distributed pre-prepared questionnaires in a local museum that housed a movie theatre, together with an accompanying information sheet that invited participants to send letters and emails to my university office. The first letter arrived on the second day of the survey, hand delivered by a lady who had completed the questionnaire the day before. Her letter, and those which followed, demonstrated a tendency also evident in the questionnaire responses to draw a strong connection between memories of cinema and events in the respondent's personal life. This connection was so strongly assumed by participants that many began both letters and questionnaires with a version of the *jiko shōkai* or self-introduction used when meeting a new person in Japan. This standard format includes the following personal information: name, place of birth, place of residence and perhaps year of birth or job description. Several participants and interviewees also produced personal life narratives structured like the published biographical information that one might find in a magazine or newspaper. These were delivered by post or in person, with an accompanying personal letter or a completed questionnaire.

These participant-created documents had some very practical uses: the Japanese language has many homophones and it is not always possible to discern the kanji characters used in the writing of a name or place from the pronunciation of the same word. A written set of notes was very useful to help make sense of interview recordings and notes taken during conversations. At the same time, however, interviewees also used the life-narrative documents almost as one might in a formal job interview or similar situation. Details of which schools had been attended and when might seem extraneous to a project on cinema memory, but they were presented almost like credentials, in that participants would refer back to specialist knowledge that they held about an area or period relevant to cinema production on the basis of having lived there then. I was impressed with the sense that my study participants approached their role in the research project as an opportunity to communicate their lives and experiences in such a holistic aspect and as a means to crafting a particular sense of self.

While the questionnaire survey and follow-up interviews included a number of questions related to each respondent's personal history, these were all specific to cinema culture and viewership. Questions such as, 'At what age did you first go to a cinema theatre?' and 'Who is your favourite actor?' do not directly suggest the requirement for a life narrative or resumé. However, my study participants were largely of the generation who attended school during the 'life-narrative movement' of the 1950s (Avenell 2010: 50) and this may have had some impact on how they chose to represent their histories and experiences. During this decade, the *Yamabiki gakko* (Echo school) book of children's life narratives was taught in schools and 'life composition' essays by children were published frequently (Avenell 2010: 51). It is possible that the instinct to respond to a question about cinema experiences of the past with a formalised account of one's background and origins was formed in such early schooling experiences.

Writing of the life-narrative movement, cultural scholar Tsurumi Kazuko argued, 'The people who make history, write history, and through writing they remake themselves' (quoted in Avenell 2010: 51). By weaving personal stories of their lives and their families' lives into a larger historical narrative about the conditions of everyday life in the early postwar period, study participants situated themselves as 'people who write history' and therefore, inevitably, people who rewrite history. Rewriting or reimagining a historical moment is itself a generative act, as Tessa Morris-Suzuki notes: 'By remembering a particular piece of the past, by making it our own, we create our sense of belonging to a certain group of people – whether a nation, local society, ethnic minority, or religious group . . . Indeed, it is the very act of historical commemoration that calls group identity into being' (2005: 23). Both alone in the crafted communication materials analysed here, and in groups in the events and activities discussed in the second part of this chapter, study participants called into being a group of memory-keepers engaged in an ongoing relationship with cinema culture.

While the histories written by my study participants were created in response to questions about cinema, they were also informed by cinema content. A number of study participants also supported their memory narratives with photographs and other material documents relating to the period under discussion. As Morris-Suzuki observes, this is not uncommon in oral histories and imaginaries of the historical more broadly.

> Our visions of history are drawn from diverse sources: not just from the narratives of history books, but also from photographs and historical novels, from newsreel footage, comic books and, increasingly, from electronic media like the internet. Out of this kaleidoscopic mass of fragments we make and remake patterns of understanding which explain the origins and nature of the world in which we live. And doing this, we define and redefine the place that we occupy in that world. (Morris-Suzuki 2005: 2)

My interviewees were concerned with communicating about the situation of Japan and their hometowns at the time, and mixed pictures of stars and film ephemera with historical photographs showing the poverty and devastation of the local areas. While photographs of stars were often used to prompt recollections, they also demonstrated regular memory failures, for example when the name of a star or how a photograph came to be included in a collection could not be recalled. Viewing photographs and film fan yearbooks and anthologies together with interviewees often brought up references to historical events outside the speaker's direct experience. Like the life narratives and resumés discussed above, I came to understand the sharing of archives of historical photographs as a kind of demonstration of the speaker's 'expert witness' status. Many interviewees referred to these photographs as confirmation that the memories they were sharing were based in historical fact. In this respect, these materials played a similar role to the references to shared family memories discussed in Chapter 4, wherein interviewees referred to 'checking' their memories with family members to ensure their perceived accuracy before offering these memories as part of my study.

The input of family members was also present in a smaller group of interviewees' materials which demonstrated engagement with cinema culture that extended to making things inspired by cinema content and taking part in film production at an amateur level. A small number of interviewees shared still photographs of films that were made in their local areas, in some cases featuring family members acting as extras or background actors. One interviewee, Koyama san, wore a jacket to our meeting which had been handmade by her mother, who loved to copy the fashions that they saw together in Hollywood films. While Annette Kuhn observes that the cost of copying a film star's clothing may have been the reason why her British interviewees recalled 'relatively few memories involving clothes' (2002: 114), she notes that 'the loving detail with which clothes and hairstyles are described and the often anecdotal manner of their description' can 'suggest a high degree of affective and imaginative investment in these memories' (2002: 130). Koyama san was careful to explain that her mother had made the jacket from offcuts of discarded fabric rather than new cloth, and that it had been handed down to her. Interviewees in Kanako Terasawa's study of Japanese women watching Hollywood films in the postwar era similarly recalled adopting actresses' styles because other people around them also did so, and 'there were other people in the same clothing' (2010: 252). By contrast, Koyama san wore her mother's jacket to our interview to emphasise her mother's unique taste and skill in creating the clothing herself and to perform a love of cinema culture that ran through her family line.

While Koyama san's handmade jacket was perhaps the most elaborate crafted material shared in my study, a number of participants drew diagrams and sketches to illustrate their memories. Interviewees often used hand-drawn maps to locate their family homes within the local surroundings, as they remembered them during the early postwar. Like Kuhn's interviewees, this also seemed to be an opportunity for many to suture themselves into a cinematic history, as the maps formed the beginning of a narration in which the historical imaginary of the interviewee was structured like a cinematic narrative in the use of testimonies of walking to the cinema from home as a kind of opening sequence. A number of interviewees in both my own project and Annette Kuhn's formative study of 1930s British cinema began their accounts with a detailed description of walking to the cinema from their home or place of work:

> A number of informants provide discursive 'memory maps' of the parts of town, the neighbourhoods or the suburbs where they first went to the pictures. These maps vary in style and detail, but their function is always to lay out a mise en scene for the recollections which follow. They are 'establishing shots', in a sense; and like establishing shots in films, they work at the service of a story or stories. In mapping out the locations of their memory stories, informants will either insert themselves fully into the past, or speak from the standpoint of the present, or they may 'shuttle' discursively between past and present. (Kuhn 2002: 18)

Kuhn has noted that these descriptions were not unlike a kind of 'establishing shot' for the interviewee's account of memories of viewership. The 'guided tour' that the interviewee gives the interviewer around the recreated map in their minds develops this cinematic metaphor in Kuhn's study into a 'sequence composed of a montage of shots' (2002: 22–3).

> The informant guides the listener through a memory landscape not so much joined up by lines on a mental map . . . as constructed around a series of anecdotes prompted by remembered places ('And then we had another place'). In cinematic terms, this

might be a sequence composed of a montage of shots as opposed to a single tracking shot or sequence shot. (Kuhn 2002: 22–3)

As my own study developed, these similarities with Kuhn's project, set almost twenty years earlier in 1930 and in the UK, far away from Japan, became more apparent. At the same time, it seemed to me that my project also had a degree of regional specificity, in that while my interviewees' testimonies took a similar form to the participants in Kuhn's study, the material nature of their engagements differed slightly, as did their relation to me, the interviewer. In addition to a 'memory map' created through narrative, my interviewees often sent material information in advance of our interview, such as a hand-drawn map of one interviewee's home. After the first interview, a number of participants in my study sent follow-up materials, including more maps, both printed and hand-drawn, showing the location of the cinema theatres in their local area relative to frequently visited sites such as schools, shopping districts and homes.

A number of study participants also kept a close watch on the local newspapers for any articles that could be of relevance to my study and I received regular packages over the course of the four-year project containing marked-up newspaper clippings. For example, in response to my enquiries about cinema access in the postwar era, one study participant sent me a marked-up copy of a local newspaper in which Matsuoka Isao, former chairman of Tōhō studios (1995–2009), recorded his memories of cinema culture in 1957, the year he joined Tōhō (Matsuoka 2016). Matsuoka recalled that the average entrance fee for an adult in 1957 was 150 yen, with discounted rates of 62 yen for children. This seemed to support the participant's memories of accessing cinema theatres as a child, when the discounted rate could still be difficult to obtain for a child trying to get into the cinema alone. Instead, he recalled that it was easier to go with family members who would pay the entrance fee for him or to work with a group of male children to find free access by paying for one ticket and then having the ticket-holder open a side door for the other children, echoing the memories of interviewees discussed in Chapters 2 and 3.

By creating, collecting and donating materials of relevance to their cinema memories, a core group of study participants greatly advanced not only my ethnographic research project but my collection of supporting documents and scholarly materials. Five study participants, including one who co-organised the monthly film club discussed in more detail below, sent academic articles related to events and people that they had discussed during our formal interviews. In fact, around 30 per cent of the materials that formed the literature review for Chapter 6 were contributed by this dedicated group, including a package of academic articles on the topic of Kansai film clubs. Imai san, who had developed quite a high-profile public persona, sent clippings and a DVD of his own media appearances, discussed in more detail below. Several interviewees introduced me to friends who were also willing to be interviewed, to film centres and archives around Kansai and to perceived expert interviewees such as producers and actors active in the period under study.

This scholarly activity on the part of volunteers who are not academics is not uncommon in Japan among the two groups of which my study participants are part: retirees and film fans. While one's sixties marked the retirement from full-time work for the majority of participants in my study, a second stage of life known as *kanreki* is thought to begin from age sixty-one in Japan, as elderly people enter a period of greater freedom:

> *Kanreki* was often regarded as the beginning of one's second childhood . . . Japanese people of 60 years of age and over were permitted to be dependent on others . . . In other words, *Kanreki* signified a social sanction, permitting entry into *inkyo* 'retired life', if this was desired. In reality however, most Japanese older people continued to work, either for money or for the satisfaction of continuing to have a meaningful role in life. (Maeda and Ishikawa 2002: 115)

Many participants in my study referred to this stage of *kanreki* as the main reason for their regular cinema attendance later in life and therefore their participation in a research project that began with a survey based in a film theatre. One interviewee even noted that since her husband's retirement, he preferred to use the home space to study Latin and French, and so she had taken to 'commuting' to a cinema specialising in retrospective screenings of postwar films as though it were a job. Another highly involved participant in my project spoke of the research activities that he conducted before and after our interview in relation to his retirement hobby, motorcycling. When I queried the connection, he explained that preparations for his seventieth-birthday motorbike trip from Kobe to Hokkaido had involved significant research about the route, accommodation and weather conditions, similar to the research he had pursued on behalf of my project.

The materials generated and archived by study participants suggest the key role of creative activities and collection practices in the development of a public identity as lay expert or keeper of cinema memories. During a casual post-interview conversation, I discussed the unanticipated level of preparedness that all interviewees displayed with Takeda san, a retired advertising producer who co-organised a monthly film screening in northwest Kyoto called the Kinugasa eiga kai (Kinugasa Film Club). Briefly describing Annette Kuhn's 'Cinema Culture in 1930s Britain' project,

I noted that while some aspects were similar to my own study, in particular participants' drawing of maps to describe locations and journey routes, the large amount of unsolicited material that I had been sent seemed unusual. Takeda san speculated that perhaps there was some relation between Japanese wartime and postwar experience and the studious approach adopted by participants in my study, suggesting that Japanese interviewees may be more worried about making mistakes in giving accounts of their personal life histories and of the wider socio-historical situation of postwar Japan. While on the one hand a sense of having been on the 'wrong side' of wartime history may create concerns about misrepresenting oneself, on the other the studious attitude often attributed to the extreme deprivation suffered by many in the aftermath of the war encouraged a passion for devoting oneself wholeheartedly to a cause or project, often education or service for others.

My research project was in a way both education and service; service to the project in the short term and to the wider goal of educating Japan's younger generations through such research in the longer term. For this reason, Takeda san speculated that interviewees may have developed a particularly *majime* (earnest or committed) relation to the project. The circulation of audience-generated materials is an active part of the creation of cinema memory, which as Takeda san suggests can tell us not only about cinema cultures of the past but about the socio-political and historical conditions in which these cultures were formed and about their impact on the communication styles used by members of a generation to give an account of themselves through cinema memory.

Takeda san was in many ways an ideal person with whom to discuss this mode of communication. A retired producer of workplace information videos for a major advertising company, he had spent most of his adult life attending and organising film clubs and discussion groups after participating in an amateur filmmaking group at university. As discussed in Chapter 6, the university filmmaking group closed due to lack of funds and disruption caused by the student movement. Takeda san went on to attend local film-viewing groups like Shidofu, discussed in Chapter 6, and to run his own workplace film club screening foreign films borrowed from embassies and cultural institutions. The memories of these groups that Takeda san shared with me, as well as his thoughts on the Kinugasa eiga kai, which he helped to run, led me to consider the effort of setting up and running such clubs as a creative activity. In order to better understand the creative practices involved in these clubs, often known as 'circles', the second part of this chapter will explore the historical background of their formation before looking more closely at the activities of the Kinugasa eiga kai.

Circle Activity in Postwar Japan

The participants in my study grew up during what was understood to be a boom in grassroots organised events focused on cultural study and discussion. As discussed in Chapter 6, during the 1950s a 'circle movement' took off, in which 'small voluntary associations called circles (*sākuru*)' were established 'within workplaces and communities throughout Japan' (Bronson 2016: 124). The focus of these groups was various: Justin Jesty notes that circles in the 1950s and 1960s were too many to categorise, whether they were affiliated with workplaces, schools or political institutions, or 'just for fun' (2018: 22–3). Larger workplaces and local areas even 'had multiple circles in a particular genre with competing identities' (Jesty 2018: 23). Andrew Gordon notes the emphasis on creative pursuits in common circle themes of the period: 'classical music appreciation, singing, poetry writing and more' (2009: 98). Many such groups 'held performances or exhibitions, or produced their own handprinted publications' (Jesty 2010: 4). A number of participants in my study who regularly attended circles such as the Kinugasa eiga kai tended also to participate in another kind of circle activity, most often choral singing or painting groups which also organised exhibitions.

Postwar circles often created materials or events to showcase or further develop their discussions, and the writings and creative productions of these circles were sometimes published as paperback volumes for mass readership or more often as mimeographed copies 'distributed within the circle and then circulated in the workplace and community' (Bronson 2016: 124). These were not understood as vanity projects, but rather as a serious attempt to grapple with the question of how cultural consumption and discussions about culture could contribute to the building of a new postwar society: 'Observers of the movement believed that this cycle of observing, writing, and discussing might produce citizens capable of realizing the promise of postwar democracy' (Bronson 2016: 124).

While the term *sākuru* was used in the 1930s to refer to 'support organs' for the 'proletarian organizations' including political parties and unions (Avenell 2010: 45), the postwar use of the term tended to focus on the development of the individual as a supporting member of society. Nonetheless, the Japan Communist Party did recognise the more creative contributions of postwar *sākuru*, calling the materials produced by *sākuru* 'creative forms of the struggle for peace' (Bronson 2016: 125). Adam Bronson argues, 'For some, democracy promised new opportunities for creative self-expression' in the postwar era (2016: 127), connected to 'a new kind of subjectivity, one that might be fashioned through active participation in a circle' (2016: 128).

The mid- to late 1950s was 'a golden age for circles of all types' (Gordon 2009: 98), marked in 1955 by the foundation of a national body to support workplace circles, managed by the Sōhyō federation. The Association for Groups (Shūdan no kai), which as Avenell points out was itself a group formed of intellectuals including Tsurumi Shinsuke, Ōsawa Shinichirō and others, was formed in 1963 to study circles and other group associations (Avenell 2010: 46). In a publication assessing group activity from 1945 to 1976, Sasaki Gen argued for 'six broad categories of circles' (Avenell 2010: 46). These included groups based on friendship, those based on common interest, study groups, civic action groups, cultural production groups and research groups. The film circles that were described to me and those that I attended in the course of my ethnographic project were perhaps closest to common-interest groups, though they often included a studious element, and like the Kyoto kiroku eiga o miru kai discussed in Chapter 6, could develop into cultural production groups.

A number of the participants in my study were engaged with, helped to organise or joined the study through film circles and my own ethnography included participant observation at three film-viewing circles in Kyoto and Osaka. In this respect, circle creation and organisation is of significance for this study. However, I am also interested in exploring Tsurumi Kazuko and Tsurumi Shunsuke's insistence on circles as 'spaces for remaking the self (*jiko kaizō*)' (Avenell 2010: 58). In addition to their focus on understanding the role of cultural consumption and amateur production in the formation of a democratic postwar self, circle activities could also give participants an enhanced or further developed sense of self through learning new skills or uncovering previously unobserved talents. It was also an opportunity to meet people outside one's usual social sphere and to perform a self slightly different to that performed in everyday life: 'Circles were forums for people to meet, away from their usual social roles' (Jesty 2010: 4).

The Position of Film Circles in Postwar Life

As the previous chapter discussed with reference to a specific film circle turned production unit, organised film circles and their related activities, such as group-based cinema-going and ticket-buying groups, were a major feature of the early postwar cinema landscape in Japan. A number of film circles were affiliated with studios, theatres, workplaces, businesses, educational establishments and political groups. Film circles also developed cross-organisational links with one another, and the close associations between cinema viewership, education and political and personal development articulated by these larger organisations suggests an understanding of film circle activities as key to understanding how a sense of self could be crafted through cinema culture in postwar Japan.

The first major nationally recognised film circle organisation of the postwar era was the Tokyo Film Circle Convention (Tokyo eiga sākuru kyōgikai, shortened to Tokyo eisakyō), which formed in 1948 with the goal of making 'good' films available to watch cheaply, raising the taste and education level of working people who participated and using circle activity to encourage the creation of democratic films (Uryū [1958] 1994: 748). This focus on raising public awareness of social and political issues was not confined to Tokyo, but appeared in the manifestos and advertising materials of film circles in Kyoto and Osaka as well as other areas. The number of film circles, studio 'friendship' groups (*tomo no kai*) and cinema study or research groups (*kenkyūkai*) continued to increase throughout the 1950s and showed 'no sign of stopping' (Uryū [1958] 1994: 748).

In 1958 a special section of *Kinema Junpō* (*Film Record*, or *The Movie Times*) was devoted to 'Film and Circles: The Power Advancing Japanese Cinema' (*Eiga to sākuru: Nihon eiga o zenshinsaseru chikara*). Critics Okada Susumu, Hatano Kanji and Uryū Tadao recalled their own participation in film circles of various types dating back to the 1920s. In his account of his workplace film circle, Okada noted that one of the most important aspects of the circle for the members that he spoke with was the opportunity to hear other people's impressions of the films screened there ([1958] 1994: 743–4): 'Like all film fans, I think about film. I talk about film. That's why audiences make opportunities to gather together. This is where audiences' ideas and independent expression are born' (Okada [1958] 1994: 744). Okada posited his workplace film circle as a space where new ideas emerged and were developed in conversation with others and argued that the film circles of the late 1950s 'were born from the liberation of film audiences' expression immediately after the war' ([1958] 1994: 744).

Okada also noted an economic imperative for the creation of workplace film circles that was consistent across the film circles discussed within this special section of *Kinema Junpō*: 'A popular slogan for many film circles today is, "Making good films cheap"' (*yoi eiga o yasuku*) (Okada [1958] 1994: 744). This same goal was reiterated in the contributions of

Hatano Kanji and Uryū Tadao, who connected the affordable provision of 'good' films with an attempt to educate working- class and impoverished groups within the wider Japanese public. The often poverty-stricken viewers of the organisations discussed in Hatano's article were students who formed film research groups (*eiken*) in order to invite film previews and filmmakers to university campuses ([1958] 1994: 744–6). Yet based on his experience in two or three university *eiken*, Hatano warned that it was 'easy for *eiken* to become elitist' ([1958] 1994: 746). While the majority of *eiken* aimed to renounce the capitalist ideals and practices common within filmmaking, Hatano argued that many *eiken* themselves 'became flavoured with the most prevalent film capitalism' by selling discounted cinema tickets and hosting large recruitment drives at the beginning of the academic year to capture new students and grow the organisation ([1958] 1994: 746). Instead of practising these high-capitalist activities, Hatano argued, *eiken* should focus on the personal development of the student body: 'We shouldn't stop only at selling cinema tickets, but taking film as a key, students should undergo self-reformation, or self-reinvention (*jiko kaizō*) by enjoying good films amongst themselves' (Hatano [1958] 1994: 746).

Many film circles had adopted the slogan 'Support the development of good films, boycott worthless films' (*yoi eiga o sodate, kudaranai eiga wa boikotto suru*) (Uryū [1958] 1994: 748). By the late 1950s the number of *eiken* was also steadily increasing and those formed at Kyoto University and Tokyo University had begun to produce film industry professionals such as directors and film critics as well as publish their own journals (Uryū [1958] 1994: 747). In this way the professional film industry and non-professional film organisations overlapped and influenced one another. Film circles and viewers' organisations produced the film industry professionals of the future.

Uryū made a distinction between *eiken* (film research groups), *eiga kanshōkai* (film viewing meetings), *eiga sākuru* (film circles), *shokuiki sākuru* (workplace circles), film theatre friendship groups (*eigakan no tomo no kai*) and other organisations created to bring film to groups of viewers and host discussions about those films. Collectivising these varieties of film organisations under the term *eisa*, Uryū argued that because these organisations brought together people of various genders, ages, employments, ideologies and feelings, 'not investigating the nature of these organizations and circles would really be a waste' (Uryū [1958] 1994: 749). In the spirit of Uryū's call for a deeper investigation into film-viewing organisations and their activities, this chapter explores the creative activities of film circles and those who frequented them.

The Development of the Postwar Film Circle Format

In his short article titled 'Nihon eigakai ni okeru eiga sākuru no ayumi' (The development of film circles within the film world), Uryū Tadao argued that 1947 can be seen as a rough starting point of postwar film circle and club activities (Uryū [1958] 1994: 747). He noted two key elements in this development: the first was the adoption of the 6-3-3-4 schooling system which created a new high school system and a new university system where pupils and students could freely watch films and were able to discuss and theorise about them (Uryū [1958] 1994: 747): 'As this developed, the *eisa* was given an organizational form and rapidly expanded' between high schools and universities (Uryū [1958] 1994: 747). *Eisa* were used to encourage film viewers to think about Japan's future in this early stage of the postwar era and to invest in both personal and national developmental ideals: 'This involved reflecting the good and bad of real life. There was material poverty – no film, no electricity, cinema entrance fees were not affordable for all, but there was also a poverty of imagination as the film world could not envision the new age it was burdened with showing' (Uryū [1958] 1994: 747).

At this time, *eisa* were authorised to distribute discounted cinema tickets (Uryū [1958] 1994: 749), which must have increased their popularity among people keen to attend the cinema more cheaply as well as those interested in joining film circles' discussion sessions and creative activities: 'Some members supported this, and some did not, being more concerned with artistry than economics' (Uryū [1958] 1994: 749). In 1957 the Tokyo eisa kyō's successor, Tokyo Eiga Aikōkai Rengokai (Association of people who love film), stopped the distribution of discounted tickets (Uryū [1958] 1994: 749). As a result, membership fell from 50,000 to 30,000, stabilising at 40,000 in 1958 (Uryū [1958] 1994: 749). This suggests that while discounted cinema tickets were doubtless a draw for many, the other creative and social activities of the film circle were still attractive to many members even without this financial incentive.

'The Audience is Organized' and Also Excellent

These creative and social activities took some organisation, recalling Kondo's point above about the satisfaction of discharging one's tasks, whether in the official workplace or in a leisure or hobby space involving some creative or organisational labour. In his contribution to the *Kinema Junpō* feature titled 'The Audience is Organized' (*Kankyaku wa soshiki suru*), Okada Susumu emphasised the creative labour of bringing people together, sourcing film prints and hiring screening spaces that was central to film circle activities ([1958] 1994: 743). This acknowledgement of the work involved in creating a film circle suggests that the activity could take the place of meaningful work for those denied that experience, either due to unemployment or to a lack of ideological, political or aesthetic engagement with the work they were paid to do. This appeared to be the case for Takeda san, who had aspired to create artistic films but found himself managing the production of workplace informational videos. His interest in experimental and high-art films, often foreign-made, was expressed through the various film circles he attended and created. The opportunity to discuss such films with like-minded viewers, or at least other people willing to give their time to watching challenging films, was also a major attraction for many film circle attendees. This discourse also situated discussions about film in a privileged position, as a means of expanding consciousness and freeing the mind. Its legacy was apparent in the attitudes of participants in my study who spoke of cinema viewership as a high-minded pursuit and even a social responsibility.

With a focus on education in his contribution 'University film study and film culture' (*Daigaku eiken to eigabunka*), Hatano Kanji argued, 'It is said that the Japanese film audience is excellent, of a high level unmatched anywhere in the world' ([1958] 1994: 745). Hatano agreed that this was true, yet he noted that there was still little in the way of alternative opportunities for entertainment in Japan aside from cinema ([1958] 1994: 745). For a long time in Japan, Hatano argued, students had cultivated a diligent (*majime*) approach to engaging with the arts ([1958] 1994: 745): '*Eiken* give them the opportunity to discuss with teachers, who attend in large numbers' ([1958] 1994: 745). Hatano's observations were based on his own experience of 'two or three university *eiken* groups', in which goals for self-development and the development of the student body were closely tied to the aim of further developing the Japanese cinema (*Nihon no eiga no hatten ni tsunagaru*) ([1958] 1994: 745). His use of the term *majime* echoes the words of my interviewees, who regularly brought up this approach to cinemagoing. For example, Kobayashi san remembered, 'It may sound strange, but the films that seemed appealing at that time were very intellectual.' Tilting his head as though marvelling at the preferences of postwar audiences, he recalled, 'Even themes like pure literature or serious works like that attracted a big audience.' He nodded vigorously with direct eye contact, emphasising their commitment: 'People at that time had a desire for intellectual things, and that feeling was extremely strong.'

Hatano argued for an 'organizational theory' (*soshikiron*) of amateur film cultural activity: 'The organizational theory of culture and the arts is that people who love arts and culture have to find these for themselves.' He proposed a 'second principle' for 'deepening the theory of activities' (*rironkatsudō no fukaka*) ([1958] 1994: 745):

> While 30 or 50 people might attend at first, after 5 or 6 weeks the number suddenly declines, in effect, becoming something like a regular social education course. Core members, after some years, get interested in bringing in more people (2 or 3 years on), but as the group expands it is often without aim or endeavour. On that point, would it not be good to use film study surveys within the *eiken* to enhance the model? There are models available, based on the surveys used to analyse audience demographics . . . Although this is research kind of work, it will offer an opportunity for committed members around the fringes, and for studious members to come to the fore. Furthermore, students in that class or phase with a committed disposition will surely grasp the correct way of appreciating film. (Hatano [1958] 1994: 745)

Hatano's 'third principle' related to filmmakers and particularly what he called 'the principle of the amateur spirit' ([1958] 1994: 745). Arguing that 'experimental film is losing its important position in Japanese film culture', Hatano opined that 'amateur sensibilities are needed at this point' ([1958] 1994: 745): 'I want to see a focus on amateur freshness, artlessness, eccentric conception, their shocking angles of genius and different perception. *Eiken* films have the feeling of clumsy genius' ([1958] 1994: 745). Hatano suggested that *eiken* could not only foster future filmmakers but also film critics: 'you could say the place is an "egg" for film critics' ([1958] 1994: 745). Regardless of the outcome, however, he surmised that 'a wider orientation towards the issue of 'film appreciation and humanity' is desirable: 'The larger part of the *eiken* membership will not become critics, not to mention art critics. If we can learn how to enjoy film, and to enrich one's life from film, can't we become an attractive student society for the whole student body?' ([1958] 1994: 745).

Like retirees, cinema enthusiasts in Japan have long been understood as a potentially scholarly group. Hiroshi Kitamura notes that as commercial screenings revived in cities after Japan's defeat and Occupation, 'filmgoers increasingly took part in group activities to share their excitement and passion in larger communal settings' (H. Kitamura 2010: 174): 'In 1948 a local trade paper made note of the "nationwide eruption" of these student-run organisations' (H. Kitamura 2010: 174). Kitagawa Kazuo interprets these activities as attempts to 'resurrect selfhood' during the rapid social change of the postwar era (Kitagawa 2000: 50). My ethnographic findings largely support Kitamura and Kitagawa's assessment of the close relationship of film circle activities to an idea of developing the self. Participants in my study expressed their memories of their encounters with film as a kind of extending of the self, both into imagined spaces and as a form of self-cultivation and self-improvement.

At the same time, however, participants expressed surprise and even ridicule when I suggested to those who were members of film circles that they might visit a public cinema with other group members or spend time together socially. This was particularly interesting given that many continued to attend public screenings of films they could easily find on DVD shown on temporary equipment not much bigger or better than the kind they could have at home. I am not sure that the 'excitement and passion' that Kitamura's early postwar viewers were keen to share is exactly what is being shared in film circles today by those who grew up in the postwar years. Furthermore, I wonder whether participants in my own study would agree that the selves they are cultivating at retrospectives and film circles are in any sense 'resurrected' from an earlier time. Rather, a significant number of participants expressed the desire, as people born during and immediately after the war, to relive the memories and experiences of elder generations through films produced between 1930 and 1950. For these participants, film viewing was not an attempt to resurrect something past, but to stage and restage an encounter with the past.

Eiga Sākuru and Talking About Cinema

Memories of past film circles exerted a significant influence on the film circles and similar activities attended and created by my study participants in the mid- to late 2010s. Study participant Imai san recalled the *eiga sākuru* at his workplace as a formative influence on his attitude to cinema culture. At the time of our interview he ran a regular event called the Meeting to Talk about Cinema (Eiga o kataru kai). Imai san had worked for the Special Post Office in Shiga prefecture for thirty-four years, where the workplace club activities (*kurabu katsudō*) included *eiga dokushō* (film reading/ film literacy), at which everyone watched films on an assigned subject or topic and discussed them while eating and drinking, so it had the feeling of a 'talk session' (*kataru kai*). Imai san recalled, 'After retirement, I decided to set up my own film talk session. I managed to do this two years ago [in 2014], in association with the Kyoto Shinbun newspaper office in Shiga after chatting to them for an occasional section on cinema.'

Imai san held such 'cinema talk session' events in Osaka, Kyoto and in Ōtsu city in Shiga prefecture. He described the event as mainly comprised of 'talking about cinema, not only Japanese cinema but also films from overseas. I take questions and I don't only answer in a one-sided way from my own view, but rather consider the film from many angles, listening to what is thought to be good about a particular film.' He connected this activity to the continuation of his life and goals, using the word *shōgai*, which can be variously translated as one's whole life, one's career or lifetime: 'I want to continue this [activity] throughout my whole life (*shōgai*). Yes. More than that, this is my purpose in life, or reason for living (*ikigai*) . . . There are so many good films, both Japanese and from overseas, and so few people watch them nowadays.'

The three creators of the Kinugasa eiga kai also emphasised a lack of viewers for films perceived to be 'good' as a motivating factor in their decision to set up a film circle in contemporary Kyoto. It was during participant observation at Kinugasa eiga kai that I first heard about the Kyoto kiroku eiga o miru kai, the film viewing club turned filmmaking collective that had made the film *Nishijin* (Matsumoto Toshio, 1961) discussed in detail in Chapter 6. Kinugasa eiga kai was the third incarnation of that film viewing club, after both the original and its successor folded due to lack of funds, a fire at the membership office and various internal issues. Kinugasa eiga kai met on the third Saturday of every month in the north-west of Kyoto near the Kinugasa campus of Ritsumeikan University, though the group had no affiliation with the school. Between ten and thirty members from an overall membership of 150 met each month to view two or three films selected by a rotating *zachō* or meeting leader, followed by a discussion session, with beer and snacks offered at 100 yen each, subsidised by the group's 500 yen participation fee. The majority of the Kinugasa eiga kai members were aged over seventy; nonetheless, the long *zadankai* discussion session after each monthly screening would run for two hours, totalling around seven hours altogether.

The three founding member-organisers and the rotating *zachō* would prepare an intricate three- to five-page document each month with details of the films screened, reasons for choosing those films and plans for the following months, as well as a short history of the club. From 2015 to 2018 the screening was held in a Western-style house designed by the architect Motono Seigo in 1924 (see Figure 7.1), though in late 2018 the group moved to the Art Space Number One hall (*Āto supēsu ichiban kai*) near Imadegawa metro station. Motono's son and his wife were founding members of the Kinugasa eiga kai and had offered the use of the house once each month. Located at Tōji in Kitamachi, the Motono house is situated within the 'Kinugasa ekaki mura' or 'painting village', home to a group of Japanese modern artists since 1918. In a small shrine to the south, a statue commemorates Makino Shōzo (1878–1929), the film director, film producer and businessman known as a pioneer of Japanese cinema (see Figure 7.3). Takeda san, one of the organisers, noted that the house itself

Figure 7.1 The Motono house, home to the Kinugasa eiga kai until 2018.

was key to the cultural atmosphere of the club: 'People want to see these films, and they want to see them here.'

Kinugasa eiga kai members and organisers were largely concerned with bringing films that they considered to be good, high-art or groundbreaking to a broader viewership. Members expressed the desire to draw in younger film viewers to educate them about cinema history. There were attempts at programming to attract younger viewers, for example screening *Shin Godzilla* (*Shin-Gojira*, Anno Hideaki and Higuchi Shinji, 2016) alongside *Godzilla* (*Gojira*, Honda Ishirō, 1954) to draw local students to the viewing club towards the end of the university term time (see Figure 7.2). However, the members were disappointed when the five students who turned up left during the break after watching the 2016 film, showing little interest in the 1954 original.

Figure 7.2 The Kinugasa eiga kai hosts a screening of *Godzilla* (1954) and *Shin Godzilla* (2016).

Figure 7.3 On Senbon street, a plaque commemorates the 'father' of Japanese cinema, Makino Shōzo.

From my first attendance at the Kinugasa eiga kai meetings in September 2016, I was struck by the significant amount of time that the elderly members would devote to viewing two or three films in this historic building, boiling in summertime and, as I would later learn, freezing in winter. I was invited to distribute questionnaires at this meeting; one was returned during the meeting itself, and another three later by post. However, it was the lively discussion session at the end of the meeting that provided an opportunity to listen to a frank exchange of opinions on often sensitive topics which drew me back to the meeting every month for the next two years.

Talking About Cinema at the Kinugasa eiga kai

At the first meeting I attended, sixteen members watched the director's cut of Sam Peckinpah's *The Wild Bunch* (1969). The *zachō* for that meeting was Takeda san himself, and he had set aside time at the beginning of the session for me to introduce my project to the membership and obtain permission to study the group. Takeda san was seventy-three at that time and his organising activities were supported by the other two founders, Kubo san, aged ninety-three, and Watanabe san, the youngest at sixty-something. While Takeda san or Watanabe san took charge of the post-meeting analysis notes which were sent to the membership list by email each month, and Takeda san tended to open the discussion session while Watanabe san managed the distribution and payment for the subsidised drinks and snacks available, it was clear that Kubo san was in charge of the discussion and its direction.

Watanabe san and Takeda san referred to themselves as *sewanin* or 'caretakers' of the Kinugasa eiga kai. In his post-meeting analysis for the September 2016 meeting, Watanabe described the 'spirited discussion' (*danron fūhatsu*) held by the 'lovers of hardcore cinema' (*sujiganeiri no eiga suki*) as lively 'as always'. Noting the many 'derailments and digressions' (*dassen itsudatsu*) of the discussion, he recalled that participants had agreed that Peckinpah's film had broken new ground in its era for the level of violence, yet that his surprisingly careful and deliberate crafting of the film nonetheless left a sense of the orthodox Western genre about it. The beautiful scenery, slow-motion depictions of violence and judicious cutting were praised by discussants, demonstrating a knowledge of film language and filmmaking technique that recalls the educational aspirations of the film circles discussed by Hatano above. A perceived fidelity to the historical setting in the 1910s was also commended, particularly in the gendered characterisations. Summarising the group discussion, Watanabe san wrote, 'the sense of the era and the masculinity and femininity depicted in the film, and so on, is a little difficult to put into words' (*kotoba ni tsuduru to komuzukashi sō desu*). Takeda san raised the question of gender during the discussion in relation to whether his choice of film had been appropriate. A number of female attendees, around 30 per cent of the group aged between fifty and ninety years old, agreed that the content was challenging and many had not particularly liked the film. Nonetheless, a number noted their appreciation of the opportunity to engage with a film outside their sphere of interest. Watanabe san closed his summary with the observation, 'Even still, when a person watches a film like this, understanding its breadth and freedom, that is the attraction.'

The question of gender was raised again in a later meeting in January 2017. Willi Forst's *Burgtheatre* (1936) and David Lean's *Hobson's Choice* (1954) were the slightly unlikely film pairing for this meeting, and seventeen attendees joined the screening and discussion. *Zachō* Ishihara san explained his choices as motivated by a love of Western arts and stories about psychology and premeditated crimes. While a number of discussants used the date of Forst's film to demonstrate their knowledge of the development of sound in film history, study participant and Kinugasa circle member Yamashita san was particularly interested in the difference between male and female experiences of mixed-gender age-gap relationships and asked the group a number of questions related to their personal experience within the framework of discussions about the romantic and familial relationships depicted in the films. She recalled her school years and her teachers' lessons on postwar gender relations, and wondered about the impact of American and British gender norms on postwar Japanese behaviours. At this point, Kubo san redirected the discussion as group members began to share personal and friends' experiences of age-gap marriages. She reminded the group of the intended focus on film and steered them away from personal disclosures.

This had happened before, in a meeting in December 2016 with nineteen attendees. A second-year student from the film arts programme at the local Doshisha University had obtained permission to film the meeting to practise documentary filmmaking techniques and so I had expected the discussion to be quite tame. The screening films were *12 Angry Men* (Sidney Lumet, 1957) and *For Kayako* (Oguri Kōhei, 1984), with a uniting theme of justice and injustice. The narrative featuring *zainichi* Korean characters living in Japan in Oguri's film gave rise to a characteristically frank discussion about Japanese–Korean relations and the legacy of the Fifteen Years War and the Second World War. One group member brought up her perception that there was widespread anti-Japanese teaching and sentiment in Korea and China, which began a debate about war responsibility that got very heated. Another group member argued that Japan had not really lost the war directly to America or to China, as the kind of direct combat seen in Vietnam had not occurred in Japan. A third speaker dismissed this as 'stupid thinking' (*ahoteki kangaekata*) and soon the insults 'stupid' and its more insulting variants (*baka, aho*) were being thrown around generally in the group discussion. The atmosphere was definitely heated, but not explicitly angry. People laughed incredulously at others' statements and appeared more excited than offended by the debate. Kubo san sat with eyes closed and a look of mild irritation throughout. When Takeda san asked her opinion (not explicitly noting that she would have been the only adult during the wartime of those present in the room), she firmly expressed her belief that the film club was no place for talking about politics or historical truth and that discussion should be centred on the film itself. Takeda san deferred to her opinion and rerouted the discussion.

These three vignettes of discussion sessions at the Kinugasa eiga kai demonstrate how the use of cinema as a prompt or pretext for giving an account of the self can occur in group settings. While the majority of the quotations and descriptions relating to participants' statements and memories in this book occurred during private discussions between one participant and myself or a small group discussion between an interviewee, myself as interviewer and my research assistant or partner as camera operator, as well as some moments observed during discussions among old friends, the Kinugasa eiga kai offered an opportunity to observe a larger group of acquaintances communicating together about and through cinema. The result appeared little different to the more private or small group conversations, with participants readily applying issues and themes perceived through cinema content and style with elements of their own lives and memories that they wished to discuss. In this respect, the use of talking about cinema to give an account of oneself appeared as prevalent in acquaintance groups like film circles as it was in friendly, familial or interviewer–interviewee communications.

Creating Connections to and through Cinema

This chapter has considered the work of making or creating in the shaping of a sense of self through engagement with cinema culture, analysing material created and collected by study participants as well as the events and gatherings organised by participants in order to bring film fans together in discussion. Arguing for the study of discourses and communication practices, including the creation and collection of film ephemera, as an essential element in our understanding of film history, I have explored how the self is crafted through narratives about a relationship to cinema, embodied by the physical materials that my study participants collected, archived, created and donated. As the conclusion will show, however, the social activities, media appearances and dedicated speaking events that key participants organised to share their stories about cinema which have been discussed in this chapter may have been the last in a closing chapter on grassroots cinema culture organisation by elderly Japanese people. The COVID-19 pandemic, which began for Japan in January 2020 and is ongoing at the time of writing, has forced the circles and activities discussed in this chapter to close. While study participants continue to communicate about cinema online, the nature of their cinema-themed discourse is changing, as are the accounts that they give of themselves and their lives.

Conclusion
Giving an Account of Oneself through Talking About Cinema

> There is no reason to call into question the importance of narrating a life, in its partiality and provisionality. I am sure that transference can facilitate narration and that narrating a life has a crucial function, especially for those whose involuntary experience of discontinuity afflicts them in profound ways. No one can live in a radically non-narratable world or survive a radically non-narratable life. (Butler 2005: 59)

This book has investigated the role that talking about cinema culture, memories of film viewing and the feelings that cinema stirs in oneself can play in making oneself more knowable to a listener. Throughout the previous chapters we have explored how cinema is used to discuss feelings about particular times and places in one's life as well as how the film theatre itself could shape the daily experiences of audience members. Stories about engaging with cinema have been used to support perceptions or senses of memories from the very early years of survey respondents' and interviewees' lives, suggesting that talking about cinema can be part of the creation of 'prosthetic memory' (Landsberg 2002) as well as a means to attempt to conjure and vicariously experience historical moments lived by elder family members. Turning cinema engagement into political engagement, or into a form of labour, by organising film-related events or even producing films themselves builds another layer around the kind of self that can be formed by a relationship to cinema culture and stories about that relationship. The preceding chapters have each made a case for talking about cinema, in a variety of aspects, as a mode of representing something about the self to another, and at the same time bringing that self into being through its very description.

As Judith Butler writes, giving an account of oneself is no small matter in the project of a human life. Butler argues that an un-narratable life can be considered unliveable, in that it is not recognised by interlocutors: 'After all, no one survives without being addressed; no one survives to tell his or her story without first being inaugurated into language by being called upon, offered some stories, brought into the discursive world of the story' (Butler 2005: 63). To find one's way in the world and 'in language', Butler argues that we must become part of 'a web of relations in which affectivity achieves articulation in some form' (Butler 2005: 63). This book has proposed talking about cinema and engagement in cinema culture as one form of such articulation of affectivity.

Understanding talking about cinema as formative of a sense of self in this way suggests the importance of paying attention not only to the possibilities of engaging with cinema culture but also to what happens when that engagement is no longer possible. For some, engagement with cinema culture and the narratives around it may become impossible for financial, physical or circumstantial reasons such as not being able to afford a cinema ticket, travel to a theatre or meeting event, or to make time for film viewing and discussion. For those who participated in this study, which ended in April 2018, the global pandemic which arrived in Japan in January 2020 was to significantly change cinema culture, film viewing and how audiences talked about cinema, to whom and via what media. As the participants in this study were aged between seventy and ninety-five at the time of the research, they found themselves more isolated from film culture than most, as many did not engage with streaming platforms or online communication platforms like Zoom, Skype and Line.

The Impact of COVID-19 on the Japanese Cinema Landscape

At the time of writing, the pandemic is ongoing and its impact on almost every aspect of daily life remains unclear. Guidance and initiatives for behavioural change are still adapting, often abruptly, and there are quite significant differences across and between countries. While Japan was forced to confront the immediate implications of the spread of COVID-19 earlier than many other countries, with the arrival of the British-registered *Diamond Princess* luxury cruise ship and its 691 infected passengers in Yokohama on 3 February 2020 (Nakazawa et al. 2020), it was not until April 2020 that major cities began to shut down. Then-Prime Minister Abe Shinzō declared a state of emergency on 7 April 2020 for Tokyo, Chiba, Kanagawa, Saitama and Osaka, Hyogo and Fukuoka, affecting 56 million people or around 45 per cent of the total population of Japan (Kyodo News 2020). Cinemas, including small independent 'mini-theatres' as well as large multiplex theatres, closed temporarily and citizens were asked to refrain from non-essential outings.

Almost immediately, a range of industry and citizen-organised petitions, support systems and crowdfunding initiatives sprang up to aid the closed cinema theatres, stalled production units and disrupted distributors. Film director Irie Yu began by using her popular blog to list small theatres that patrons could continue to fund by buying membership or merchandise (Irie Yu Film 2020). In the Kansai region, theatre owners set up a crowdfunding campaign called Save Our Local Cinemas which ran from 6 April to 12 April 2020. Selling T-shirts designed by the Kyoto Minami Kaikan cinema theatre director, the initiative collected 4,805 donations and 13,227 T-shirt orders, which enabled each cinema theatre to receive 2.8 million yen in support (Save Our Local Cinemas Project 2020). Thirteen cinema theatres participated, including Kyoto Minami Kaikan, Demachiza, Fukuchiyama Cinema and Kyoto Cinema in Kyoto; Cine Nouveau, Theatre Seven and Seventh Art Theatre in Osaka; Motomachi Movie Theatre, Kobe Planet Film Archive and Pal Cinema Shinkoen in Kobe; Takarazuka Cine Pipia and Toyooka theater in Hyogo, and Maizuru Yachiyo Hall in Maizuru.

Directors Fukada Koji and Hamaguchi Ryusuke founded the Mini-Theatre Aid Fund, sponsored by a variety of cultural producers, networks, galleries and actors and working in tandem with other movements to protect cinema culture, including Save the Cinema, Do It Theatre, Asian Documentaries and Stay Home Mini-Theatre. Volunteers supported a Motion Gallery crowdfunding initiative that ran from 13 April to 15 May 2020 and collected 331,025,487 yen from 29,926 individual donors (Motion Gallery 2020). The project offered a range of products, from a 3,000 yen 'support' option which included a message of gratitude from the famous founders, to a 5,000 yen 'future ticket' option which allowed a donor to attend a future showing in the participating theatre of their choice anytime until 2022, and to stream four films from the online Sunkus Theatre which was set up to aid distribution during the pandemic. With 117 participating theatres, each received around 3 million yen, which mini-theatre owner Asai Takashi noted made up only a small percentage of each theatre's loss (Gerow 2020). The associated Save the Cinema petition, which called for emergency assistance for all film efforts during the pandemic, recruited 91,523 supporters (Change.org 2020). Distributors also received support from the Help the Distributors project, which was launched by an independent movie distribution company on 15 May 2020 to address difficulties in distribution.

The charming and effective websites which fostered this activity combined offers of merchandise and future event tickets with questionnaires seeking to understand audiences' preferences for future events, informational articles such as 'What is an independent distribution company?' (Help! The Movie Distributor Project 2020) and recordings of online events such as interviews with cinema owners, filmmakers and critics. Some websites had dedicated areas which documented the reach of the initiatives by archiving print media mentions of their efforts and interviews with key personnel. Other common themes included message boards or video areas which showcased messages of support, reviews of new and classic films and actors, and links to creative projects undertaken by filmmakers during periods spent at home.

The Motion Gallery page for the Mini-Theatre Aid Fund included some emotive writing on the history and experience of mini-theatres that recalled the language used by participants in my own study of memories of cinemagoing. Describing the key qualities of cinema theatres that can be defined as mini-theatres, one section begins by noting that when we have a feeling that we want to see a film being shown at 'that particular movie theatre', then we are probably thinking of a 'mini-theatre' (Motion Gallery 2020). From 'the unique selection of films to be screened, pamphlets and goods lined up at ticket offices and shops, light meals, and introductory articles about the movies being shown in the lobby' to the 'flyers and posters of past screenings of films that are called masterpieces, and in-house displays handmade by staff', the description of the mini-theatre ideal recalled the stories told by my study participants of their favourite film experiences, and particularly Takeda san's observations about the draw of the Motono house as a screening space for the Kinugasa eiga kai in Chapter 7. While 'the screen, the feel of the chair, and the staff who create the environment' ensure that 'every element that makes up a mini-theater has its own personality', the website text argues that the mini-theatre is also 'a mirror-like place that reflects the culture of the city' (Motion Gallery 2020). Echoing the observations of my study participants in the preceding chapters, the writers conclude that 'the films that capture various countries, regions, ages, and themes that are shown there have taught us the diversity of culture . . . Encounters with unique works screened in the mini-theater are an unforgettable memory' (Motion Gallery 2020). Hearing the words and sentiments of my study participants echoed in this call to save the cinema in Japan underscored the importance of film culture and finding places to talk about film culture for the formation of a sense of self in everyday life. At the same time, however, as these formative discussions moved online I was conscious that the voices of the age groups represented by my study participants were largely missing.

CONCLUSION

The Kinugasa Eiga Kai Responds to a Global Pandemic

Having moved from the Motono house to the Art Space Ichibankan building near Imadegawa metro station in central Kyoto, the Kinugasa eiga kai held its 78th meeting in February 2020 with fourteen members. On 27 February 2020, Takeda san wrote to the membership by email to announce an 'extraordinary adjournment' of the meeting scheduled for 21 March due to the spread of the new coronavirus. The short message was signed '*sewanin*' or 'caretaker'. On 21 March, Takeda san wrote to the membership again, noting that the date was that of the previously cancelled meeting. While the Kinugasa eiga kai was only 'temporarily closed', he sounded alarm on the part of the 'caretakers' about the increasing severity of the pandemic: 'The spread of the new coronavirus has not stopped even now. On 12 March the WHO admitted that the outbreak is a pandemic.' Characteristically, Takeda san was attentively following developments around the world as well as in Japan. He wrote, 'In Italy, the death toll of up to 19 people a day has reached a total of 3,405 people. It is the largest total in the world, surpassing China.' Turning to Japan, he quoted a government expert who had said, 'Although Japan is holding up, there is still a risk of spreading the infection.' 'Recently,' Takeda san observed, 'it seems that the number of cases where the source of infection and the route of infection are unknown is increasing.' He had therefore contacted the caretakers of Kinugasa eiga kai to ask their opinion on continuing the 'temporary recess' of meetings from April 2020 onwards. While the caretakers had agreed that, 'It is a pity that there is no prospect of a reunion for a while', they resolved to retain the scheduled programming for a future meeting, which they anticipated may not be too far away.

I heard nothing further from Takeda san or the Kinugasa eiga kai until June 2020, when he wrote to note that three months had passed since the recess began. Citing the 'historic' nature of the ongoing pandemic, he asked, 'How are you doing, everyone who is forced to live a life of long-term withdrawal (*hikikomori*)?' While the government had lifted the state of emergency by June, and the Kinugasa eiga kai members were theoretically free to meet again, it seemed that the experience had scared many. Takeda san wrote to communicate that after surveying fifteen core members, including the caretakers and experienced chairpersons, only three people had expressed a willingness to restart the screening meetings, using new measures to safeguard attendees from transmission of infection. The other twelve warned that reopening was 'premature' and advised that they continue to monitor the situation. Perhaps the long screening and discussion sessions, close quarters and use of older buildings, as well as the age of many participants, added to their concern.

Takeda san himself seemed very worried about the effect of the pandemic on everyday life. Referring to the virus as a 'silent killer', he noted that the lack of PCR testing available in Japan in June 2020 and the predominance of asymptomatic cases made it hard to trace infection. 'We caretakers have a duty to give due consideration to safety,' he wrote. 'Participants cannot be exposed to the risk of viral infection. After all, safety and security are the major premise on which we can resume our activities.' He concluded that the temporary adjournment should continue, closing with a short paragraph that seemed to me to communicate the deeply engaged nature of the Kinugasa group's use of cinema to understand everyday life. Combining a near-scholarly approach with endless curiosity about the natural world and a philosophical outlook, Takeda san wrote:

> In the first place, it is said that there are 1.6 million kinds of viruses in nature. This Corona problem has been exacerbated and pushed by global economic growth. For human beings who do not care about artificial climate change and the destruction of our ecosystem, it may be a warning from the natural world. If you have any opinions or criticisms regarding the above, please feel free to send them to the caretaker. Lastly, please continue to be vigilant against infections and spend your time wisely during the disaster. (Takeda 2020)

He wrote again in August to continue the postponement, using language that seemed designed to cheer the membership on: 'Now, patience is key. Everyone, please lovingly take care of yourself (*gojiai*).' Then silence followed.

In January 2021 a new year message arrived and it transpired that Takeda san himself had been ill. The Kinugasa email brought new year congratulations, but it held a darker tone than previous messages: 'The current spread of infection has reached a record high, including the peak of the third wave, the number of infected people and the number of deaths. The Japanese government has unabashedly continued its two-pronged policy of infection prevention and economic policy. We will continue to be at the mercy of the new coronavirus, which repeatedly mutates.' Takeda san noted that coronavirus continued to be 'a very scary illness for late-stage elderly people such as myself who have heart disease'. Elderly people in Japan appear to have cancelled plans for gathering during the pandemic at a rate 5.9 times higher than younger people (Kashima and Zhang 2021). Kinugasa screenings would not restart, and the names of the other two 'caretakers' had disappeared from the email signature. Finally in November 2021 Takeda san wrote again to say that members had been contacting him to ask about restarting the screenings. 'As a caretaker, I'm thinking of observing the situation for a while,' he wrote.

> The number of infected people in Japan has settled down, but the cold weather will be severe this winter, and the spread of the sixth wave of infection is still widespread. In Europe, where the second vaccination was in progress, breakthrough infections due to highly infectious mutant strains are increasing. Anyway, we don't want to create a cluster at our movie venue. We ask for the understanding of all the participants regarding the postponement of the resumption. (Takeda 2021)

It seemed notable that none of the caretakers nor the membership had suggested a replacement online meeting or even recommended some of the online movie events or screening platforms discussed above. While a number communicated personally via Facebook and Line, the Kinugasa screenings seemed to be imaginable only as in-person events where viewers could cluster together, drinking and chatting during breaks and the long discussion session. I was reminded of Takeda san's insistence that 'Members want to see films *here*' and considered that in light of the pre-pandemic change in location from the Motono house to the Art Space venue, the 'here' might have referred to the Kinugasa group setting itself rather than the physical building or space in which members gathered.

Cinemagoing after 2021

Developments within the Kinugasa eiga kai membership suggest the deep importance for many of the 'going' part of 'going to the cinema' – leaving the house, sitting with others and talking about what one has seen together. In a 15 July 2021 article titled 'The Movies Are Back, But What Are Movies Now?', critic A. O. Scott of *The New Yorker* observed that 'the pandemic-accelerated fear that streaming would kill moviegoing has been proven wrong. People like to leave the house.' Yet that 'doesn't mean the status quo has been restored' (Scott 2021). Instead, Scott argues, we may be living through an era of 'seismic alteration' in cinemagoing and film production, similar to the introduction of sound or the collapse of the studio system. Yet Scott worries that online viewing may be 'circumscribing our taste and limit[ing] the range of our thought' (Scott 2021). Like the participants in my study quoted in previous chapters, he associates the cinema with learning as well as stimulation and entertainment, and expresses concern that the algorithm-driven suggestion and advertising systems of small-screen streaming practices will lead us to consume content based on its similarity to our existing preferences, rather than challenging our viewing habits and thereby our view of the world and our place in it.

'The more you watch', Scott argues, 'the harder the algorithm works to turn its idea of you into a reality' (2021). If the two sets of responses to cinemagoing during the pandemic surveyed above are contrasted, one shifting online and one resolutely remaining offline, we might become concerned that while younger and middle-aged viewers find their 'you' or 'self' shaped not by the cinemagoing experience and their encounter with other viewers but by an algorithm, older viewers and their memories simply disappear. Both results are troubling, though film critics to date appear to be more concerned about the impact and influences of algorithm-driven streaming sites and private at-home viewing patterns on participating viewers rather than the dropping off of those who choose not to consume cinema content in this way. Yet as the previous chapters have sought to demonstrate, top-down narratives about controlling populations through cinema content rarely meet their own objectives at the saturation level to which they aim. Whether we research the reception of censored content shaped for ideological purposes by an occupying bureaucracy or the access and advertisement arrangements of cinema theatres and film studios, studying audiences shows us that they use and access cinema in divergent ways for their own means. There is always a work-around for the resourceful viewer.

The long arc of audience behavioural change, if we can conceive of one, may situate the innovations and shifts of the pandemic more in line with changes in viewing habits like the introduction of assigned seating in cinemas, for example, or the banning of smoking. Perhaps 'double screening' will become as accepted in future cinemas as smoking is not, and audiences of the future will scroll through their phones while keeping one eye on the big screen. Or maybe theatres will veer in the opposite direction and create ever more focused avenues for cinema viewing, with private stations and personal sound systems, like the personal headsets envisioned as part of everyday cinema culture in the early years of the development of headphones (Roquet 2022: 40). While we cannot predict the future of viewership, we know that audiences always find ways to surprise us. It would also be ahistorical to think of a unilinear shift from one mode of viewing to another when audience studies tell us that viewers often access multiple modes of engagement at once. Just as the gift was not replaced by the commodity but continued to exist alongside it (Tsing 2013), the Kinugasa eiga kai existed alongside mini-theatres and multiplexes, which suggests that the future of cinema will at least be varied if not hybrid.

These are just some of the aspects in which studying the audience allows us to think through pressing problems that face us today. An ethno-historical approach to audience studies and cinema memory can give us the nuanced and multi-layered view that we will need to rethink cinema culture, and how we engage with it, as we reform many aspects of our societies and everyday lives from 2021 onwards. I hope that the preceding chapters have presented a convincing case for the cinema as not simply a means of entertainment, but a part of a bigger and deeply meaningful project of making ourselves, as viewers and sensory beings feeling alongside one another, more knowable to ourselves and to each other. Whatever happens to the cinema, in whichever form we imagine 'cinema' taking, an understanding of its meanings and uses in our larger life projects will ensure that we understand saving the cinema as a means of saving ourselves, or at least an expression of ourselves that can be perceived and recognised by others.

Bibliography

Ahmed, Sara (2004), 'Affective Economies', *Social Text* 22: 118–39.
Akiyama, Kiyoshi (1968), 'Yakuza eiga wa sara ni manpukukan o ataeyo: eiga shūkan to narutakiizumu' [Yakuza movies give a feeling of satisfaction: Emerging movie-going habits], *Eiga Geijutsu* [Film Art] 16(5) (1 May): 64–5.
Alekseyeva, Julia (2017), 'Butterflies, Beetles, and Postwar Japan: Semi-documentary in the 1960s', *Journal of Japanese and Korean Cinema* 9(1): 14–29.
Allen, H. W. (1945), 'Elimination of Japanese Government Control of the Motion Picture Industry', SCAPIN 146, 16 October 1945. Box 8565, Folder 31, SCAP records, National Archives (and online): http://dl.ndl.go.jp/info:ndljp/pid/9885209
Allison, Anne (1996), *Permitted and Prohibited Desires: Mothers, Comics, and Censorship in Japan*. Boulder: Westview.
Allison, Anne (2002), 'Playing with Power: Morphing Toys and Transforming Heroes in Kids' Mass Culture', in J. M. Mageo (ed.), *Power and the Self*, Cambridge: Cambridge University Press, 71–92.
Ang, Ien (1991) [1985], *Watching Dallas: Soap Opera and the Melodramatic Imagination*. London and New York: Routledge.
Ang, Ien (1996), *Living Room Wars: Rethinking Media Audiences for a Postmodern World*. London and New York: Routledge.
Annavajhula, J. C. B. (1989), 'Japanese Subcontracting Systems', *Economic and Political Weekly* 24(8): 15–23.
Anon. (1957), 'Josei kankyaku-sō no kenkyū' [A Study of the Female Audience], *Kinema Junpō* [The Movie Times] (October): 145–9.
Anon. (1968), 'Kōgyōkai: Yakuza bangumi ni gaika', *Kinema Junpō* [The Movie Times] 481 (11 November): 83.
Aoyama, Tomoko (2008), 'The Girl, the Body, and the Nation in Japan and the Pacific Rim: Introduction', *Asian Studies Review* 32(3): 285–92.
Armstrong, Peter (2011), 'Architecture in the Mono-no-nai-jidai', in Roman Rosenbaum and Yasuko Claremont (eds), *Legacies of the Asia-Pacific War: The Yakeato Generation*, 216–28. London: Routledge.
Asahi Shinbunsha (1963), 'Editorial', *Asahi Shinbun* (15 April). Tokyo: Asahi shinbunsha.

Asai, Eiichi (1961a), 'Kyoto kiroku eiga o miru kai no rekishi' [A History of the Kyoto kiroku eiga o miru kai], *Eiga Hyōron* [Film Criticism] 18(10): 21–30.
Asai, Eiichi (1961b), 'Nishijin o seisakushite' [Making Nishijin], *Me: Kyoto kiroku eiga o miru kai kikanshi* [Eye: Bulletin of the Kyoto kiroku eiga o miru kai] (June): 18.
Avenell, Simon Andrew (2010), *Making Japanese Citizens: Civil Society and the Mythology of the Shimin in Postwar Japan*. Berkeley: University of California Press.
Bae, Catherine Yoonah (2008), 'Girl Meets Boy Meets Girl: Heterosocial Relations, Wholesome Youth, and Democracy in Postwar Japan', *Asian Review* 32(3): 341–60.
Baskett, Michael (2008), *The Attractive Empire: Transnational Film Culture in Imperial Japan*. Honolulu: University of Hawaii Press.
Benedict, Ruth (2005) [1946], *The Chrysanthemum and the Sword: Patterns of Japanese Culture*. Boston: Houghton Mifflin Harcourt.
Berlant, Lauren (2008), 'Thinking about Feeling Historical', *Emotion, Space and Society* 1(1): 4–9.
Boltanski, Luc and Eve Chiapello (2005), 'The New Spirit of Capitalism', *International Journal of Politics, Culture, and Society* 18(3): 161–88.
Bourdieu, Pierre (1984), *Distinction: A Social Critique of the Judgement of Taste*. Translated by Richard Nice. Cambridge, MA: Harvard University Press.
Brandon, James R. (2006), 'Myth and Reality: A Story of Kabuki during American Censorship, 1945–1949', *Asian Theatre Journal* 23(1): 1–110.
Bronson, Adam (2016), *One Hundred Million Philosophers: Science of Thought and the Culture of Democracy in Postwar Japan*. Honolulu: University of Hawaii Press.
Butler, Judith (2005), *Giving an Account of Oneself*. New York: Fordham University Press.
Campbell, Jan (2005), *Film and Cinema Spectatorship: Melodrama and Mimesis*. Cambridge: Polity Press.
Cather, Kirsten (2014), 'Policing the Pinks', in M. A. Nornes (ed.), *The Pink Book: The Japanese Eroduction and Its Contexts*, 93–148. Ann Arbor: Kinema Club.
Cazdyn, Eric (2002), *The Flash of Capital: Film and Geopolitics in Japan*. Durham, NC: Duke University Press.
Certau, Michel de (1984), *The Practice of Everyday Life*. Translated by Steven Rendall. Berkeley: University of California Press.
CIE 1949a – CIE(D) 05299. 1949. GHQ/SCAP 834/870. 000006766450. Motion Picture Code of Ethics by Motion Picture Association of Japan 1949. National Diet Library, Tokyo: Records of the Supreme Commander for the Allied Powers.
CIE 1949b – CIE(D) 01446-01451. 1949/01-1949/12. GHQ/SCAP 035.4/870. 000006753043. Conference Reports.
Coaldrake, William H. (2003), *Japan from War to Peace: The Coaldrake Records 1939–1956*. London and New York: Routledge Curzon.

Coates, Jennifer (2016), *Making Icons: Repetition and the Female Image in Postwar Japanese Cinema, 1945–1964*. Hong Kong: Hong Kong University Press.
Coates, Jennifer (2017), 'Socializing the Audience: Going to the Cinema in Postwar Japan', *Participations* 14(2): 590–607.
Conde, David (1945), Consolidated Report of Civil Information and Education Section Activities, Daily Report to Brigadier General Ken R. Dyke, Chief of CI & E, November 16, 1945, from Mr. D. Conde, Motion Picture and Visual Media Section. GHQ/ SCAP Records, National Diet Library, Tokyo.
Conde, David (1965), 'Nihon eiga no senryōshi' [The Occupation History of Japanese Cinema], *Sekai* 237 (August): 251.
Crockett, Lucy Herndon (1949), *Popcorn on the Ginza: An Informal Portrait of Post-war Japan*. New York: W. Sloan Associates.
Deleuze, Gilles (1989), *Cinema II: The Time-Image*. Translated by Hugh Tomlinson and Robert Galeta. Minneapolis: University of Minnesota Press.
Desser, David (1988), *Eros Plus Massacre: an Introduction to the Japanese New Wave Cinema*. Bloomington: Indiana University Press.
Doane, Mary Anne (2002), *The Emergence of Cinematic Time: Modernity, Contingency, the Archive*. Boston: Harvard University Press.
Dollase, Hiromi Tsuchiya (2008), 'Girls on the Home Front: An Examination of Shōjo no tomo Magazine 1937–1945', *Asian Studies Review* 32(3): 323–39.
Dyer, Richard (2004), *Heavenly Bodies: Film Stars and Society*. London and New York: Routledge.
Eiga geijutsu nenkan (1947), *Eiga geijutsu nenkan* [Motion Picture Arts Yearbook 1947]. Tokyo: Jijitsu shinsha.
Eiga junpō (1941), 'Kankyaku dōtai chōsa' [Audience Demographic Survey]. *Eiga junpō* [Film Report] (1 December): 54–6.
Eiga no tomo (1951), Fan Letters. *Eiga no tomo* [Film Friend] (April): 37.
Fooken, Kristin (2020), 'Inabata and the Lumières – Exploring the Transnational Foundations of Cinema in Japan', in Marcos Centeno Martin and Norimasa Morita (eds), *Japan beyond Its Borders: Transnational Approaches to Film and Media*, 187–201. Tokyo: Seibunsha.
Fujiki, Hideaki (2011), *Kankyaku e no apurōchi* [Approaching the Audience]. Nagoya: Nagoya University Press.
Fujiki, Hideaki (2013), *Making Personas: Transnational Film Stardom in Modern Japan*. Cambridge, MA: Harvard University Asia Center; Harvard University Press.
Fujiki, Hideaki (2014), 'Creating the Audience: Cinema as Popular Recreation and Social Education in Modern Japan', in Daisuke Miyao (ed.), *The Oxford Handbook of Japanese Cinema*, 78–382. Oxford: Oxford University Press.
Fujiki, Hideaki (2019), *Eiga kankyaku to wa nani mono ka: media to shakai shutai no kin-gendaishi* [Who is the Cinema Audience?: A History of Media and Social Subjects, 1910s–2010s]. Nagoya: Nagoya University Press.
Fukui, Nanako (1999), 'Background Research for The Chrysanthemum and the Sword', *Dialectical Anthropology* 24(2): 173–80.

Fukuoka, Takeo (1950), 'Eigakan ni okeru abekku no seitai' [Lifestyles of couples in the movie theater], *Chūō kōron* [Central Review] (December): 162–7.

Furuhata, Yuriko (2013), *Cinema of Actuality: Japanese Avant Garde Filmmaking in the Season of Image Politics*. London and Durham, NC: Duke University Press.

Galbraith, Patrick W. (2013), 'Maid Cafes: The Affect of Fictional Characters in Akihabara, Japan', *Asian Anthropology* 12(2): 104–25.

Geertz, Clifford (1973), *The Interpretation of Cultures*. New York: Basic Books.

George, Timothy S. (2001), *Minamata: Pollution and the Struggle for Democracy in Postwar Japan*. Boston: Harvard University Asia Center.

Gerow, Aaron (2010a), *Visions of Japanese Modernity: Articulations of Cinema, Nation, and Spectatorship, 1895–1925*. London: University of California Press.

Gerow, Aaron (2010b), 'The Process of Theory: Reading Gonda Yasunosuke and Early Film Theory', *Review of Japanese Culture and Society* 22: 37–43.

Gerow, Aaron (2014), 'From "Misemono" to Zigomar: A Discursive History of Early Japanese Cinema', in Jennifer M. Bean, Anupama Kapse and Laura Horak (eds), *Silent Cinema and the Politics of Space*, 157–85. Bloomington: Indiana University Press.

Gerow, Aaron (2015), 'Documentarists of Japan #9: Matsumoto Toshio', Documentary Box. Interview and translation by Aaron Gerow. Online. Available at: http://www.yidff.jp/docbox/9/box9-2-e.html

Gerow, Aaron (2020), 'Japanese Film and the COVID Pandemic – Remotely in Space and Time'. *Tangemania* blog. Online. Available at: http://www.aarongerow.com/news/japanese-film-and-the-covid.html

Gonda, Yasunosuke (1914), *Katsudō shashin no genre oyobi ōyō* [The Principles and Applications of the Moving Pictures]. Tokyo: Dojinsha.

Gonda, Yasunosuke (1922), *Minshu goraku no kichō* [The Foundations of Popular Entertainment]. Tokyo: Dojinsha.

González-López, Irene (2019), 'Marketing the Panpan In Japanese Popular Culture: Youth, Sexuality, and Power', *US-Japan Women's Journal* 54(1): 29–51.

Gordon, Andrew (2009), *The Wages of Affluence: Labor and Management in Postwar Japan*. Boston: Harvard University Press.

Hamaguchi, Eshun (1988) [1977]. *'Nihonjin Rashisa' no sai hakken* [A Rediscovery of 'Japaneseness']. Tokyo: Kodansha.

Hankins, Joseph D. (2014), *Working Skin: Making Leather, Making a Multicultural Japan*. Berkeley and Los Angeles: University of California Press.

Hansen, Miriam Bratu (2000), 'The Mass Production of the Senses: Classical Cinema as Vernacular Modernism', in Christine Gledhill and Linda Williams (eds), *Reinventing Film Studies*, 332–50. London: Arnold.

Hareven, Tamara K. (2002), *The Silk Weavers of Kyoto: Family and Work in a Changing Traditional Industry*. Berkeley and Los Angeles: University of California Press.

Hatano, Kanji (1994) [1958], 'Daigaku eiken to eigabunka' [University film study and film culture], *Kinema Junpō* [The Movie Times] (15 November), reprinted in *Best of Kinema Junpō*, 744–5. Tokyo: Kinema Junpōsha.

Hatano, Kanji (1950), 'Eiga wa gakkō e shinnyū suru' [Cinema Intrudes into School], *Eiga Kyōshitsu* [Film Classroom] 4(2): 8.
Help! The Movie Distributor Project (2020), 'Help! The Movie Distributor Project', *Note Website*. Online. Available at: https://note.com/help_the_dsbtrs
High, Peter B. (1984), 'The Dawn of Cinema in Japan', *Journal of Contemporary History* 19(1): 23–57.
High, Peter B. (2003), *The Imperial Screen; Japanese Film Culture in the Fifteen Years War, 1931–1945*. Madison: The University of Wisconsin Press.
Hirano, Kyoko (1992), *Mr. Smith Goes to Tokyo*. Washington, DC: Smithsonian Institution Press.
Hojo, Nobuhiko (1970), 'Yakuza eiga no kōryoku' [The Efficacy of Yakuza Films], *Kinema Junpō* [The Movie Times] 517 (1 March): 50–1.
Hori, Hikari (2002), 'Eiga o mirukoto to katarukoto: Mizoguchi Kenji "Yoru no onnatachi" (1948) o meguru hihyō, jendā, kankyaku' ['Women of the Night' (1948) as Framed by the Occupation Era in Japan: Negotiations between Text, Critics and Female Spectators], *Eizōgaku* [Japan Society for Image Arts and Sciences] 68: 47–66.
Hori, Hikari (2017), *Promiscuous Media: Film and Visual Culture in Imperial Japan, 1926–1945*. New York: Cornell University Press.
Ichida, Yoshihiko (2020), 'The Ethics of the Agitator: On Hiroshi Nagasaki's *The Phenomenology of Politics*', in Gavin Walker (ed.), *The Red Years: Theory, Politics, and Aesthetics in the Japanese '68*, 38–56. London and New York: Verso.
Ijima, Tetsuo (1969), 'Nihon eiga hihiyō: Hibotan bakuto' [Japanese Film Criticism: The Red Peony Gambler], *Kinema Junpō* [The Movie Times] 509 (15 November): 70.
Iles, Timothy (2008), *The Crisis of Identity in Contemporary Japanese Film: Personal, Cultural, National*. Leiden and Boston: Brill.
Inabata, Katsutarō (1897), *Inabata Katsutarō no Lumière kyōdai ate shokan 4tsū* [Inabata Katsutaro's Four Letters to the Lumière Brothers]. Online. Available at: https://www.inabata.co.jp/ik/digital/
Itakura, Fumiaki (ed.) (2019), *Kōbe to eiga: eigakan to kankyaku no kioku* [Kobe and cinema: film theatres and audience memories], Kobe: Kōbe Shinbun Sōgō Shuppan Sentā.
Iwamoto, Kenji (2006), 'Nashonarizumu to kokusaku eiga' [Nationalism and the National Policy Film], in Iwamoto Kenji (ed.), *Nihon eiga to nashonarizumu* [Japanese Film and Nationalism 1931–1945], 7–28. Tokyo: Shinwasha.
Iwasaki, Akira (1978), 'The Occupied Screen', *Japan Quarterly* 25(3): 302–22.
Jansen, Marius B. (1965), 'Changing Japanese Attitudes Toward Modernization', in Marius B. Jansen (ed.), *Changing Japanese Attitudes Toward Modernization*, 43–98. Princeton, NJ: Princeton University Press.
Jesty, Justin (2010), 'Arts of Engagement: Art and Social Movements in Japan's Early Postwar', PhD diss., The University of Chicago.
Jesty, Justin (2018), *Art and Engagement in Early Postwar Japan*. Ithaca, NY: Cornell University Press.

Kaffen, Philip (2020), 'Jidaigeki: The Duplicitous Topos of Jidaigeki', in Hideaki Fujiki and Alastair Philips (eds), *The Japanese Cinema Book*, 285–97. London: BFI; Bloomsbury Publishing.

Kashima, Saori and Zhang, Junyi (2021), 'Temporal Trends in Voluntary Behavioural Changes During the Early Stages of the COVID-19 Outbreak in Japan', *Public Health* 192: 37–44.

Katō, Mikiro (1995), 'Eigakan to Kankyaku no Rekishi: Eigatoshi Kyoto no Sengo' [A History of Film Theatres and Audiences: Postwar Kyoto as Cinema City], *Eizōgaku* [Japan Society for Image Arts and Sciences] 55: 44–58.

Katō, Mikiro (1996), 'A History of Movie Theatres and Audiences in Postwar Kyoto, The Capital of Japanese Cinema', *Cinemagazinet!* No. 1. Online. Available at: http://www.cmn.hs.h.kyoto-u.ac.jp/NO1/SUBJECT1/KYOTO.HTM

Kawahara, Michiko (1947), 'Hara Setsuko ron' [Discourse on Hara Setsuko], *Eiga Fan* [Film Fan] 7(6) (June): 30–1.

Keene, Judith (2010), 'Cinema and Prosthetic Memory: The Case of the Korean War', *PORTAL Journal of Multidisciplinary International Studies* 7(1): 1–18.

Kersten, Rikki (1996), *Democracy in Postwar Japan: Maruyama Masao and the Search for Autonomy*. London and New York: Routledge.

Kimura, Bin (1972), *Hito to hito no aida: seishun byorigakuteki Nihon ron* [The relations between people: psychopathological Japanese theory]. Tokyo: Kobundo.

Kinema Junpōsha (1952), 'Film Industry', *Kinema Junpō* [The Movie Times] (1 January): 54.

Kitagawa, Kenzō (2000), *Sengō no shuppatsu: Bunka undō, seinendan, sensō mibōin* [Postwar Beginnings: Cultural Movements, Youth Groups, War Widows]. Tokyo: Aoki shoten.

Kitamura, Hiroshi and Keiko Sasagawa (2017), 'The Reception of American Cinema in Japan', *Oxford Research Encyclopedia of Literature* (November): 1–15.

Kitamura, Hiroshi (2004), '"Home of the American Movies": The Marunouchi Subaruza and the Making of Hollywood's Audiences in Occupied Tokyo, 1946–9', in Melvyn Stokes and Richard Maltby (eds), *Hollywood Abroad: Audiences and Cultural Exchange*, 99–120. London: BFI.

Kitamura, Hiroshi (2010), *Screening Enlightenment: Hollywood and the Cultural Reconstruction of Defeated Japan*. Ithaca, NY and London: Cornell University Press.

Kitamura, Kyōhei (2017), 'Sukurīn ni tōeisareru "seishun": Kurosawa Akira "Waga seishun ni kui nashi" no ōdiensu" [Projected Youth on the Screen: The Audience of Kurosawa Akira's No Regrets for Our Youth], *Masu komyunikēshon kenkyū* [Journal of Mass Communication Studies] 90: 123–42.

Kitaura, Hiroyuki (2020), 'The Studio System: The Japanese Studio System Revisited'. Translated by Thomas Kabara. In Hideaki Fujiki and Alastair Philips (eds), *The Japanese Cinema Book*, 109–25. London: BFI; Bloomsbury Publishing.

Koikari, Mire (2002), 'Exporting Democracy? American Women, "Feminist Reforms," and Politics of Imperialism in the U.S. Occupation of Japan 1945–1952', *Frontiers: A Journal of Women's Studies* 23(1): 23–45.

Komatsu, Hiroshi (1996), 'The Lumière Cinématographe and the Production of the Cinema in Japan in the Earliest Period', *Film History* 8(4): 431–8.

Kondo, Dorine (1990), *Crafting Selves: Power, Gender and Discourses of Identity in a Japanese Workplace*. Chicago: University of Chicago Press.

Kondo, Kazuto (2020), *Eigakan to kankyaku no media ron: senzenki Nihon no 'eiga o yomu/ kaku' to iu keiken* [Film theatre and audience media theory: prewar Japan and the experience of 'reading a film']. Tokyo: Seikyusha.

Kuhn, Annette (2002), *Dreaming of Fred and Ginger: Cinema and Cultural Memory*. New York: New York University Press.

Kuriyama, Shigehisa (2002), 'The Enigma of "Time is Money"', *Japan Review* 14: 217–30.

Kyodo News (2020), 'Japan PM Abe declares state of emergency amid widespread virus infections', *Kyodo News* (8 April). Online. Available at: https://english.kyodonews.net/news/2020/04/ac4415709921-abe-to-declare-state-of-emergency-amid-widespread-virus-infections.html

Kyoto Kūshū o Kiroku Suru Kai [Kyoto Air Raid Memorial Society] (1979), *Kakusareteita kūshū* [Hidden Bombings]. Kyoto: Kyoto Air Raid Memorial Society.

Kyoto Media Support Center (2019), 'Kyoto's Film Culture and History vol. 4', Kyoto Media Support Center website. Online. Available at: http://kanko.city.kyoto.lg.jp/support/film/en/culture/volume/04.php

Laird, Colleen (2012), 'Sea Change: Japan's New Wave of Female Directors', PhD diss., University of Oregon.

Landsberg, Alison (2003), 'Prosthetic Memory: The Ethics and Politics of Memory in an Age of Mass Culture' in Paul Grainge (ed.), *Memory and Popular Film*, 144–61. Manchester: Manchester University Press.

Landsberg, Alison (2004), *Prosthetic Memory: The Transformation of American Remembrance in the Age of Mass Culture*. New York: Columbia University Press.

Lewis, Diane Wei (2019), *Powers of the Real: Cinema, Gender, and Emotion in Interwar Japan*. Boston: Harvard University Press.

Lowery, Shearon (1995), *Milestones in Mass Communication Research: Media Effects*. USA: Longman Publishers.

Lummis, C. Douglas (1982), *A New Look at The Chrysanthemum and the Sword*. Tokyo: Shohakusha.

MacArthur, Douglas and staff (1994), *Reports of General MacArthur: MacArthur in Japan: The Occupation: Military Phase* vol. 1. Department of the Army.

MacDougall, David (2005), *The Corporeal Image: Film, Ethnography, and the Senses*. Princeton, NJ: Princeton University Press.

Maeda, Daisaku and Hisanori Ishikawa (2002), 'Ageing in Japan', in David R. Phillips (ed.), *Ageing in the Asia-Pacific Region: Issues, Policies and Future Trends*, 131–50. London and New York: Routledge.

Marks, Laura (2000), *The Skin of The Film: Intercultural Cinema, Embodiment, and the Senses*. Durham, NC: Duke University Press.

Martin-Jones, David (2006), *Deleuze, Cinema and National Identity: Narrative Time in National Contexts*. Edinburgh: Edinburgh University Press.

Maruyama, Masao (1965), 'Patterns of Individuation and the Case of Japan: A Conceptual Scheme', in Marius B. Jansen (ed.), *Changing Japanese Attitudes Toward Modernization*, 489–532. Princeton, NJ: Princeton University Press.

Matos, Christine de (2007), 'A Very Gendered Occupation: Australian Women as Conquerors and Liberators', *US-Japan Womens' Journal* 33: 87–107.

Matsubara, Ichirō (1948), 'Iroke to Joyū' [Actresses and Sex Appeal], *Eiga Goraku* [Film Entertainment] 2(2): 13.

Matsuoka, Isao (2016), 'Watashi no rirekisho' [My Personal History], *Nihon keizai shinbun* [Japan Economics Newspaper], 11 June.

Mayne, Judith (1993), *Cinema and Spectatorship*. London: Routledge.

Mayo, Marlene (1984), 'Civil Censorship and Media Control in Early Occupied Japan: From Minimum to Stringent Surveillance', in Robert Wolfe (ed.), *Americans as Proconsuls: United States Military Government 1944–1952*, 263–320. Carbondale: Southern Illinois University Press.

McLelland, Mark (2010), 'Kissing is a symbol of democracy! Dating, Democracy, and Romance in Occupied Japan, 1945–1952', *Journal of the History of Sexuality* 19(3): 508–35.

Metz, Christian (1975), *The Imaginary Signifier: Psychoanalysis and the Cinema*. Translated by Celia Britton, Annwyl Williams, Ben Brewster and Alfred Guzzetti. Bloomington and Indianapolis: Indiana University Press.

Miller, Laura (2008), 'Japan's Cinderella Motif: Beauty Industry and Mass Culture Interpretations of a Popular Icon', *Asian Studies Review* 32(3): 393–409.

Mini Theatre Aid Project (2020), Mini Theatre Aid Crowd Funding Report Website. Online. Available at: https://minitheater-aid.org/

Ministry of Internal Affairs and Communications (2017), Official Statistics of Japan. Online. Available at: http://www.e-stat.go.jp/SG1/estat/List.do?bid=000001007702&cycode=0

Morishita Akihiko (2009), 'Eizō bunka no soshutsu: Kyoto kiroku eiga o miru kai no katsudō o furikaeru. Dai nibu: Mitai eiga o tsukuru: senki ni okeru "Nishijin" no jishu seisaku' [Creation of New Culture: Activities of 'Kiroku-eiga wo miru kai', Kyoto Part 2: Making films: independent production of 'Nishijin' in the late period], *Kobe geijutsu kōka daigaku kiyō geijutsu kōgaku* [Kobe University of Design Report]. Online. Available at: http://kiyou.kobe-du.ac.jp/08/thesis/05-01.html

Morris-Suzuki, Tessa (1997), *Re-Inventing Japan: Time, Space, Nation*. London: M. E. Sharpe.

Morris-Suzuki, Tessa (2005), *The Past Within Us: Media, Memory, History*. London: Verso.

Motion Gallery (2020), 'Let's connect to the future!!! Supporting mini-theaters nationwide that have nurtured diverse movie cultures Mini-Theater AID Fund', Motion Gallery website. Online. Available at: https://motion-gallery.net/projects/minitheateraid

Motion Picture Producers Association of Japan (Eiren) (2021), Statistics of Film Industry in Japan. Online. Available at: http://www.eiren.org/statistics_e/index.html

Mulvey, Laura (2006), *Death 24x a Second*. London: Reaktion Books.

Murakami, Yasusuke, Kumon Shumpei and Satō Seizaburo (1979), *Bunmei to shite no ie-shakai* [The Ie-Society as a Civilisation]. Tokyo: Chuokoron-sha.

Nakai, Rei (1958), 'Sākuru no undō no iku saigetsu' [The Period of the Circle Movement], *Eiga hyōron* [Film Criticism] (November): 60.

Nakazawa, Eisuke, Hiroyasu Ino and Akira Akabayashi (2020), 'Chronology of COVID-19 Cases on the Diamond Princess Cruise Ship and Ethical Considerations: A Report from Japan', *Disaster Medicine and Public Health Preparedness*, 14(4): 506–13.

Narita, Ryūichi (1999), *Sensō wa dono yō ni katararete kita ka* [How did the war come to be narrated?]. Tokyo: Asahi Shimbunsha.

Nishijin Textile Center (2020) Online. Available at: http://nishijin.or.jp/eng/nishijin_textile_center

'Nishijin' seisaku jōei kyōkai (1961), '"Nishijin" seisaku' [Documentary Film: Nishijin']. Promotional handbill, March.

Nornes, Markus (2002), 'The Postwar Documentary Trace: Groping in the Dark', *positions: east asia cultures critique* 10(1): 39–78.

Oguma Eiji, Ken'ichi Uzuoka and Takahashi Naoki (2009), *1968*. Tokyo: Shinyōsha.

Ohnuki-Tierney, Emiko (1990), 'The Ambivalent Self of the Contemporary Japanese', *Cultural Anthropology* 5(2): 197–216.

Oka, Kunio (1937), 'Eiga to josei: eiga ni taisuru josei no tokushitsu' [Movies and women: Women's characteristics in relation to movies], *Nihon eiga* [Japanese Film] (June): 25.

Okuda, Susumi [1958] (1994), 'Kankyaku wa soshiki suru' [The audience is organised], *Kinema Junpō* [The Movie Times] (15 November), reprinted in *Best of Kinema Junpō*, 743–4. Tokyo: Kinema Junpōsha.

Orbaugh, Sharalyn (2007), *Japanese Fiction of the Allied Occupation: Vision, Embodiment, Identity*. Leiden: Brill.

Orr, James J. (2001), *The Victim as Hero: Ideologies of Peace and National Identity in Postwar Japan*. Honolulu: University of Hawaii Press.

Ōshima, Nagisa [1963] (1964), *Sengo Eiga: Hakai to Sōzō* [Postwar Cinema: Destruction and Creation]. Tokyo: San'ichi Shobō.

Ōshima, Nagisa (1978), *Dōjidai sakka no hakken* [Discovery of contemporary writers]. Tokyo: San'ichi Shobō.

Radway, Janice (1984), *Reading the Romance: Women, Patriarchy, and Popular Literature*. Chapel Hill: University of North Carolina Press.

Raine, Michael (2012), 'Introduction to Matsumoto Toshio: A Theory of Avant-garde Documentary', *Cinema Journal* 51(4): 144–54.

Rokurō, Hidaka (1984), *The Price of Affluence: Dilemmas of Contemporary Japan*. Tokyo, New York and San Francisco: Kodansha International Ltd.

Roquet, Paul (2016), *Ambient Media: Japanese Atmospheres of Self*. Minneapolis: University of Minnesota Press.
Roquet, Paul (2022), *The Immersive Enclosure: Virtual Reality in Japan*. New York: Columbia University Press.
Saito, Ayako (2014), 'Occupation and Memory: The Representation of Woman's Body in Postwar Japanese Cinema' in Daisuke Miyao (ed.), *The Oxford Handbook of Japanese Cinema*, 327–62. Oxford: Oxford University Press.
Sanada, Shiini (1949), 'Yasashiku utsukushiku; Takamine Mieko' [Gentle and beautiful: Takamine Mieko], *Eiga Fan* [Film Fan] 9(2): 6–7.
Satō, Yō (2013), '"Kyoto kiroku eiga o miru kai" ni tsuite sono zenshi' [An essay on Kyoto kiroku eiga o miru kai], *Engeki Eizōgaku* [Theatre and Visual Arts]: 41–55.
Save Our Local Cinemas Project (2020), Save Our Local Cinemas Project Shop website. Online. Available at: https://localcinema.base.shop/
Save The Cinema Project (2020), '#SaveTheCinema "Save the Mini Theater!" Project Petition', Change.org website. Online. Available at: https://www.change.org/p/savethecinema
SCAP (Supreme Commander of the Allied Powers) General HQ (1945), 'Indication of Production Principles of IDS.' Draft Memorandum to Japanese Empire, issued by General Headquarters of Allied Powers, 22 September 1945, Box 8563.
SCAP (Supreme Commander of the Allied Powers) General HQ (1946–9), '000.076 Women's Affairs', February 1946–January 1949, Folder 28, Box 2879.
SCAP (Supreme Commander of the Allied Powers) General HQ (1948), 'Political Information-Education Program', National Archives II at College Park, Maryland, RG 331, GHQ/SCAP, CI&E, Box 5305, files 12 and 15.
Schilling, Mark (2001), 'Kon Ichikawa at Eighty-Six: A "Mid-Career Interview"', in James Quandt (ed.), *Kon Ichikawa*, 409–28. Toronto: Cinemathetique Ontario.
Scott. A. O. (2021), 'The Movies Are Back. But What Are Movies Now?', *The New York Times* (15 July). Online. Available at: https://www.nytimes.com/2021/07/15/movies/streaming-theater-hollywood.html
Seigworth, Gregory J. and Melissa Gregg (2010), 'An Inventory of Shimmers', in Melissa Gregg and Gregory J. Seigworth (eds), *The Affect Theory Reader*, 14–25. Durham, NC: Duke University Press.
Seraphim, Franziska (2006), *War Memory and Social Politics in Japan, 1945–2005*. Cambridge, MA: Harvard University Press.
Shigematsu, Setsu (2012), *Scream from the Shadows: The Woman's Liberation Movement in Japan*. London: University of Minnesota Press.
Shōjo bakari no zadankai: risō no shōnen, risō no kōsai' [Shōjo-only Roundtable: Ideal Boys, Ideal Friendships] (1951), *Shōjo no tomo* [Girls' Friend], 44(10) (September): 72–7.
Skoggard, Ian and Alisse Waterston (2015), 'Introduction: Toward an Anthropology of Affect and Evocative Ethnography', *Anthropology of Consciousness* 26(2): 109–20.

Sobchack, Vivian (1992), *The Address of the Eye: A Phenomenology of Film Experience*. Princeton, NJ: Princeton University Press.
Sobchack, Vivian (2004), *Carnal thoughts: Embodiment and Moving Image Culture*. Berkeley: University of California Press.
Sorensen, Lars Martin (2009), *Censorship of Japanese Films During the U.S. Occupation of Japan: The Cases of Yasujiro Ozu and Akira Kurosawa*. Lewiston, NY: Edwin Mellen Press.
Stacey, Jackie (1994), *Star Gazing: Hollywood Cinema and Female Spectatorship*. London and New York: Routledge.
Stacey, Jackie (2013), 'On Being Open to Difference: Cosmopolitanism and the Psychoanalysis of Groups', in Jackie Stacey and Janet Wolff (eds), *Writing Otherwise: Experiments in Cultural Criticism*. Manchester: University of Manchester Press.
Staiger, Janet (2000), *Perverse Spectators: The Practices of Film Reception*. New York and London: New York University Press.
Standish, Isolde (2000), *Myth and Masculinity in the Japanese Cinema: Towards a Political Reading of the 'Tragic Hero'*. London: Curzon.
Standish, Isolde (2005), *A New History of Japanese Cinema*. New York: Continuum.
Standish, Isolde (2011), *Politics, Porn and Protest: Japanese Avant-Garde cinema in the 1960s and 1970s*. London: Continuum.
Sutton, Damian (2009), *Photography, Cinema, Memory: The Crystal Image of Time*. Minneapolis: University of Minnesota Press.
Suzuki, Takao (1984), *Words in Context: A Japanese Perspective on Language and Culture*. Tokyo: Kodansha International.
Takada Hideki (1949), 'Hara Setsuko san ni sasaguru koibun' [A Love Letter to Setsuko Hara], *Eiga Fan* [Film Fan] 9(10) (October): 31–3.
Takahashi, Toshie (2016), *Audience Studies: A Japanese Perspective*. London: Routledge.
Takebe, Yoshinobu (2016), *Ōsaka 'eiga' koto hajime* [At the start of the movies in Osaka]. Tokyo: Sairyūsha.
Taylor, Helen (1989), *Scarlett's Women: Gone with the Wind and its Female Fans*. New Brunswick, NJ: Rutgers University Press.
Terasawa, Kanako (2010), 'Enduring Encounter: Hollywood Cinema and Japanese Women's Memory of the Post-war Experience', PhD diss., University of London.
Toki, Akihiro and Kaoru Mizoguchi (1993), 'A History of Early Cinema in Kyoto, Japan (1896–1912).' *Cinemagazinet!* No. 1. Online. Available at: http://www.cmn.hs.h.kyoto-u.ac.jp/NO1/SUBJECT1/INAEN.HTM
Tsing, Anna (2013), 'Sorting Out Commodities: How Capitalist Value is Made Through Gifts', *HAU: Journal of Ethnographic Theory* 3(1): 21–43.
Tsuchiya, Yuka (2002), 'Imagined America in Occupied Japan: (Re-)Educational Films Shown by the U.S. Occupation Forces to the Japanese, 1948–1952', *The Japanese Journal of American Studies* 13: 193–213.
Tsukada, Yoshinobu (1980), *Nihon eigashi no kenkyū* [A Study of Japanese Movie History]. Tokyo: Gendai Shokan.

Tsukamoto, Jirō (1947), 'Dare ka ichiban oshare ka?' [Who is the most stylish?], *Eiga Bunko* 2: 42–4.
Tsumura, Hideo (1939), 'Eiga kankyaku wa henbō suru' [The Movie Audience Transforms], *Chūō kōron* [Central Review] (February): 89.
Tsunoda, Takuya (2015), 'The Dawn of Cinematic Modernism: Iwanami Productions and Postwar Japanese Cinema', PhD diss., Yale University.
Tsurumi Kazuko (1947), 'Kiku to Katana: Amerikajin no Mita Nihonteki Dotokukan' [The Chrysanthemum and the Sword: Japanese Morals as Seen by an American], *Shiso* [Thought] (April): 221–4.
Tsurumi, Kazuko (1970), *Social Change and the Individual: Japan Before and After Defeat in World War II*. Princeton, NJ: Princeton University Press.
Ueda, Manabu (2007), 'Kankyaku no tomadoi: Eiga sosoki ni okeru shinematekku no kogyo o megutte.' [The Audience's Confusion: On the Exhibition of the Cinematheque in the Formative Period of Cinema], *Ato risachi* [Art Research] 7: 129–39.
Ueda, Manabu (2012), *Nihon eiga sōsō-ki no kōgyō to kankyaku: Tōkyō to Kyōto o chūshin ni* [Exhibitions and Audiences in the Early Years of Japanese Cinema: Focus on Tokyo and Kyoto], Tokyo: Waseda University Press.
Ueda, Manabu (2020), 'Exhibition: Screening spaces: A history of Japanese film exhibition', in Hideaki Fujiki and Alastair Phillips (eds), *The Japanese Cinema Book*, 126–39. London: BFI; Bloomsbury Publishing.
Uryū, Tadao [1958] (1994), 'Nihon eigakai ni okeru eiga sākuru no ayumi' [The development of film circles within the film world], *Kinema Junpō* [The Movie Times] (15 November), reprinted in *Best of Kinema Junpō*, 747–9. Tokyo: Kinema Junpōsha.
Uryū, Tadao (1967), 'Eiga fukkō wa josei no dōin kara: josei kankyaku genshō no donsoko wa sugita' [Cinema Recovery Begins with Women's Mobilisation: Female Audience Decrease Hits Bottom], *Kinema Junpō* [The Movie Times] 450: 88–91.
Voelcker, Becca (2021), 'Land Cinema in the Neoliberal Age', PhD diss., Harvard University.
Wada-Marciano, Mitsuyo (2007), 'Teshigahara Hiroshi's Woman in the Dunes (1964)', in Alastair Phillips and Julian Stringer (eds), *Japanese Cinema: Texts and Contexts*, 180–92. London: Routledge.
Wada-Marciano, Mitsuyo (2008), *Nippon Modern: Japanese Cinema of the 1920s and 1930s*. Honolulu: Hawaii University Press.
Wada-Marciano, Mitsuyo (2014), 'Reading Nishijin (1961) as Cinematic Memory', in Daisuke Miyao (ed.), *The Oxford Handbook of Japanese Cinema*, 363–82. Oxford: Oxford University Press.
Whitehead, Derek H. (2003), 'Poiesis and Art-making: A Way of Letting-Be', *Contemporary Aesthetics* 1(1): 5.
Yomota, Inuhiko (2000), *Nihon no joyū* [Japanese Actresses]. Tokyo: Iwanami Shōten.

Yoshimura, Kōzaburō et al. (1952), 'Dai issen yondai kantoku gendai nihon fūzoku o kataru' [Four Japanese Directors Talk about Contemporary Japanese Customs], *Kinema Junpō* [The Movie Times] 29 (1 January): 36.

Zahlten, Alexander (2017), *The End of Japanese Cinema: Industrial Genres, National Times, and Media Ecologies*. Durham, NC: Duke University Press.

Index

12 Angry Men (Sidney Lumet, 1957), 181
1947 Constitution of Japan, 49, 88, 89, 98, 121, 122, 132
47 Loyal Retainers (*Chūshingura*), 87

Abashiri Prison series (*Abashiri bangaichi*, 1965–8), 153
Allied Occupation of Japan (1945–52), 2, 3, 4, 7, 18, 21, 25, 27, 31, 33, 34, 46–50, 72, 76, 79, 86–8, 90–1, 97–100, 107–10, 120–137, 150, 151, 160, 175
Art Theatre Guild, 73, 111, 150
Asai Eiichi, 138, 141–2, 144–8
audience and reception studies, 1, 5, 14, 22, 25, 27, 35, 44, 65, 72, 78, 143, 190

Boyhood (*Shōnenki*, Kinoshita Keisuke, 1951), 130
Buñuel, Luis, 145
buraku, burakumin, 118, 144, 157
Burgtheatre (Willi Forst, 1936) 180
Butler, Judith, 19, 26, 28–9, 75, 161–2, 183–4

Carmen Comes Home (*Karumen kokyō ni kaeru*, Kinoshita Keisuke, 1951), 72
censorship, 2, 7, 21, 46–8, 72, 87, 97, 100, 106, 118, 120–2, 125, 131, 134, 137, 190
Central Motion Picture Exchange (CMPE), 126, 131
Children Calling Spring (*Haru o yobu kora*, 1959), 146
Children of the Bomb (*Genbaku no ko*, Shindō Kaneto, 1952), 87
Cinderella (Geronimi et al., 1950), 131–2

cinema theatre, 10, 20, 37, 44, 52–67, 71–2, 75–6, 79–85, 89, 112–13, 124, 128–30, 134–6, 150, 156, 159, 162–3, 172, 185–6
Civil Censorship Detachment (CCD), 47–8, 87
Civil Information and Education Section (CIE), 46–8, 87, 125
Company Production Materials Survey Group (Hōga rokusha seisaku shiryo chōsa kai no nichiyō kankyaku chōsa), 134
Conde, David, 46–7, 130, 137

Daiei, 61, 152
Death by Hanging (*Koshikei*, Ōshima Nagisa, 1968), 154

Early Summer (*Bakushū*, Ozu Yasujirō, 1951), 98
Edison, Thomas, 36–7, 40, 42–3
Eirin (Film Ethics Regulation Control Committee, Eiga Rinri Kikō), 47–8, 59, 134
ethno-history, 2, 5–6, 14, 19, 25, 53, 103, 107, 122, 161, 190

Fifteen Years War, 150, 181
For Kayako (Oguri Kōhei, 1984), 181
Fuji Junko, aka Fuji Sumiko, 105

Gate of Flesh (*Nikutai no mon*, Suzuki Seijun, 1964), 87
Godzilla (*Gojira*, Honda Ishirō, 1954), 178, 179
Godzilla (*Shin-Gojira*, Anno Hideaki and Higuchi Shinji, 2016), 178, 179

Gonda Yasunosuke, 43–5
Gone with the Wind (Victor Fleming, 1939), 72
Great Kantō Earthquake, 4

Hani Susumu, 62
Hara Setsuko, 69, 96–7, 101, 104–5, 109, 116–18
Hiroshima (Sekigawa Hideo, 1953), 87, 89
Hobson's Choice (David Lean, 1954), 180

Ichikawa Kon, 3–4
Imamura Shōhei, 149, 154
In This Corner of the World (*Kono sekai no katatsumi ni*, Katabuchi Sunao, 2017), 112
Inabata Katsutarō, 37–42
Ishihama Akira, 89
Ishihara Yujirō, 69, 103, 105
Iwasaki Akira, 47

Japan–Korea Treaty (1965), 151
Japan–US Security Treaty (Anpo), 34, 151

Kawakita Kashiko, 73
Kido Shiro, 132
Kikuchi Kan, 31
Kinema Junpō (*Film Record*, or *The Movie Times*), 65, 93, 108, 130, 131, 135, 137, 152, 154, 171
Kinoshita Keisuke, 62, 72, 87, 91, 130, 154
Kinugasa eiga kai (Kinugasa Film Club), 13, 138–43, 158, 167–9, 177–82, 187–9
Kishi Keiko, 108
Kitahara Mie, 68, 69
Kitaōji Kinya, 103
Kobayashi Masaki, 87, 154
Korean War, 85, 140
Koreeda Hirokazu 73
Kurosawa Akira, 73, 87, 95, 97, 117, 133, 156
Kyoto kiroku eiga o miru kai (Kyoto documentary film viewing group, 1955–62), 21, 138, 141–58

Late Spring (*Banshun*, Ozu Yasujirō, 1949), 98
Listen to the Voices from the Deep (*Kike wadatsumi no koe*, Sekigawa Hideo, 1950), 140
Little Women (Mervyn LeRoy, 1949), 126

Los Olvidados (The Forgotten Ones, Luis Buñuel, 1950), 145
Lumière, 37–42, 67

MacArthur, Gen. Douglas, 46, 49, 50
Makino Shōzo, 177
Matsumoto Toshio, 142, 145–7, 151, 177
Mifune Toshirō, 105
Mikuni Rentarō, 92, 104–6
mini-theatre, 184–6, 190
Mini-Theatre Aid Fund, 185–6
Mito Mitsuko, 109
Miyajima Yoshio, 146
Miyoshi Akira, 146
Mizoguchi Kenji, 87, 95, 118, 154
Murakami Haruki, 70–1

New Faces, 125
Nikkatsu, 4, 61, 149
Nishijin, 143, 146–9
Nishijin (*Nishijin*, Matsumoto Toshio, 1961), 138, 142–3, 148, 177
No Regrets for Our Youth (*Waga seishun ni kui nashi*, Kurosawa Akira, 1946), 45, 97, 100

One Wonderful Sunday (*Subarashiki nichiyōbi*, Kurosawa Akira, 1947), 87, 133
Orimono no machi, Nishijin (*The Weaving Town of Nishijin*, 1961), 148
Ōshima Nagisa, 62, 149–51, 154
Ozu Yasujirō, 77, 93, 95, 98

'pink' genre, 121, 134–5

Red Peony Gambler series (*Hibotan bakuto*, 1968–72), 152
Red Purge, 140

sākuru (circle), 6, 13, 50, 140, 169, 171–6
Second World War, 85, 106, 117, 150, 181
Sekine Hiroshi, 146
Shi dokyumentari shinema (Shidofu), 142, 148
Shin Riken, 146
Shindō Kaneto, 62, 87, 154
Shintōhō, 61
Shōchiku, 4, 61, 68–9, 73, 110, 113, 132, 149
Soldier Gokudo (*Heitai Gokudo*, Saeki Kiyoshi, 1968), 152

Supreme Commander for the Allied
    Powers (SCAP), 2, 3, 33, 44–7, 49,
    59, 74, 87, 98, 100, 118, 120, 123–7,
    130–4, 137
Suzuki Seijun, 149

taiyōzoku (sun tribe), 68–9, 103
Takakura Ken, 100–1, 152–3
Takamine Hideko, 105
Takamine Mieko, 107–9
Tanaka Kinuyo, 105, 109
television, 45–9, 52–3, 57, 61–7, 69, 94,
    104, 121, 136–137, 149, 156
Teshigahara Hiroshi, 73
The Ceremony (*Gishiki*, Ōshima Nagisa,
    1971), 154
The Human Condition (*Ningen no jōken*,
    Kobayashi Masaki, 1959–61), 87
The Idiot (*Hakuchi*, Kurosawa Akira,
    1954), 117
The Insect Woman (*Nippon konchūki*,
    Imamura Shōhei, 1964), 154
The Living Desert (James Algar, 1953),
    69–72, 111, 114
The New Earth (*Atarashiki tsuchi* / *The
    Daughter of the Samurai* [*Die Tochter
    des Samurai*], Itami and Fanck, 1937),
    99
The Red Shoes (Michael Powell and Emeric
    Pressburger, 1948), 58, 111, 115
The Wild Bunch (*Sam Peckinpah*, 1969),
    179

The Wizard of Oz (Victor Fleming, 1939),
    72
Tōei, 13, 61–2, 68, 113, 135, 152
Tōhō, 61, 68, 110, 113, 140, 146, 166
Tōhō strikes (1946–9), 140, 146
Tokyo Story (*Tokyo monogatari*, Ozu
    Yasujirō, 1953), 98
Tower of Lilies (*Himeyuri no tō*, Imai
    Tadashi, 1953), 88
Tsuchimoto Noriaki, 142
Twenty-Four Eyes (*Nijūshi no hitomi*,
    Kinoshita Keisuke, 1954), 87, 91

Uchida Tomu, 105
Ugetsu (*Ugetsu monogatari*, Mizoguchi
    Kenji, 1954), 118, 154
United Productions of America (UPA), 110

Wada Tsutomu, 142
war-retro genre, 87, 88
Waterloo Bridge (Mervyn LeRoy, 1940), 72
Woman Gambler series (*Onna tobakushi*,
    1967–71), 152

Yamabiki gakko (Echo school), 163
Yamada Isuzu, 109
Yoshinaga Sayuri, 117
Your Name (*Kimi no na wa*, Makoto
    Shinkai, 2016), 112
Yukishiro Keiko, 103

Zenkyōtō, 155

EU representative:
Easy Access System Europe
Mustamäe tee 50, 10621 Tallinn, Estonia
Gpsr.requests@easproject.com